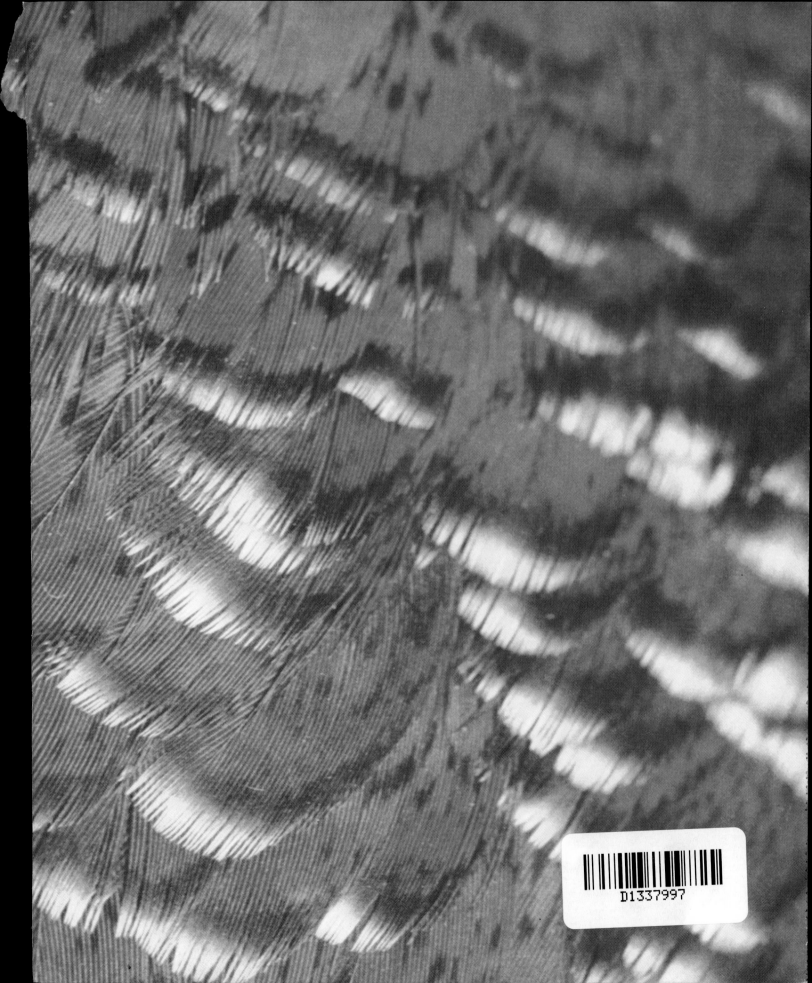

game : a cookbook

This book is dedicated to our Dads,
Kevin Hilferty and John Butterworth.
They are, quite simply, the kind of
writers we aspire to be.

game : a cookbook

trish hilferty and
tom norrington-davies

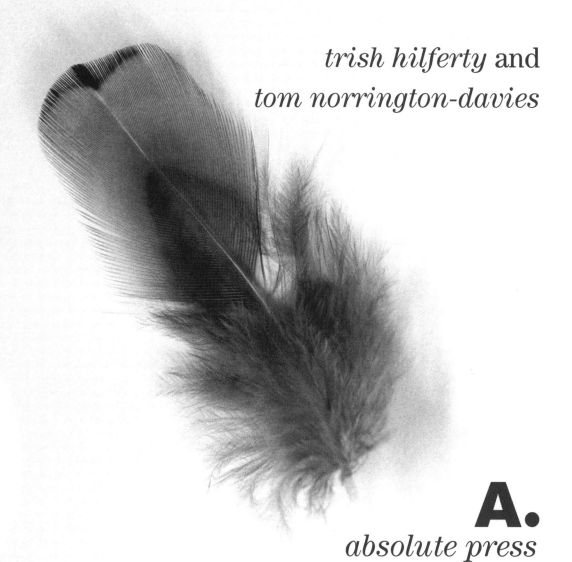

A.

absolute press

First published in Great Britain
in 2009 by

Absolute Press
Scarborough House
29 James Street West
Bath BA1 2BT
Phone 44 (0) 1225 316013
Fax 44 (0) 1225 445836
E-mail info@absolutepress.co.uk
Website www.absolutepress.co.uk

Photography copyright © Jason Lowe
(except page 9 by Lara Holmes)

Publisher
Jon Croft
Commissioning Editor
Meg Avent
Editor
Lucy Bridgers
Art Director & Designer
Matt Inwood
Design Assistant
Claire Siggery
Indexer
Gill Tebbutt
Photographer
Jason Lowe
Food Stylist
Trish Hilferty
Props Stylist
Liz Belton

A catalogue record of this book is available
from the British Library

ISBN 13: **9781906650100**

Printed and bound in Slovenia on behalf of
Latitude Press

A note about the text
This book is set in Century and Helvetica
Neue. The first Century typeface was cut in
1894. In 1975 an updated family of Century
typefaces was designed by Tony Stan for
ITC. Helvetica was designed in 1957 by
Max Miedinger of the Swiss-based Haas
foundry. In the early 1980s, Linotype
redrew the entire Helvetica family.
The result was Helvetica Neue.

Reprinted 2010

Contents:

intr

Whenever we are asked what kind of food we like to cook most, we are bound to reply, almost in unison, 'game'.

We are both seasoned and seasonal cooks. We love the ins and outs of the culinary calendar, whether that means waiting for our first handful of asparagus in spring, or a glut of tomatoes and pumpkins come early autumn. Even the so-called bleak midwinter provides a bounty of food, which extends far beyond cabbages and root vegetables, if you want it to. And, in fact, the reason we don't spend those colder months dreaming too much about the summer is probably because our cooking is dominated by the huge choice of game on offer. Game is not winter food by any means, but it is the best thing about that time of year. Why do we love it so much?

First up, it is the most unbelievably tasty food, naturally. That's not naturally as in 'of course'. Perhaps we should have said that it is naturally tasty! Next time you find yourself slathering a chicken breast with a marinade to save it from mediocrity, try swapping it for something that has literally walked on the wild side, and tastes like it.

Next time you find yourself worrying about the way your pork chop was treated on the farm, consider the genuinely free-range lifestyle of a rabbit, or a deer, or any number of other critters that roamed where they liked, and ate what they wanted.

Worried about cholesterol? Additives? Cost? Provenance? Game is, by and large, lean, unadulterated, cheap and local.

Bored of turning to the same recipes again and again? If you are new to game, you are about to discover a wealth of quick, easy, simple and delicious dishes that, despite being staggeringly uncomplicated, manage to thrill the taste buds on several levels all at once. Game never seems to taste the same twice. Just like a brilliant wine and its terroir, or a spankingly fresh oyster and its riverbed, game has such a close relationship with nature that it manages to delight and surprise you on some level every time you cook and eat it.

Before we go any further, we ought to roughly explain what we mean by 'game'. If we were the types to rely on dictionary definitions we would simply describe game as 'wild animals now or formerly hunted for food and sport', then crack on with the bit you really bought this book for, the recipes. However, if you are reading this book curled up on a sofa and you fancy a bit of background to this marvellous subject then read on.

Introduction

What's in a name?

In Britain and most of Europe the word 'game' is a purely culinary term used to describe wild (or at least wild-ish) meat and fish. You might still hear the word being used in other parts of the world to describe large, usually dangerous animals, hunted for trophies. Elephants in Africa, tigers in Asia and bison in the Americas were all once known as 'big game'. This sport is, at least in theory, a dwindling practise, since many of those species that were once seen as 'big game' are endangered and protected by anti hunting laws.

In the British Isles, where we have never had many big beasts to contend with; most hunting has been about pest control, and / or providing food. Now that hunting foxes with hounds has been banned, just about all the wild animals Britons trap and shoot are considered fit for the table. To understand why this food source is still known as 'game', you need to look at our ancient past.

Once upon a time man was a hunter-gatherer who lived entirely on what he could find or catch. As most humans morphed into agrarian societies who grew or raised their food, the wild stuff changed from being a staple to a supplement. In countries like this one, where pretty much the entire population has come to rely on well-established animal husbandry and industrially farmed crops, hunting has become, for better or worse, a much more leisurely pursuit. Your average modern hunter-gatherer indulges in little more than the occasional mushroom hunt or an afternoon's blackberry picking. Some people are not exactly stimulated by the idea of pouncing on a patch of bramble and, for them, a far more exciting prospect involves quarry that presents some jeopardy. i.e. it will try and run away or, in some more extreme cases, put up a fight. However you feel about hunting, it is this very jeopardy or thrill factor that has given us the word 'game'. When modern, well-fed humans hunt, they are not all that dissimilar to dogs chasing sticks.

The wild and the not-so-wild

Most of the game eaten in the British Isles, Europe and North America falls into one of three distinct groups. The first is a pretty motley crew of truly wild animals, but in such densely populated parts of the world, its members live in direct competition with humans, especially those who farm cereals, fruit or vegetables. Rabbits, pigeons, some deer and a whole host of less famous delinquents might be seen as game in the kitchen, but they could also be quite accurately described as vermin. Thanks doubtlessly to this wholly unappetising label, such animals are no longer widely eaten in the UK. More's the pity, because they are all delicious. What's more, they are extremely common and, as a result, incredibly cheap to buy for those of us who do not hunt. If we had a mission statement as both cooks and authors, it would probably be to get more people eating this confoundingly underrated food source.

The second group is probably the most famous and definitely the most popular. Most members of this group are related to (or at least taste like) animals that mankind has domesticated over the centuries. Grouse, pheasant and partridges all descend from ancient ancestors of the modern chicken. Wild ducks and other waterfowl are distant cousins of the farmyard goose. Venison is an herbivore that will provide meat to rival the best beef and lamb. All of the above can and do live wild in this part of the world. But, in Britain at least, mankind profoundly influences their lives and habitats.

Because these animals are either naturally shy, or migratory (or both) and tend to give humans a wide berth, finding and catching them presents a number of challenges, and they have become the darlings of the hunting community as a result. Because so much land in the UK is privately owned, hunting provides a valuable income to many farmers and estate keepers. Over the centuries they have learned to manage and control the local populations of those animals that attract the sporting hunter. In the case of birds like pheasant and partridge, it is common practise to rear chicks in a protective environment and release them into the wild as adults (and targets). The last Highland moor you hiked across may have been carefully manicured to encourage grouse. The same might be true of wetlands favoured by wild ducks and waders. We will deal with this management of Britain's most popular game in each individual chapter but, for now, it is suffice to say that not all of our favourite 'wild' food is particularly wild.

The third group is likely to cause contention amongst some game aficionados as to whether we should have included it at all. Some formerly wild animals that, for one reason or another, no longer proliferate in this country have been reintroduced on what can only be described as farms. They are raised, fed, managed and slaughtered for the table as a purely commercial venture. It is possible to buy farmed versions of nearly all Britain's wild animals. Venison, rabbits, salmon and guinea fowl are the most obvious examples. But it is also possible to buy 'game' that is not available in its wild form at all, such as 'wild' boar or quails.

There is another type of game that might be available to you if you live outside the UK, Europe or North America. Occasionally, you might come across what we call exotic game (i.e. kangaroo, ostrich, alligator etc). Such items are hard to find in the British Isles and, for that reason alone, we have not included them in this book. Our humble apologies, should you be reading this on the other side of the world. It is worth noting that some 'exotic' game can be adapted to the recipes in this book. For example some African hoofed game like springbok could be cooked using recipes for venison or roe deer.

Introduction

A matter of taste

Even if you have never eaten game, you have probably heard a myriad of expressions used by people trying to describe its flavour. Venison tastes like beef; rabbit and pheasant are not a million miles from chicken, and wild boar is, unsurprisingly, quite 'porky'. But it becomes harder to describe the flavour of animals that taste only of themselves, like hare or pigeon, for example. And this is when you are most likely to come across a word that both attracts and repels people in equal measure. That word is 'gamy'.

Two major factors that cause an animal to taste gamy are its lifestyle and diet. Animals that are farmed for meat get fed and watered to fatten them up for the table. They are also subjected to what you could call enforced idleness. This lazy lifestyle supplements their diet, aiding the 'fattening up' process. The most pronounced form of this practise can be seen in the marbling on a good beefsteak, or the crackling on a loin of pork. If the same animals were living wild, their meat would be markedly different. The difference would be most pronounced in terms of leanness. Wild animals expend an enormous amount of energy looking for food and avoiding predators. Their muscles work hard, making the meat behave quite differently to their farmed counterparts. This is most obvious when you compare the breast meat on flying birds like wild duck to the same cut on farmed versions. The wild animal's diet, which in farmed animals is mostly cereal based, is much more varied. This has a huge impact on the taste of an animal's meat. These lean and strongly flavoured results of living wild are what we call 'gamy'.

There is a tendency, especially amongst the uninitiated, to assume that gamy means strong or even overpowering. This is not necessarily the case. There are meats that have a very strong gamy flavour but, in most cases, it is more of a hint than anything. The myth that all game is the carnivorous equivalent of blue cheese is one of many that needs busting, in our opinion.

We have said that the taste of wild meat is largely down to its lifestyle and diet, but there is a much stronger influence on the flavour of any meat whether wild or farmed, and that is how it is kept after it has been dispatched. With the possible exception of fish, no meat is particularly good to eat immediately after slaughter. Purveyors of the finest beef, lamb or pork often like to boast that their meat has been 'hung' for several days (if not weeks) before it hits the butcher's block.

Hanging meat allows the muscle fibres to relax (which encourages tenderness), but it also leads to moisture loss (which intensifies flavour). Lots of game is hung for exactly the same reasons. But, because the carcasses tend to be smaller, and left intact as a result, the effects of hanging tend to be much more pronounced. This is especially true of game that is hung without being skinned or eviscerated. Some game enthusiasts claim that it is best eaten after it has been hung until it actually tastes 'high'.

The same people might, with the best of intentions, be under the misapprehension that game is tough and inedible until it is, for want of a better word, rotten! This misunderstanding probably stems from a belief that the hard working muscles of wild animals will not tenderise in the same timeframe as their farmed counterparts. Luckily, these people are in a pretty small minority. You can safely assume that this minority does not include game dealers or butchers who are in the business of selling the stuff. No butcher in his or her right mind would want a stock of near-rotten meat on his or her hands. Nor would your average chef. In all our years of buying game we have never been duped or bullied into buying anything 'high'. Neither will you.

A meat for all seasons

In 1831 an Act of Parliament decreed that the shooting of various forms of game be restricted to fixed seasons. This Act, still in force today, was designed to protect some species of game during their mating and nesting times, ensuring the sustainability of hunting, whether for sport or dinner. It just so happens that most animals mate and breed in the warmer months. As a result, some wild food is off limits during spring and summer. This is why you may have read that game is out of season if there is no 'R' in the month (the same rule of thumb, notably, is applied to shellfish, which spawns during the same period). Whilst this is a convenient soundbite, it isn't strictly so. Many unprotected species (mainly pests like rabbit, pigeon, some deer and wild boar) have no closed season and some fish, especially salmon, are at their best during the summer months. We have said earlier that game is not necessarily restricted to autumn or winter. With this in mind, if our recipes suggest using meat that is only available seasonally (especially between September and April), we have taken care to provide you with a suggested substitute that isn't. There is plenty of summery cooking in this book!

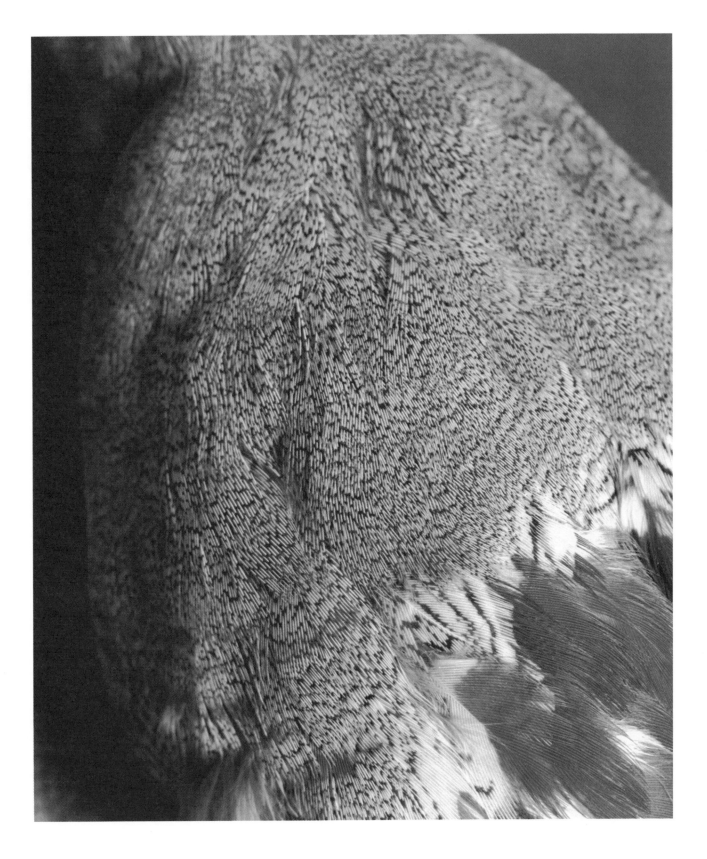

Introduction

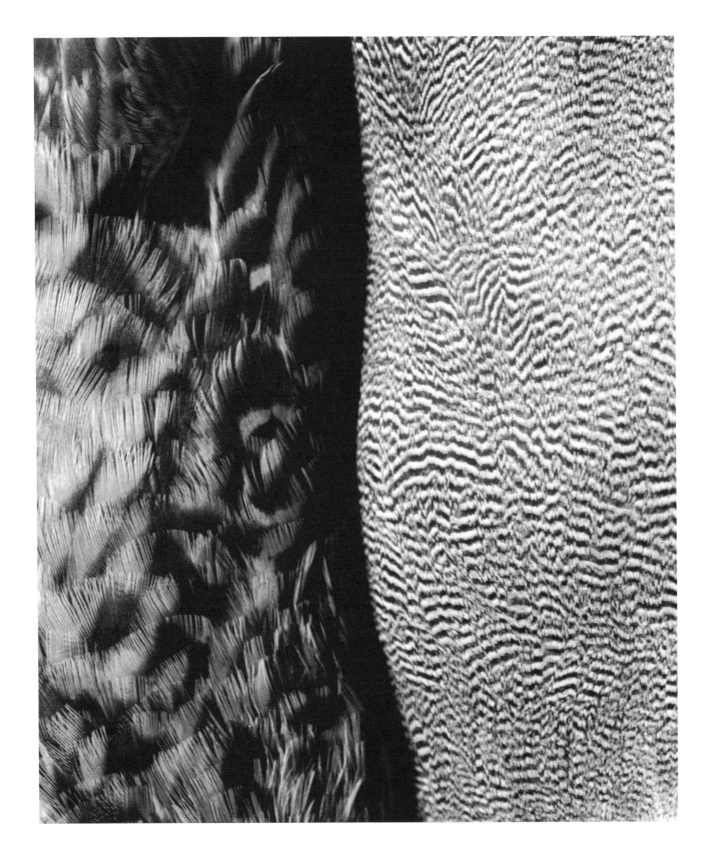

14

A buyer's market

Another myth that needs busting is the notion that game is off limits unless you own a shotgun or are good mates with someone who does. You might not be able to wander into your local supermarket and expect to find the entire canon of game represented on the shelves but it is around, and, in the case of some savvy retailers, there seems to be more choice available every year. In the twenty-first century two mediums have probably empowered the adventurous shopper more than any other. The first (and most convenient) is surely the Internet. It is not a massively gross exaggeration to say that much of what you want is only a click away: just try typing your heart's desire into the world's favourite search engine and you will see what we mean. The other (which requires a little more leg work) is your nearest farmers' market or farm shop. Farmer's markets, in particular, seem to be very game friendly. It should, but sadly doesn't, go without saying that few better business relationships are worth nurturing more than the one between you and your nearest high street butcher. Nothing seems to delight most butchers more than a request that they get something special in for you.

How to use this book

This book is quite different to other collections of game recipes. To make it as user friendly as possible we have grouped certain types of game together, not necessarily because they live like each other, which might be the most logical approach, but because they cook like each other. Those cookery-based definitions neatly fall into three general groups. These are:

a) Game birds
b) Mammals, or furred game
c) Fish

Within each of these groups are sub-groups that cook and eat quite similarly to one another. For example, guinea fowl and pheasant are quite large birds, with white meat. They can be prepared and cooked in roughly the same way as each other. This is an obvious example. Some subgroups are not so immediately apparent. For example, many people might instinctively think that rabbit and hare are almost the same. In fact, hare is much more like venison, with its dark, red meat. Although it is smaller than a deer, hare can be jointed, prepared and cooked in much the same way as venison and, for this reason, it will appear in the same section as deer. If the main aim of the book is to entice you to cook our delicious and user-friendly recipes, it helps to know that each recipe can be adapted for other, similar meats or fish. This is especially useful when you consider that various types of game come in and out of season at different times to one another. All the animals in any given sub-group can be jointed or filleted in exactly the same way even if, as in the case of hare and venison, they are not the same size.

The recipes

Because we really want you to appreciate that natural flavour of game we are so in love with, each chapter will open with a simple guide to classic roasts and suggested trimmings. Do bear with us if you read lots of exhortations to simply throw something in the oven with a sprinkle of salt, pepper and not much else. We are not trying to skimp on recipes and, to prove the point, we hope you will find plenty of eclectic and quite surprising treatments for a group of meats and fish that are, rightly or wrongly, seen as overtly traditional. You will find plenty of light salads, stir fries, pasta and rice dishes, and the odd bit of charcuterie, in amongst the 'meat and two veg'.

Introduction

Broadly speaking, game birds can be divided **3** *into main groups.*

The most common, and the most popular, are the wild or at least semi wild fowl birds of the galliform group. The galliform birds have decorative plumage, loud mating calls and fairly questionable flying skills, since they tend to feed off the ground. This has always been good news for humans since it has made them easy to hunt. As if that weren't enough, galliform birds tend to provide their hunters with lots of pale ('white') meat. If all this sounds familiar, that is because chicken is a member of this group. All modern forms of hen are direct descendants of an ancient bird known in Asia and Africa as jungle fowl. Distant cousins of modern-day chicken include peacocks, pheasants, guinea fowl, grouse and quail.

For the purposes of this book we have divided the galliform (or chicken like) birds into three main groups. The first group is pheasant and guinea fowl. This is because they are similar in both size and flavour. Partridge and quail are both portion-sized birds and they will appear in a shared chapter, too. Grouse, with its darker meat and exclusive price tag, merits a chapter all of its own, and we'll come to that later.

Pheasant

Ask most people to name a game bird and they are more than likely to say pheasant. It's the most commonly sighted, edible wild foul in Britain, as you probably know if you have caught a flash of its brilliant plumage out walking or driving along country lanes. In fact this bird is not all that wild. Most pheasant is 'managed'. This means it has been raised by a farm or country estate, primarily for sport. The pheasant eggs are incubated and hatched just like farmed hens. They are reared in a protected environment until they are old enough to fend for themselves. At this point they become game in the true sense of the word. Once the shooting season starts in the first autumn of a pheasant's life, it will be hunted, either for pleasure, or the dinner table, or both. The popularity of pheasant shoots means that the meat is incredibly plentiful whilst in season, making it one of the cheapest forms of game you can buy.

There is an issue, albeit minor, to contend with when buying pheasant. In our opinion, you can roughly divide the pheasant season into two halves; falling neatly between the autumn (up to and including christmas) and the winter (January and February, when the season officially ends). When pheasant is young, at the top of the season, it is smaller and, as a result, more tender all over. At this point it is good for pretty much anything, including roasting (see below). But once these birds have spent a couple of months running around and developing very strong legs, they can become somewhat tougher. By then, they are really best saved for pot-roasts and braises. Even in the autumn, there is the outside chance that your pheasant is a survivor from the last season, which will make it a right old bruiser. The best advice we can give you when buying pheasant is to ask the butcher or game dealer how old the pheasant is.

If he or she doesn't know (or doesn't want to tell you!) there is a test you can conduct yourself. If you are buying the pheasant 'long legged', or unbutchered, examine the claws and beak. If they are soft and pliable, the bird is a young one. If they are well developed and hard, it is probably older. If the bird is oven ready, (i.e. fully plucked, without its head or claws) you can take a look at the breastbone. A hard, protruding breastbone indicates that the bird is well into its first or second year.

Some cooks believe that there is also a marked difference between cock (male) and hen (female) pheasants. They might claim that cock meat will be tougher. We haven't found this to be the case. Cock pheasants are bigger than hens, but this doesn't necessarily make them any trickier when it comes to roasting. If you buy your game oven ready, as most people do, you will have a hard time guessing the sex of any of it. When buying pheasants we base our decision on how to cook them on the age of the bird and the time of year. This really is a much more reliable guideline.

Guinea fowl

Is guinea fowl a game bird? Strictly speaking, the answer is no. In its native Africa, guinea fowl is a wild bird, but if you buy it in the UK it will certainly have been farmed. Like it or not, today's cook can choose between wild and farmed versions of nearly all game (see page 12 for a more detailed discussion of this issue). If you are troubled by the idea of any animal being raised for sport, you might wish to choose guinea fowl over pheasant, since it will most certainly have been raised specifically for the dinner table. However, guinea fowl comes with a few issues of its own, because sadly, like all farmed birds, it is possible to buy intensively reared guinea fowl.

However, many suppliers are committed to a truly free-range version. When bred well, guinea fowl is as tasty as pheasant, with a slightly less gamey and more 'corn-fed' flavour due to its grainy diet. You can swap any of our recipes for pheasant with guinea fowl and vice versa. What's more you can joint pheasant and guinea fowl in exactly the same way, and that is why we include them both in this chapter.

Jointing pheasant and guinea fowl

This will be easy if you have ever dealt with a whole chicken, as pheasant and guinea fowl are like hens, only slightly smaller and leaner. Place the bird on its back on a chopping board with its breast facing up and its legs to the right.

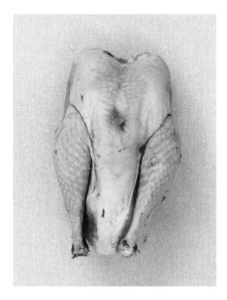

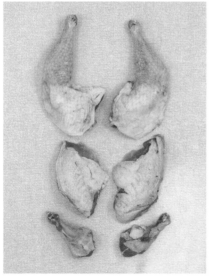

The easiest way to joint all birds is to start by removing the legs. Ease the leg nearest you gently away from the breast and, with a sharp boning knife, cut the stretched skin, near to the thigh (this avoids you cutting the skin over the breast meat). Now the leg falls naturally away from the breast. Hold it down on the board with the palm of your left hand, which will expose the socket, or joint. Work the tip of the knife delicately around this socket and the leg will come neatly away. You can now swing the other leg around to the front of your board and repeat the process.

You can further joint pheasant and guinea fowl legs to isolate the thigh meat. Lay the leg out with the thigh end to the left. Find the knee joint with your fingers and place your knife into the middle of the joint. You will be able to push the knife through this joint on any poultry. Now you have the two legs, divided into thighs and drumsticks. Guinea fowl drumsticks are very much like those on a chicken. Pheasant drumsticks are much trickier to cook and eat, due to the bird's very well developed tendons. We find the best way to deal with jointed pheasant legs is confit or casserole them (and sometimes, if we feel very flush, they go straight into the stock pot).

You are now left with the two breasts, left attached to the backbone. Using a cleaver or cook's knife, chop off the wing tips (don't discard them as they make good stock). Keep the bird breast up, with the (now exposed) 'parson's nose' or rump to the right. Using a large cooks knife again, work the blade under the breastbone towards the neck until you can lift the breasts clean away from the backbone. Keep the backbone for stock. You now have two breasts, on the breastbone. Some chefs and butchers call this the 'crown'. Some recipes in this book will call for game

birds to be cooked on the crown but if you want to separate the two breasts, here is how to do it: turn the breasts over so that the skin side is down, and the wishbone (two protrusions where the bird's neck would have started) is to your right. Hold the heel of your knife in the middle of the wishbone and, applying some leverage from heel to tip, cut the crown in half lengthways.

Breast meat is nearly always better cooked on the bone but to remove the meat from the breastbone switch back to a small boning knife and gently run it along the bone, easing the flesh away as you go. What you are left with will resemble a smaller, gamier version of a chicken supreme with the stub of the wing attached.

Spatchcocking guinea fowl

This is a term used to describe removing the backbone of poultry, thereby 'flattening' the meat, allowing the legs and breast to make contact with a grill or pan all at once. We do not spatchcock pheasant as a rule, because the legs are not great on or under a grill, but this is a great way to treat guinea fowl as well as partridge and quail (see page 45). Hold the bird breast-side down, in your right hand, with the neck cavity facing you. Using a pair of robust scissors (or even poultry shears) snip away at either side of the backbone from the neck downwards, finishing either side of the thighs. The backbone will lift clean away. Ease the legs and wings apart and place the bird on a chopping board, now breast-side up. Gently press the breast with the palm of your hand until the bird is flattened. You might hear a slight pop, as the wishbone breaks. This is normal.

Classic roasts and suggested trimmings

Roast pheasant

In our opinion, pheasant is the trickiest of game birds when it comes to roasting. The reason? Pheasant looks a lot like chicken and it can, on occasion taste a lot like chicken. But it will never behave like chicken in the oven. It simply doesn't have the requisite fat content, either in its skin or its flesh. That is why many people describe it as dry meat. In many ways, pheasant is more akin to turkey than any other meat. They have hard working legs, with tasty brown meat on them, but if you roast the pheasant conventionally, by the time those legs are cooked and yielding, the pale meat on the breast can be overdone. So, we have devised a cooking method that gets round this problem with no faffing about.

You will need
Half a pheasant per person (based on pheasants between 800g and 1kg)
1 medium to large onion per pheasant
duck fat, lard or unsalted butter
salt and freshly ground black pepper

Preheat your oven to 200°C / Gas Mark 6. Season the cavity of each pheasant generously with the salt and pepper. Rub about half a teaspoon's worth of salt on the skin of each bird. Peel and halve the onion.

You start cooking the pheasant on the stovetop. In a large-ish ovenproof pan or roasting tray, warm the fat as gently as possible over a low heat. Park the pheasant in this fat, on one side and cook the leg, gently, for about 10 minutes.

Whilst this happens, place the onion halves in the same pan, face down. You should keep checking the meat and the onion every couple of minutes to make sure the leg doesn't brown too quickly. Barbecue-like patches of carbonised pheasant skin (or onion for that matter) are not going to help this dish: you want to give the leg a very slow tan. Once this has been achieved, turn the pheasant over and repeat the process on the other leg.

Once both legs are browned nicely they will have been given a good head start on the breast, so now the pheasant can go into the oven. Place it on the backbone, and stabilise it by placing the onion halves either side of the carcass. This stops the pheasant from wobbling or falling onto one side whilst cooking.

Cooking times will depend on the size of the bird. 20 minutes should be plenty for an 800g pheasant, but add 5 minutes to the cooking time for every extra 100g. And do not forget to rest the pheasant after cooking. You should turn it onto the breastbone (i.e. upside down) and rest it for at least 10 minutes before jointing or carving, and serving.

Trimmings and stuffings
As with the smaller game birds, we find that cooking and serving stuffings on the side of the roast (as opposed to putting them in the cavity) is much better for the meat. This is especially true for pheasant, which is dry when the breast meat is cooked for too long (see roasting section above). If you really fancy stuffing a pheasant we highly recommend the ballotine recipe on page 35.

Pheasant and chestnuts are natural partners, with similar seasons, so the chestnut stuffing on page 234 is perfect with this bird. Given its mild similarity with turkey meat, pheasant actually makes a fine centrepiece for Christmas dinner and will go with any of the classic Christmas trimmings. Try it one year.

Roast guinea fowl

Although it looks similar to pheasant, guinea fowl behaves much more like chicken. Being a largely domesticated bird, it has the fat content of chicken in both its skin and meat. This has led some game aficionados to damn it as 'game lite' (or, worse still, as an out and out impostor). In fact we would characterise guinea fowl as having all the attributes of a really good, tasty version of corn fed chicken, due to its largely grain based diet. It can even taste a bit 'nutty' which makes it a great bird for roasting, with few embellishments.

You will need
half a guinea fowl per person (approximate weight 700–900g per bird)
100g unsalted butter per bird, at room temperature
salt and freshly ground black pepper

Preheat your oven to 200°C / Gas Mark 6. Season the cavity of each guinea fowl generously with salt and pepper. Working from the neck downwards, with your hands, carefully detach the skin away from the breast meat. This will leave a little pocket under the skin, into which you want to smear the butter, as gently as possible. Smooth the skin back over the butter and rub it, even more gently now, with about half a teaspoon of salt per bird. Rub the salt onto the legs too.

Place the bird, on its backbone, in a heavy-bottomed, ovenproof pan or roasting tray. Roast it for 30 minutes, if it is a 700g bird, but add 5 minutes per 100g above this weight. You can test guinea fowl for readiness just as you would a chicken; carefully insert a sharp knife or skewer into the deepest part of the thigh meat (where it meets the breast). If the juices run clear, with no pink tinge of blood, then the bird is ready. Unlike many game birds, we rest guinea fowl breast up: this is because the classic roasting method should give you a nice, 'chickeny', crispy skin. Rest the bird for at least 10 minutes before carving and serving.

Trimmings and stuffings

The lemon and mascarpone stuffing on page 237 is a classic way to treat a guinea fowl. For once we actually recommend putting this stuffing into the cavity of the bird. It is a very loose stuffing and you will need to 'sew' up the leg end of the cavity, using a toothpick or skewer. Up the cooking time from 30 minutes to 45.

Grilled guinea fowl

Guinea fowl is also a great bird for grilling or barbecuing. You can spatchcock it following the method in the jointing section of this chapter (page 22). Note that you don't need any oil for the seasoning or cooking; because the skin of guinea fowl is naturally fatty, like corn fed chicken.

You will need
half a guinea fowl per person
salt and freshly ground black pepper
4 sprigs of thyme per bird, leaves pinched off

Combine the seasonings and rub them over the inside and outside of the spatchcocked guinea fowl. Allow the meat to rest for half an hour with the seasoning. Heat a grill or barbecue until it is red hot and cook the guinea fowl, starting skin down until it is as marked as you wish. Then turn it over and cook for 10–15 minutes, depending on the intensity of the heat and the size of the bird. Make sure you test it for doneness. Carefully insert a sharp knife or skewer into the deepest part of the thigh meat (where it meets the breast). If the juices run clear, with no pink tinge of blood, then the bird is ready. Rest the guinea fowl for 10 minutes before serving.

Roast pheasant breast with lentils and green sauce

You can use pheasant or guinea fowl breast for this recipe. The lentils and green sauce would also pair very well with the traditional roast recipe on page 24. If you prefer to, you could buy ready-cooked puy lentils. These can simply be added to the cooked vegetables in place of the dried lentils and warmed through. You will need about 400g of pre-cooked lentils to match the dried amounts in this recipe.

serves 4

For the pheasant
200g puy lentils
2 tablespoons mild vegetable oil for
   cooking
1 shallot
1 carrot
1 stalk celery, finely diced

4 boned breasts of pheasant, skin on
4 more tablespoons mild olive oil for
   cooking
salt and fresh ground black pepper
125ml (a glass, really) of dry white wine

For the green sauce
1 garlic clove
2 anchovy fillets
1 shallot or small red onion
1 teaspoon capers
4–5 cocktail gherkins (cornichons)
1 tablespoon Dijon mustard
150ml olive oil
1 tablespoon wine (or sherry) vinegar
a large bunch of parsley (flat-leaf is
   best)
a small bunch of tarragon
salt and freshly ground black pepper

Make the green sauce first. Start with the base. Chop the garlic and anchovies together until they form a rough paste. Pop them into a mixing bowl. Dice the shallot or red onion as finely as possible and add it to the bowl. Chop the capers and cornichons and add them to the bowl with the mustard, oil and vinegar. This is now the base of the sauce and, in effect, the dressing for the leaves. Chop the parsley and tarragon together as roughly or as finely as pleases you really. Green sauce can be served almost as a rough, chopped salad, or as cohesive as a pesto. Whatever you do, don't blitz it, or you will end up with something like lawn clippings. Stir the herbs into the base and check the seasoning. You might like to add salt. You might want to sharpen it with more vinegar or loosen it with a splash more olive oil. The choice is yours: green sauce is a very adaptable recipe. Set the sauce aside, but don't refrigerate it.

Set your oven to 200°C / Gas Mark 6. Check the lentils for any small pieces of grit and place them in a good-sized saucepan. Cover them with a litre of water and bring them to a rapid boil. Keep a close eye on the lentils for the first 10 minutes of their cooking time. Remove any foam that comes to the water's surface. Reduce the heat after 10 minutes and allow the lentils to simmer gently. They can take anything from 30–40 minutes to cook from here on in, depending on their freshness. If the water level reduces too much you can top it up with a splash more from a boiled kettle.

While the lentils simmer, heat the oil gently in a wide-bottomed pan and add the diced vegetables, all at once. Add half a teaspoon of salt, stir it in, lower the heat as much as possible and cover the pan. Allow the vegetables to sweat this way for about 20 minutes, until they are sweet and tender. Do not let them brown. If they look like they might catch at any point you can add a splash of water (literally 2 tablespoons' worth). Once the lentils are cooked to your liking (they should be soft with just a little bite), stir in the vegetables and season with a little more salt and freshly ground black pepper if you wish. The lentils are quite plain but, remember, there is a lot going on in the green sauce. Now pour the lentils onto a wide dish (we use a fairly shallow-sided roasting tray), so that they cool and stop cooking. Set them to one side.

Place the pheasant breasts in a large mixing bowl and toss them with 2 tablespoons of the mild cooking oil, plus a seasoning of salt and pepper for each bird. Heat a wide-bottomed frying pan (preferably with an ovenproof handle) and add the final 2 tablespoons of oil. Fry the pheasant breasts fairly briskly, skin-side down, until they are golden brown. Turn them over and add the wine to the pan. Let the wine bubble for a few minutes, then transfer the pan to the oven and roast the pheasant breasts for about 12 minutes. Test them after this time by piercing them to see if the juices run clear. If they don't, give the birds 5 more minutes. Once done, remove them from the pan, but leave any roasting juices behind. Rest the pheasant breasts in a warm but not hot place.

Now add the lentils to the pheasant pan and warm them through. As you warm them, the lentils will pick up any extra flavours from the pan, which is lovely. Serve the rested pheasant breasts on top of the lentils. You can either adorn each portion with a dollop of green sauce, or pop it on the table and let people serve themselves.

Pot-roast guinea fowl legs with apple and cider

This recipe works better with guinea fowl than pheasant, as guinea fowl legs tend to be more succulent. However, you could also try the same recipe with whole partridges or quails.

serves 4

a small bunch of sage
2 tablespoons plain flour
salt and freshly ground black pepper
4 guinea fowl legs
2 large apples (Bramleys are excellent for this)
2 tablespoons mild olive oil for cooking
50g dry-cured streaky bacon or pancetta, diced
2 medium onions, diced finely
3 stalks celery, diced finely
2 tablespoons tomato purée
250ml strong cider (scrumpy is best)
1 litre (approximately) chicken stock or water
2 tablespoons unsalted butter

Chop the sage as finely as possible and mix it with the flour, salt and pepper. Toss this seasoned flour with the guinea fowl legs and set aside. Peel and core the apples, then cut them into rough sections (about eight pieces per apple is ideal).

Heat the cooking oil gently, in a wide bottomed pot or casserole and add the bacon. Cook it gently for a couple of minutes, or until it starts to colour and release fat. Remove with a slotted spoon and set it aside. Use the same pan to brown the chunks of apple. You can turn the heat up a little for this, as the apple pieces will caramelise slightly. Remove them and set them aside. Now use the same pan to brown the guinea fowl legs all over. Remove them and set aside, too.

Now add the diced onion and celery to the pot, with about half a teaspoon of salt. Lower the heat dramatically, stir in the bacon and cover with the lid so that the vegetables get a chance to sweat for 10–15 minutes. Do not let them brown. After this time, raise the heat, add the tomato purée and cider, stir them until combined and allow the mix to simmer rapidly for about 5 minutes.

Return the guinea fowl legs to the pot. Add just enough stock to cover the meat and slot in the apple pieces. Cover the pot and allow the casserole to simmer gently for about 40 minutes, or until the meat is good and tender, but not about to fall off the bone.

Finally, remove the legs, and then stir in the butter. Check the seasoning. You can either return the legs to the pot, and serve this dish as a slightly brothy casserole, or you can reduce the juices a little before either pouring the sauce over the legs on a serving dish.

Pheasant tagine

Moroccan tagines are slow cooked braises; the spicy cousins of European *potages* and casseroles. A tagine is a clay pot, which allows meat to braise slowly, until it can literally be pulled apart and eaten with fingers. You can use any ovenproof pot if you don't own a tagine, but in our experience cast iron, 'Le Creuset' type dishes and terracotta oven dishes are the best substitutes.

You can swap the pheasant in this recipe for guinea fowl, chicken or indeed whole quails and partridges. Many tagines have an element of fruit in them, and quince is ideal for this one, coming into season at around the same time as pheasant. If you can't get hold of a quince, substitute dried apricots, figs or dates instead.

serves 4–6

3 tablespoons mild olive oil for cooking
2 large-ish pheasants (ask for cocks if you have a friendly butcher or game supplier)
2 onions, diced finely
4 cloves garlic, chopped
salt and freshly ground black pepper
½ teaspoon saffron threads
½ teaspoon ground ginger
2 sticks cinnamon
1 quince, apple or pear
1 lemon
a small bunch parsley
a small bunch coriander

Joint the pheasants, following the instructions on page 22. Set them aside. You don't need stock for this recipe but, if you like, you can use the wings, backbones and the very ends of the legs (drumsticks) to make one.

Preheat your oven to 180°C / Gas Mark 4.

Heat the oil in your designated 'tagine pot' or casserole dish and brown the pheasant pieces all over, fairly briskly. Set them aside.

Add the onion and garlic to the remaining fat and juices, season with a generous pinch of salt, stir a couple of times and lower the heat as much as possible. Allow the onion mix to sweat like this for 10-15 minutes. Do not let it brown.

Dissolve the saffron threads in about 2 tablespoons of warm (but not boiling) water. Add them to the onions and garlic along with the ginger and cinnamon. Return the pheasant pieces to the pot. Cover them with water and season with salt and pepper. Do not stir the pot now. Peel and core the quince, then dice it roughly. Arrange the quince over the top of the pheasant and squeeze the lemon juice over everything. Now put the lid on the pot and put it in the oven. Bake the tagine for 40 minutes before checking the meat and quince for tenderness. If it is done to your liking, check the seasoning and adjust it if you wish.

Just before serving, chop the parsley and coriander and scatter them generously over the tagine. You could serve this with couscous, but we think the best accompaniment is naan-type flat bread, or even a crusty baguette.

2 Legs

Pheasant, Savoy cabbage, chestnuts and bacon

This pot roast could just as easily be done with guinea fowl or duck. You can throw it together very quickly, but it will taste like it took forever.

serves 4

1 large or 2 small pheasants
1 sprig rosemary
2 cloves garlic
125g soft butter
2 tablespoons olive oil for cooking
6 shallots, diced
1 stalk celery, diced
2 carrots, diced
1 small Savoy or round cabbage, cored and shredded
120ml (small glass) white wine
2 tablespoons brandy
1 tablespoon tomato purée
200ml water or stock (you could make your own from the pheasant)
6 rashers dry-cured smoked streaky bacon
salt and freshly ground black pepper, to taste
100g peeled, cooked chestnuts

Wash the pheasant, inside and out and pat it dry, thoroughly. Chop the rosemary and garlic and mix it with the butter. Smear the pheasant inside and out with the butter.

Heat the oil in a casserole or large pot with a tight-fitting lid and brown the pheasant(s) all over. Remove the bird(s) from the pot, leaving the oil. Add the shallots, celery and carrots and fry them quite briskly, allowing them to caramelise slightly. Stir in the cabbage. Add the wine, brandy, tomato purée and water or stock, and then return the bird(s) to the pot, breast-side up. Cover the breasts with the bacon rashers and season the dish well with salt and pepper. Cover the pot tightly with the lid or with tin foil and cook for about an hour on a gentle simmer on top of the oven.

After this time remove from the heat and test the bird(s) for readiness. If it is done, the leg(s) can be tugged away from the breast(s) with ease. Allow the cooked bird(s) to rest in the juices for at least 10 minutes before serving. You can remove the bacon rashers from the breast(s), chop them and combine them with the other ingredients before serving if you like, since they will probably fall off the bird(s) as soon as you start portioning!

Guinea fowl saltimbocca

'Saltimbocca' means, literally, 'to jump in the mouth'. It is a dish traditionally made from veal escalope or even white-fleshed fish such as red mullet. It works well with pheasant and guinea fowl or any white-fleshed bird. Tell your butcher you need the bird jointed, with the breast filleted. Keep the carcass to make stock.

serves 4

2 guinea fowl, jointed into breasts and legs
salt and freshly ground black pepper
12 large sage leaves
8 slices of Serrano ham
4 tablespoons light olive oil
100ml white wine
400ml chicken stock
1 tablespoon unsalted butter

Preheat the oven to 200°C / Gas Mark 6.

Season the breasts and legs with a little sea salt and freshly ground black pepper. Press two leaves of sage onto the skin of the breasts then one onto the thigh.

On a clean work surface lay out one slice of ham, place the first breast on top, skin-side down and carefully wrap the slice around the breast, finishing with the ham ends on the underside of the breast. Continue with each of the breasts and then come to the legs, again finishing on the underside. You can secure the ham with a toothpick if you wish.

In a wide non-stick pan, warm half of the olive oil and gently fry the legs for 2–3 minutes until the skin and ham is lightly crisped all round. Remove them to a roasting tray and bake for 10–12 minutes until the drumstick feels firm.

Meanwhile, heat the remaining olive oil in the pan and place the breasts skin-side down and gently fry over a low heat until the skin and ham have crisped and browned, about 5 minutes. Most of the cooking of the breasts is done on the skin side, so after this time the breasts should be about three- quarters done. Turn the breasts and fry on the underside for a further 3–4 minutes until the flesh is slightly springy. Transfer the breasts to a warm plate.

Take the legs from the oven and place them on the plate with the breasts. Tip the oil from the pan, then pour in the wine, letting it bubble for a few seconds, to be swiftly followed by the stock. Let this sauce reduce by about a quarter then whisk in the butter. Check the seasoning, it may need a touch of pepper but probably not salt, as the ham is quite salty.

Divide the breasts and legs between four plates and pour the reduced sauce over them. Serve with something soft and luscious like buttery mash or, proper Italian-style, with lentils.

2 Legs

Pheasant ballotine

'Ballotine' is a French term for boned, stuffed and rolled meat, mainly applied to chicken and game birds. At a push it can apply to large fish such as salmon or trout. You could use any of the stuffings in the condiment section of this book, but we favour the prune and pistachio version since the flavours complement the bird nicely. Though the ballotine can be served hot, it is equally good cold with preserved fruits or pickle.

serves 4–6

2 hen pheasants, boned
salt and freshly ground black pepper
Prune and pistachio stuffing (page 236)
1.5 litres of stock, made from the
  pheasant bones

Bone the birds first. Start by removing the wishbone, just at the neck opening, being careful not to pierce the breast. Turn the bird onto its breast and cut along either side of the backbone from the neck down. Gently run your knife along the bone and ease the flesh away from the carcass until you get to the thigh and wing joints.

Place the knife in between the ball and the sockets of the joint and give it a little twist to release, the wings and legs should still be intact, and then continue along the skeleton on either side until reaching the breast fillet. Scraping the knife along the bone, carefully detach the fillets, ensuring you don't puncture the skin.

Now lift the bird, slice away the remaining flesh from the skin and lay flat on a board. To remove the leg and wing bones, scrape the flesh away from the bone keeping the skin as intact as possible. Your bird is now ready to stuff. Repeat with the second bird.

Season the skin side of the birds with salt and pepper then lay them out on a board, flesh-side up, and lightly season the meat. Halve the stuffing mixture, form each half into sausage shapes and place in the middle of the birds. Pull up the edges, wrap the skin around the stuffing and you should have an even larger sausage. Tie with string at intervals of 2cm apart, also securing any loose edges with toothpicks.

Bring the stock to a simmer in a pan just large enough to hold the 2 birds. Slip the birds into the pot, bring the stock back to the simmer and gently poach, covered, over the lowest heat for 40 minutes or until tender.

To serve hot, slice the ballotine into 2cm rounds, remove the string and lay into warmed bowls. Ladle a little of the hot stock into the bowl. If you're serving it cold, leave the ballotine to cool completely in the stock. Once cold, slice the ballotine into thin rounds and serve with pickles and salad.

Confited pheasant with fennel and satsuma salad

You can confit pretty much any bird leg, from chicken right down to tiny quails, although that would be fiddly. If a recipe calls only for a bird's breast meat, we often preserve the legs for later, to use in salads, soups or to shred through beans and lentils. The amounts for the confit salt can be easily multiplied as it keeps for ages in a sealed jar, ready for your further confit needs.

serves 4

8 pheasant legs
500g duck fat

Confit salt
250g coarse sea salt
1 teaspoon whole black peppercorns
6 large sprigs thyme
3 large sprigs rosemary
2 cloves of garlic
6 juniper berries
3 strips of orange peel
3 strips of lemon peel

For the salad
2 small bulbs of fennel
juice of ½ juicy lemon
salt and freshly ground black pepper
2 teaspoons Dijon mustard
200g green beans
4 satsumas, clementines or oranges
100ml olive oil
2 bunches of watercress, trimmed

Confit the meat first. Put all of the ingredients for the salt in a food processor and give them a good blast. Select a non-metallic container that will fit all of the legs snugly. Scatter an even layer of salt over the base, then lay the legs on top. Spread more salt over the legs until they are completely submerged, then cover the container and refrigerate for 12 hours or overnight. Remove the legs from the cure, wash and pat them dry.

Preheat the oven to 140°C / Gas Mark 1.

Choose an ovenproof pan or casserole that will comfortably accommodate the legs and heat the duck fat there within. Pop the legs in, bring up to a simmer then cover and transfer to the oven. Gently cook for 1 hour then check the flesh, it should be soft and yielding, yet still attached to the bone. Depending on the age of the birds, it may take a little longer.

If you are going to serve the dish immediately, remove the legs, shake off the excess fat, lay them skin-side up on a baking tray and raise the oven temperature to 180°C / Gas Mark 4. If not, let them cool in the fat, transfer them to a container and refrigerate until needed.

For the salad, it's a good idea to start the fennel a bit earlier than everything else. Trim the stalks from the bulb then split them in half lengthways. Slice the fennel as finely as you can across the grain. A mandoline is the perfect tool for the job, (mind your fingers). Place the fennel in a bowl, squeeze over the lemon juice, season with sea salt and pepper, and mix in the mustard. Leave to stand for at least 20 minutes.

Now put the legs to roast in the oven for 10–12 minutes, until the skin is lovely and crisp.

Meanwhile, bring a pot of lightly salted water to the boil, plunge in the beans and cook for 5 minutes. Drain, then refresh the beans under cold running water. Carefully peel the satsumas, ensuring that all the white pith is removed, then slice lengthways into four.

To serve, add the olive oil to the fennel, mix thoroughly, then gently turn the beans, satsumas and watercress through. Divide between 4 plates and top each with 2 roasted pheasant legs.

Pheasant and ham terrine

You could substitute guinea fowl or even chicken breasts for this recipe. If you do, 4 chicken breasts will do nicely, since they are larger.

serves 8–10

6 pheasant breasts, skinned
25g unsalted butter
2 shallots, finely diced
250g chicken livers, trimmed
salt and freshly ground black pepper
8–10 slices of Serrano ham
1 egg yolk
200ml double cream
6 sage leaves, finely sliced

Preheat the oven to 140°C / Gas Mark 1.

Place the pheasant breasts, one at a time between a couple of sheets of clingfilm, and gently pound the plumper end of the breast with a mallet until the breasts are an even thickness, about 1cm.

Heat the butter in a heavy-based frying pan over a medium heat; add the shallots with a pinch of salt and sauté for 1 minute until they have just softened. Raise the heat under the pan and introduce the livers. Season them in the pan with another pinch of salt and quickly sear them on both sides. Tip the livers and shallots and any juices onto a plate to cool.

Line a 1-litre terrine with the slices of ham, leaving enough hanging over the edge of the terrine to cover the top when the dish is filled.

Whisk together the egg yolk and the cream, adding the juice that has come off the livers. Put one layer of pheasant into the bottom of the terrine using 2 of the pounded breasts. Trim them if necessary to fill any gaps. Grind over a little black pepper, then add half of the livers, sprinkle over half of the sage and spoon over a third of the cream mixture, finally covering this with a slice of ham. Repeat the procedure again ending up with the last layer of pheasant breast on top, spoon over the remaining cream, then fold the ham slices over to cover. Seal the top of the terrine with buttered foil, place it in a roasting pan and pour in boiling water to come halfway up the sides. Place the terrine in the oven and cook for 1¼ hours.

To test for doneness, insert a metal skewer or a small sharp knife into the middle of the terrine. It should come out hot. The best test is to hold it to your lip, not for too long though. If it's not hot, leave the terrine in the oven and look at it again after 10 minutes. Repeat this again if necessary.

When the terrine is cooked, remove it from its water bath and leave it to cool for 1 hour. Weigh the top of the terrine down by placing another terrine the same size on top, filled with a couple of food tins (eg: beans or tomatoes). If you don't have another terrine, cut out a piece of cardboard so that it fits the terrine like a lid, then wrap it in foil. This can be weighted down the same way. Leave the terrine weighted until it is completely cold and then refrigerate overnight.

To serve, run a knife gently around the sides of the terrine, invert onto a plate and carefully remove the mould. Carve thick slices with the sharpest knife you have. Serve with fruit chutney or cornichons.

Guinea fowl au vin

Traditionally coq au vin would employ a boiling fowl or an older, larger bird, too tough to roast, yet just right for a long slow braising. Young and tender birds such as pheasant and guinea fowl can be cooked in two stages: starting with the legs first and adding the breasts later, so that they are cooked *a point*, leaving them perfectly moist.

serves 4

80g unsalted butter
1 tablespoon olive oil
250g piece of smoked streaky bacon, cut into 1cm lardons
250g shallots or pickling onions
2 guinea fowl, jointed (page 22)
50g plain flour, seasoned with salt and pepper
200g button mushrooms
400ml red wine
600ml chicken stock
3 cloves of garlic
3 bay leaves
a small bunch of thyme
salt and freshly ground black pepper

Preheat the oven to 140°C / Gas Mark 1.

Warm 50g of the butter and the olive oil in a heavy-based frying pan and gently sauté the bacon over a medium heat until all the pieces are browned. Transfer with a slotted spoon to a casserole dish. Add the shallots to the same pan and sauté them until they have browned, then add these to the casserole dish.

Cut the breasts in half again through the middle so that there are 8 breast pieces. Dust the thighs and drumsticks in the seasoned flour, shaking off any excess. Brown these in the same pan, turning them over a few times until the skin is crisp. Add these to the dish. Now dust and brown the breast pieces but this time set them aside. Halve the button mushrooms, peel and crush the garlic cloves and sauté in the remaining butter. Add these to the casserole dish as well.

Tip off any fat lingering in the pan and then pour in the red wine and let it bubble while you scrape the bottom and sides of the pan, dislodging any tasty morsels. Reduce the wine by about a third, then add the chicken stock. Once this has come to the boil, pour it into the dish then tuck in the herbs. Season with a good pinch of sea salt and pepper and bring the dish up to a gentle boil then cover and place in the oven. Cook these pieces for 20 minutes until they are tender. Add the breast pieces and the mushrooms and continue cooking for another 25 to 30 minutes until these, too, are tender.

Strain the sauce into another pan, bring it to the boil and reduce by about a third to thicken it slightly. Pour the finished sauce back over the guinea fowl and simmer it all together for another minute before serving.

Murgh-style guinea fowl

'Murgh' is a modern Indian term to imply that the dish came from the Moghal age. This type of curry will be recognisable to you as a korma, which on the subcontinent would be better recognised as 'Murgh-style', that is to say, rich with spices, yet smoothed out with yoghurt or butter. Chillies are optional in all kormas, but they give the mild dishes a bit of a kick.

serves 4

2 medium onions
2 tablespoons fresh ginger, grated
6 cloves garlic, grated
4–5 tablespoons vegetable oil
salt
2 guinea fowl
8 cardamom pods
2 cinnamon sticks
1 teaspoon black peppercorns
4 bay leaves
100g ground almonds
1 tablespoon ground cumin
400ml natural yoghurt
2 green chillies (optional)
½ teaspoon garam masala
1 teaspoon saffron threads, soaked in
   100ml water

Preheat the oven to 160°C / Gas Mark 3.

Slice the onions finely. Prepare the ginger and garlic. Set them all aside. Heat a large, heavy-based pan over a medium heat and pour in the oil. Lightly season the birds with sea salt, then slowly brown them all over, until the skin is nice and crisp. This should take around 5 minutes. Transfer the birds to a roasting tin.

Add the whole spices and the bay leaves to the pan and when they start to splutter add the onions. Fry them, stirring occasionally until they have softened, then add the garlic and ginger and sauté for a further 3–4 minutes. Add the almonds, cumin and yoghurt and 2 good pinches of sea salt along with 200ml of water and bring the mixture up to the boil. Split the green chillies down their length and mix them in now if you are using them. Pour the sauce over the birds making sure they are properly coated, cover with a sheet of foil and place them onto the middle shelf of the oven. Braise for 30 minutes.

Remove the lid and add the garam masala and the saffron and continue to cook for another 10 minutes. Remove the birds from the oven, loosely cover the dish and leave to rest in a warm place for 10 minutes. Serve with steamed basmati rice.

Partridge and quail

Partridge and quail are, to some extent, like mini versions of their distant cousins pheasant and guinea fowl. They have plenty of succulent white meat on their breasts, although it tends to be sweeter and more delicate than that on larger birds. With partridge at least, there is also quite a pronounced gamey note to the meat, since it is the wilder of the two. Some partridge, it would seem, are wilder than others, but we shall come to this in a minute.

The partridge is a non-migratory bird that thrives in the UK year round. However, pretty much all the partridge you can buy in this country will have been managed, like pheasant, on country estates. The chicks are hand reared then released as young adults, where, once the game season opens in September, they will be shot for sport as well as dinner. Two types of partridge are available to the cook. The most common is sometimes known as red-legged or, confusingly, French (even though it will have been raised and shot in the UK). This is because, historically speaking, the red-leg is an interloper, brought in by game breeders because it was easier to rear than our own, truly native, grey partridge. This bird never took kindly to being managed and, unlike pheasant, which obligingly hangs round the area in which it was raised, fattening itself on strategically placed feed, the grey partridge, once released, reverts to being a wild, foraging bird. It is harder work to breed grey partridge for shoots, even though aficionados claim they taste better due to their foraging habits, and they are increasingly rare as a result. Because of its scarcity, grey partridge can fetch a premium not unlike grouse (see page 66). Expect to pay two-or-three times the price of red-legged partridge if you do come across native partridge.

Quail is no longer, strictly speaking, a game bird. The species is migratory, and used to be hunted in Europe during the spring and summer, when it visited from Africa. Nowadays, most quail is a farmed, Asian variety. It has always been popular in France and Spain, but in recent years quail has become an established feature on restaurant menus in the UK. Sadly, the burgeoning popularity of quail (and its eggs) has led to some pretty intensive farming practices, and the handy, 'chef friendly', portion-sized birds can be reared in battery-like conditions. Buyer beware: a properly 'free range' quail is not easy to come by, especially in a supermarket and, when you do find it, it isn't cheap. This is because it isn't easy to farm quails if you allow them to behave naturally. They need tall aviaries in which to fly, safe from predators. Luckily, you can spot the factory farmed quail a mile off. It is a slightly insipid, scrawny specimen that looks and tastes like a titchy chicken. Good, free-range quail is a world away from the intensively farmed version. It looks robust, like a partridge, with plump breast meat and quite muscular wings. And it tastes incredibly tender and juicy. Once, when free-range quail was all but impossible to get hold of, we used to avoid it, but now we tend to think of it as summer partridge which, ironically, is what it once was. Although partridge are slightly bigger, the two birds can be cooked and served in similar ways. For that reason, all the recipes in this chapter are interchangeable.

How to prepare quail and partridge

The good news for lazy cooks (like us!) is that there isn't really any call for jointing these essentially portion-sized birds. For roasting and pot-roasting they are simply unbeatable left whole. Moreover, jointing them would compromise their juiciness and tenderness. However, they can both be 'spatchcocked' for grills and barbecues. More on that in a moment.

If you buy quail and partridge from a game dealer or local butcher, they will probably have been gutted, but the livers and hearts are likely to have been left in the breast cavity. Whilst these parts are deliciously edible, they are best removed before you do anything else as they can taint the breast meat and make it bitter, especially where it meets the bone. This is easily done: simply don a rubber glove (unless you are particularly un-squeamish) and reach into the cavity from the leg end using your fore and middle fingers. Locate any remaining offal and give it a gentle tug. It will come away easily and should remain intact. The livers and hearts of small game birds have a much more intense flavour than chicken or duck giblets. If you don't like this, you can reduce the bitterness by soaking them in milk for a couple of hours. This is also a good way of prolonging their shelf life by a day or two. You can use the giblets in any stuffings or pâtés that you might want to serve with roast game birds (see our section on stuffings, pages 234 to 237).

Spatchcocking

This is a term used to describe removing the backbone of poultry, thereby 'flattening' the meat, allowing the legs and breast to make contact with a grill or pan all at once. It speeds up cooking time, and allows marinades to permeate the flesh more easily. If you like barbecues, this is a great way to treat any bird.

Hold the bird breast-side down, with one hand, with the neck cavity facing you. With the other hand using a pair of robust scissors (or even poultry shears), snip away at either side of the backbone from the neck downwards, finishing either side of the thighs. The backbone will lift clean away. Ease the legs and wings apart and place the bird on a chopping board, now breast-side up. Gently press the breast with the palm of your hand until the bird is flattened. You might hear a slight pop, as the wishbone breaks. This is normal. Now the spatchcocked bird is ready for seasoning or marinating.

Classic roasts and recommended trimmings

Roast partridge

For roasting all small game birds we use a technique we like to call hot-pan-hot-oven. Perhaps, for want of a better name this could be described as pan roasting, although that sounds a bit cheffy!

You will need a cast-iron frying pan with an ovenproof handle. Ideally, if you are a fan of cooking small game birds, the diameter of the pan will not be much bigger than they are: this stops them wobbling around and falling on their sides in the oven, which will make them cook unevenly.

Partridge's naturally pronounced flavour and robust meat is best left unaltered when roasted and, for this reason, we tend not to marinate it or lard it by covering the breast with strips of bacon. Whilst some people might say that all game needs larding to prevent dryness, we think that the hot-pan-hot-oven method allows us to cook partridge fast enough for it to retain all its juiciness and flavour unassisted.

Allow 1 partridge per person (they are usually between 400 and 500g each); if cooking a large-ish batch, ask your butcher to have them roughly the same size for even cooking times.
duck fat, lard or unsalted butter
salt and freshly ground back pepper

Preheat the oven to 250°C / Gas Mark 9 (sometimes this will be the 'max' setting on modern electric, fan-assisted ovens).

Season each partridge inside and out with a fairly generous pinch each of salt and pepper. Set the birds aside. Heat 2 tablespoons per bird of the fat in the frying pan over a brisk flame until the fat just starts to bubble. Reduce the heat to medium and place the birds in the pan, on one side, so that you start to brown one of the legs. Allow the leg to fry for about 2 minutes then turn the bird onto the other leg and repeat the process. Next, turn the bird onto its breast so that the backbone is facing you, and fry the breast for a minute or so, until it just starts to brown. Then turn the bird all the way over again so that it is now on its back. Place it straight into the oven, carefully, so that the bird does not roll over onto a leg-side. Roast for 12 minutes. (Just in case you have a really big partridge, add a minute's cooking time per 100g over 500.) Test the partridge by pressing your thumb and forefinger on the fattest part of the breast just where it meets the wing tips. It will feel properly firm, but with a very subtle 'give'. If it feels underdone, return it to the oven but test it again every 2 minutes.

If it feels ready, turn the partridge onto its breast and allow it to rest, facing down like this for 10 minutes. This will allow it to become tender, like a steak. In fact, it is probably worth pointing out that, of all the game birds, partridge can feel the most taut when it comes out of the oven. You might think that it is going to be tough or even overcooked, but the meat will relax drastically when rested.

Trimmings for classic roast partridge
These include bread sauce (see page 238); game chips (page 242) and sage and breadcrumb stuffing (page 236). We prefer to serve stuffings on the side for partridge as filling the cavity can slow down the cooking time and make the breast meat a little too dry.

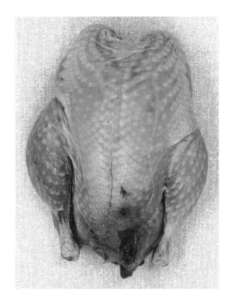

Roast quail

Quail tends to be about two-thirds the size of a partridge, which can still be good for a portion. You want the biggest quails you can get hold of for roasting. Really diddy specimens are perhaps best spatchcocked and grilled, allowing two birds per portion.

Season the quails inside and out as for partridge (see above) then follow the same hot-pan-hot-oven method, on the same temperature settings. Reduce the roasting time in the oven to 8 minutes, adding 1 minute more per 100g over the average size of 300g.

If you like, you can lard quails with thin rashers of dry-cured, streaky bacon (smoked or unsmoked). Simply wrap two rashers over each breast and secure them with a toothpick underneath the backbone. Be extra careful not to let the bacon get too dark when browning the birds in the pan. Recommended trimmings for roast quail include Boozy Prunes (page 241) or even the Prune and Pistachio Stuffing (page 236), served on the side.

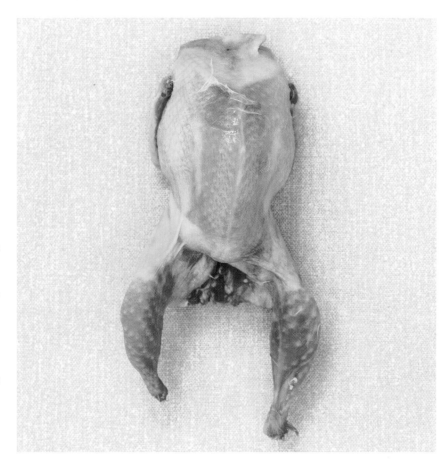

Partridge satay

Small game birds such as partridge and quail are ideal for barbecuing on skewers. 'Satay' is a popular south-east Asian marinade for grilled meat and seafood. It is also the name of the sweet peanut 'sambal' (sauce) served alongside it. If peanuts aren't your thing, you can serve the barbecued birds as they are, with wedges of lime and a simple leaf salad. This recipe requires a few special, oriental ingredients (though we list substitutes). You won't find partridge satay in Jakarta (or so we imagine), so there is no need to go for all-out authenticity.

If you live near a Chinese or oriental supermarket, it's easy to get hold of fermented shrimp paste (sold as 'kapi' or 'belachan'). If you can't, or don't fancy it, dried shrimps are a good substitute. Tamarind can also be bought in oriental (and some western) supermarkets. We prefer to use the ready-made extract, which looks like a dull version of tomato purée and is easier to keep in the fridge. Otherwise you will need to buy the seeds, soak them in warm water, and then sieve them. It is the sharp extract, not the seed that you use for cooking. The juice of a lime or lemon is a good substitute. If buying kaffir lime leaves, look for frozen rather than dried, as they have a better flavour. Lime zest is a good swap for the leaves.

serves 4

For the meat
6 partridges
skewers for barbecuing
1 level tablespoon coriander seeds
1 level tablespoon cumin seeds
400ml (roughly a tin) coconut milk
¼ teaspoon ground turmeric
2 tablespoons Thai fish sauce or light soy sauce
2 tablespoons unrefined sugar (or palm sugar)

For the sauce
2 heaped tablespoons crunchy peanut butter
1 teaspoon shrimp paste (kapi) or dried shrimps
250ml hot water
2 tablespoons soy sauce
2 tablespoons tamarind extract or the juice of a lime or lemon
2 teaspoons honey
1 teaspoon sesame oil
2 kaffir lime leaves (or grated zest of half a lime)
2 tablespoons vegetable oil
2 small shallots, diced
3 cloves garlic, chopped to almost resemble a paste
1 or 2 small red chillies, chopped to almost resemble a paste (you can chop them whole or remove the seeds depending on how hot you like your food)

Spatchcock the partridges following the instructions on page 45. Then halve them along their length as you remove the backbone. Traditionally, satay is served in three pieces so this allows three halves of a partridge per diner.

Soak the skewers in water, if they are wood or bamboo. Heat a small frying pan and dry roast the coriander and cumin seeds for about a minute, until they give off their distinctive aroma. Set them aside and, once they are cooled sufficiently, grind them with a pestle or small blender.

Combine the cumin and coriander with the coconut milk, turmeric, fish sauce and sugar. Finally, massage the marinade into the birds, then leave them in the fridge, ideally for at least a couple of hours, although one will do. While the birds are marinating, prepare all the ingredients for the sauce if you plan to serve them with it. Don't actually cook out the sauce until the meat is cooked and resting.

Once ready to cook, thread the birds onto the skewers; three halves per skewer. Heat a grill or barbecue and cook the birds, turning at least twice, for about 8 minutes. As you grill, brush them with any marinade that hasn't been absorbed. Allow the cooked satay to rest for about 5 minutes before serving.

Put the peanut butter into one small bowl and the kapi or dried shrimps into another. Divide the hot water between them and leave each bowl for a good 10 minutes or so. Drain the shrimpy bowl of all its water and either add the kapi to the peanuts or, using a pestle and mortar or small food processor, grind the shrimps until they almost resemble a paste and add them to the peanuts. Stir the peanuts and shrimps with the peanutty water in that bowl until you have a loose, murky and frankly unpromising looking paste. Never fear. Add the soy sauce, tamarind or lime, then add the honey and the sesame oil. Combine the mix thoroughly. Set aside.

Shred the lime leaf as finely as possible, if using. The easiest way to do this is to remove the leaves from their central stems, roll them into cigar shapes, then cut across the end of the little lime leaf 'cigar'. Heat the oil in a small pan or wok and, when it is hot, briskly fry the shallots, garlic and chilli. When they are starting to catch and soften, add the peanut mix and allow it to bubble fiercely. As soon as it starts to thicken and darken, move it from the heat, into a serving dish. Garnish with the lime leaves or zest and serve with the barbecued partridge.

2 Legs

game: a cookbook

Quails on toast with white onion purée and watercress

A dish that works well with partridge or quail. You can incorporate bacon if you like, just follow the instructions for larding and roasting quail on page 47.

The sweet-ish onion purée here is seasoned like bread sauce, only it sits on toast instead of being mashed with stale bread. The cooking method is actually a variation on the French onion sauce 'soubise'. You don't have to blitz it if you'd like a more rustic version. The sauce is also good with any of the classic roasts in this book, especially pheasant, wild duck and venison. The watercress is a great foil for the sweetness of the sauce, but you could swap in rocket, or pea shoots when they are in season, or a mix of all the above.

serves 4

100g soft unsalted butter
75ml whole milk
3 medium onions or 6 shallots, peeled and finely sliced
2 cloves garlic, chopped to almost resemble a paste
2 cloves
1 bay leaf
4 tablespoons crème fraîche
salt and freshly ground black pepper
4 large quails (approximately 300g each)
duck fat or lard
4 rounds good bread (we prefer sourdough for toast)
splash of white wine
2 bunches (or 1 x 85g bag) watercress or similar leaf

First make the onion purée. Heat half the butter very, very gently and, when it has melted, add the milk, then stir in the onions and garlic with the cloves, the bay leaf and a generous pinch of salt. Cover and allow the onions to sweat for 10–15 minutes, but do not let them brown. If they look as if they might, add about 3 tablespoons of water to the mix. Once the onions are soft, stir in the crème fraîche and continue to cook, as gently as is humanly possible, for about 45 minutes, or until the onion is super soft. If you have a double boiler or a good trivet, so that you can cook with indirect heat, that's even better. Allow the sauce to cool for 10 minutes, and then remove the cloves and bay leaf. Either purée the sauce or leave it as it is. Set it aside while you deal with the quails.

Set the oven to 250°C / Gas Mark 9. Generally season each bird inside and out with salt and pepper. Set the birds aside. Heat 2 tablespoons of the fat in a large frying pan over a brisk flame until the fat just starts to bubble. Reduce the heat to medium and place the birds in the pan, on one side, so that you start to brown one of the legs. Allow the leg to fry for about 2 minutes then turn the birds onto the other leg and repeat the process. Then turn the birds onto their breasts and fry for a minute or so, until they just start to brown. Then turn the birds onto their backs again and pop them into the oven, carefully, so that the birds do not roll over onto a leg-side. Roast for 8 minutes. (Just in case you have really big quails, add a minute's cooking time per 50g over 300g.) Check how cooked the quails are by pressing your thumb and forefinger on the fattest part of the breasts, just where they meet the wing tips. The meat will feel properly firm, but with a very subtle 'give'. While the quails rest, toast the bread, spread it with the remaining butter and then divide the onion purée between all the slices. Park the quails on the onion purée just before serving. If you have lots of juices in the pan you could deglaze it with a splash of white wine and anoint the quails with the juices. Garnish the plates with the leaves of your choice and serve. This is definitely a dish to eat with the fingers.

Deep-fried partridge with garlic and white pepper

Game birds respond well to deep-frying, but they tend to be on the dry side. The best way round this is an old Indonesian trick: poaching them first in a *court bouillon*. This keeps the meat incredibly tender and allows a super fast turn around the fryer. The method also works well with chicken and quail.

serves 4

4 partridges
salt and freshly ground black pepper
4 shallots
8 cloves garlic
2cm piece fresh ginger
2 bay leaves
1 level teaspoon white peppercorns
   (you can use black pepper)
50g plain flour
2 eggs
mild vegetable oil for deep-frying
2 limes or lemons (optional)

Season the partridges generously inside and out with salt and freshly ground black pepper. Set them aside. Peel the shallots and garlic. Place 2 of the shallots and 4 of the garlic cloves in a large saucepan, whole. Slice the remaining shallots and garlic cloves finely and set them aside. Add the partridges, the ginger and bay leaves, then just enough cold water to cover everything. Season the water with a teaspoon of salt. Bring the water to a vigorous simmer then remove it from the heat. Leave the partridges in the water until they have cooled enough for you to handle them easily (it should take about half an hour) and don't chill them artificially.

Remove the partridges from the water and halve them down the length. Remove the rib cage and any other sharp bones from inside the breast, using a small filleting knife. Dry the partridges thoroughly.

Grind the white peppercorns. Combine them with the flour and another half teaspoon of salt. Pop this mix into a large mixing bowl. Beat the eggs in another bowl then dip the partridge halves into the egg mixture. Remove them and coat them with the flour. Now repeat the process one more time so that they are double coated with the egg and flower mixture.

Set them aside. Heat the oil in a large pan or deep-fat fryer, to 165°C. If you are using a pan test the oil for readiness by dropping a small cube of bread into the oil. If it fizzes enthusiastically and browns within a minute, the oil is hot enough to fry. Cook the partridges in the oil until they are golden and crispy; it will take approximately 3 minutes. Set them on kitchen towel to drain. Meanwhile, fry the shallot and garlic slices briefly until they are also golden, then drain them. Serve the partridge garnished with the shallot and garlic and, if you wish, wedges of lemon or lime.

Pot-roast quails or partridges and canellini beans

Pot roasts or casseroles made with partridges or quails are very quick to put together, since the meat benefits from relatively quick cooking. The three following recipes work well with almost any white meat. You could swap in guinea fowl or rabbit.

This recipe will be even faster if you use tinned beans.

serves 4

200g dried canellini beans, soaked in
    cold water overnight and drained (or
    1 x 400g tinned canellini)
2 cloves garlic, peeled but left whole
3 leaves sage
3 tablespoons mild olive oil for cooking
4 partridges or large quails
2 onions, diced
2 leeks, diced
2 stalks celery, diced
salt and freshly ground black pepper
125ml (a glass of) white wine
1 teaspoon tomato purée
good extra-virgin olive oil

If you are using fresh beans, deal with them first. Place them in a large pot with a litre of cold water. Bring the water to a rolling boil for 10 minutes, skimming the foam that comes to the surface. Drain the beans and return them to the pot with another litre or so of water, and make sure it covers the beans by at least 2cm. Add the whole garlic cloves and sage leaves to the pot and bring the beans to a simmer until they are really tender, with no bite. It is hard to say how long this will take because it depends on the freshness of the beans. Check them after 45 minutes, then keep checking them every 20 minutes or so. Don't be shy of topping up the water, and don't add salt to the pot as this can toughen the skins.

Once the beans are fully cooked, set them aside in their stock. Heat the oil in a large pot (big enough for all the birds) and brown the partridges or quails fairly briskly on all sides. Remove them and set aside. Add the onion, leeks and celery to the pot with half a teaspoon of salt. Stir once and lower the heat as much as possible. Cover the pot and allow the vegetables to sweat for 15–20 minutes. Do not let them brown. Raise the heat. Add the white wine and let it simmer fast until it evaporates by about two-thirds. Stir in the tomato purée.

Now return the partridges to the pot with the beans and just enough of their stock to cover everything. If there isn't enough, you can use water. Season the pot, bring it up to a simmer, cover and cook for 40 minutes. Allow the birds to rest in the pot for 10 minutes before checking the seasoning, then serving them. Garnish each bowl of the bean stew with a good slug of olive oil if you wish.

Pot-roast partridge or quail with turnips and their greens

The turnip top is a sadly underrated thing. It's a flavoursome green, as delicate as spinach but with a lovely mustardy note to it. If you can't get hold of turnips with their greens attached, you can leave them out of the recipe; it will be very flavoursome just as it is. But you could swap in spinach, chard, or even rocket if you want greenery.

serves 4

4 partridges or large quails
salt and freshly ground black pepper
1 x bunch of turnips (large or small, approximately 300g), plus 1 x bunch turnip tops, if available
3 tablespoons duck fat or lard or butter
2 rashers smoked streaky bacon, diced
2 onions, diced
4 cloves garlic, chopped
2 stalks celery, diced
125ml (a glass of) white wine
1 teaspoon tomato purée
1 litre fresh chicken or game stock

Season the birds generously inside and out with salt and pepper and set them aside. Pull the green tops off the turnips and wash them thoroughly, as you would spinach. Remove about two thirds of the stalks. Set the tops aside. Dice the turnips next.

Heat the fat in a large pot (big enough to hold all the birds) and brown the bacon, fairly briskly. Remove it with a slotted spoon. Now brown the birds, briskly, on all sides. Remove them and set aside. Add the vegetables to the pot with half a teaspoon of salt, stir them once, lower the heat as much as possible and allow the vegetables to sweat for 15–20 minutes. Don't let them brown. After this time, turn up the heat, add the white wine, bacon and tomato purée. Allow the wine to simmer briskly until it has evaporated by about a third.

Return the birds to the pot with just enough stock to cover them. Bring the stock to a simmer and cook the birds for about 40 minutes. Check the seasoning and remove the birds from the casserole. Wilt in the turnip greens and return the birds to the pot one more time to serve.

2 Legs

Pot-roast partridges or quails in yoghurt

Tom's mum used to make this with chicken when he was little. You can also swap in rabbit, which is delicious.

serves 4

4 partridges or large quails
salt and freshly ground black pepper
3 tablespoons soft unsalted butter
1 tablespoon olive oil
2 onions, diced
2 cloves garlic, chopped
250ml passata (or sieved tomatoes)
100ml chicken or game stock
250ml Greek yoghurt (don't use a low-fat version)

Season the birds generously inside and out with salt and pepper. Heat the butter and oil very gently in a pot large enough to hold the birds. Brown the birds all over as gently as possible. Remove them and set them aside.

Lower the heat under the pan, add the onions and garlic with half a teaspoon of salt and stir once. Cover the pot and allow the onions to sweat for about 15 minutes. Do not let them brown. Add the passata and the stock to the onions and return the birds to the pot. Bring to a simmer and cook for 40 minutes, or until the birds feel nice and tender. Remove them from the pot at this point. If the juices seem a little brothy you can keep simmering for 5 minutes or so with the lid off, just to reduce them a little. Check the seasoning.

Finally, remove the pot from the heat and stir in the yoghurt. Return the birds to the pot or pour the juices over them onto a serving dish. Do not cook the casserole again once you have added the yoghurt. This is great with old-fashioned garlic bread, by the way.

2 Legs

Quails, snails and oak leaf

This is a dish that should be attributed to Jonathon Jones, the pioneering chef of the Anchor and Hope in Waterloo. It started its life as a delicious and robust snail and bacon salad. However, the flavours marry really well with the sweetness of the quail.

serves 4

2 tablespoons unsalted butter
4 quails
salt and freshly ground black pepper
2 thick slices of sourdough bread
3 tablespoons duck fat
250g piece of smoked streaky bacon, cut into strips or lardons about 1cm x 3cm
24 snails, out of their shells
1 banana shallot, finely sliced
1 clove of garlic, crushed
2 teaspoons good wine vinegar
1 head of oak leaf

For the vinaigrette
½ teaspoon Dijon mustard
20ml good red wine vinegar
60ml extra-virgin olive oil

Preheat the oven to 200°C / Gas Mark 6.

Melt the butter in a heavy-based frying pan large enough to hold all the birds snugly. Season the quails inside and out with a little salt and pepper, introduce them to the pan and gently brown them all over on a low heat. When the birds are sufficiently coloured, rest them on their backs and roast them in the oven for 10 minutes.

Remove the birds to a warmed plate and rest them breast-side down for another 10 minutes. Meanwhile, make the vinaigrette by mixing together the mustard, red wine vinegar and olive oil and season with salt and pepper.

Make the croûtons by cutting the bread into cubes about 1cm by 3cm and gently fry them in 2 tablespoons of the duck fat in the same heavy-based pan, then set aside.

Add the remaining duck fat to the pan and fry the lardons until they are lightly crisped. Pop the snails into the pan, toss them to coat in the fat and let them heat through. Add the sliced shallot and garlic, stirring all the time. Allow them to just slightly brown, being careful not to let them singe. Deglaze the pan with the wine vinegar and remove it from the heat.

To serve, toss the oak leaf with the croûtons and the vinaigrette in a bowl then scatter over the snails and bacon. Mix thoroughly (best done with your hands), and divide the salad between warmed plates. Nestle the quails amongst the salad and serve immediately.

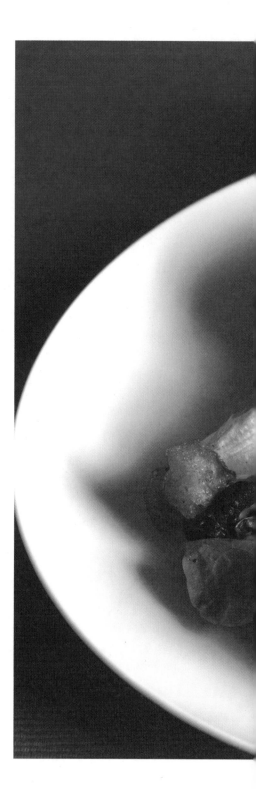

2 Legs

game: a cookbook

Raised partridge pie

An impressive centrepiece at any gathering, raised pies may look tricky to make but they are actually rather easy.

serves 8–10

500g lean pork shoulder, diced into 1cm
  cubes
375g minced belly of pork
100g smoked streaky bacon rashers,
  finely sliced
8 partridge breasts, skinned
2 blades of mace
12 sage leaves, finely sliced
1 egg, beaten

For the hot watercrust pastry
260g lard
1 teaspoon salt
750g of plain flour
1 tablespoon icing sugar
1 egg

Starting with the pastry, pour 300ml of water into a stainless-steel saucepan, add the lard and salt and bring to a simmer over a medium heat. When the lard has completely melted, add the flour and icing sugar and beat it in thoroughly with a wooden spoon. Turn the warm dough out onto a clean surface, make a well in the centre and break in the egg. Knead the egg into the dough by pulling in the sides of the pastry over the eggy surface, pushing down, turning and repeating. It will incorporate quite quickly so continue kneading until the dough is smooth, about 3 minutes.

Remove a quarter of the dough, pat it into a disc and set aside to cool. Form the remaining dough into a large disc, place that into the bottom of a 24cm spring form tin and slowly and carefully work the pastry up the sides of the pan with your finger tips, making sure there

are no holes or gaps. Cover and chill for 2 hours.

Preheat the oven to 200°C / Gas Mark 6.

Place the pork, bacon, mace and sage into a large bowl, season with a good pinch each of salt and freshly ground black pepper and mix together until all is well combined.

Place half the meat filling into the pastry shell, but don't pack it in too tightly – leave a little room around the edges. Season the partridge breasts and lay them overlapping the pork and then top them with the remaining filling, dome like, leaving a small gap around the sides to tuck the lid into.

Roll out the remaining pastry into a 25cm disc, and drape it over the top of the filling. Dampen the pastry edges with the beaten egg and pinch together to seal well all around.

Make a hole in the centre of the pie, brush the top with the beaten egg and place onto a baking tray. Bake for 30 minutes, then turn the oven down to 180°C / Gas Mark 4 and cook for a further 45 minutes. If the pie begins to colour too much, cover it with a sheet of foil.

Remove the pie from the oven and leave to rest for 5 minutes before removing the spring form ring. Brush the sides of the pie with a little more beaten egg and return to the oven for 10 minutes more. It should be crisp and a lovely golden brown all over.

Cool slightly before serving warm, or cold, with a sharp chutney or piccalilli.

Partridge escabeche

'Escabeche' is a Spanish method of marinating fish or fowl in a hot vinaigrette, essentially curing them. Escabeche is best prepared 24 hours in advance. It should be served at room temperature, with loads of crusty bread and salad. This would be perfect for an early autumn picnic.

serves 4

150ml olive oil
4 partridges, spatchcocked (see quail page 45)
salt and freshly ground black pepper
1 medium onion, finely sliced
1 bulb fennel, finely sliced
2 large cloves of garlic, finely sliced
300ml red wine vinegar
150ml water
4 sprigs of thyme
2 bay leaves
1 teaspoon black peppercorns
4 strips of orange peel

Heat 2 tablespoons of the olive oil in a wide, heavy-based frying pan. Lightly season the birds on both sides with salt and pepper and gently fry them, skin-side down, over a medium heat until the skin has browned, then turn them and seal the underside. Remove the birds from the pan and set them aside.

In the same oil add the onion, fennel and garlic and sauté for 2–3 minutes until they have softened slightly. Pour in the rest of the olive oil, vinegar, and water and add the herbs, peppercorns and peel, along with a good pinch of salt, and bring to the boil. Return the partridges to the pan and bring the whole to a gentle bubble, making sure the birds are completely covered. Simmer over a low heat for 25 minutes until the birds are tender.

Transfer the birds to a non-metallic dish, cover them with the vegetables and their cooking liquor, and let the escabeche come to room temperature. Cover and refrigerate for 24 hours before serving.

Take the escabeche out of the fridge a good half-hour before dishing up to allow it to come to room temperature.

Grouse

Grouse is legendary. This diminutive wild bird is possibly the textbook example of Brillat Savarin's theory that you are what you eat. Grouse loves moorland; moreover it loves heather, on which it feeds almost exclusively. The result is incredibly distinctly flavoured, almost bittersweet meat, which is absolutely peerless. You might be able to say that a partridge eats a bit like chicken or that teal is a tad ducky. Grouse simply tastes like nothing else. To many people, it is the first and last word in game.

Celebrity can be a terrible burden to carry and, for grouse, this is partly due to the infamous 'glorious twelfth'. The twelfth of August is the official opening day of the grouse season. Most other game birds come into season much later: partridge cannot be hunted until the first of September and pheasant is off limits until October. So naturally, there is some excitement about the glorious twelfth, since it is a sort of New Year's day for hunters and game dealers. A veritable industry (albeit exclusive) has grown up around getting grouse from its moorland habitat to the restaurant table as quickly as possible; if you know where to go, it can be on some menus the same day. The first grouse to reach the kitchen can be incredibly expensive. As a result, grouse has an unfair reputation for being prohibitively dear. In fact this is not true. It never becomes cheap, per se, but the price does drop significantly once the season is in full swing.

Ironically, all that frantic activity around the glorious twelfth misses a vital trick. Like all game, grouse is better if it is hung. In grouse's case this should be done for anything up to 10 days. The flavour deepens, and the meat becomes tenderer. As daft as this seems, the price pretty much halves within a week of the season's opening (i.e. grouse gets cheaper as it gets better!). We start buying grouse from September onwards, and it can last all the way up to December. Some years are better than others, depending on the vagaries of British weather, predators and parasites.

We think the best way to look at this much talked about (and widely misunderstood) bird is as a somewhat indulgent, seasonal treat. We strongly recommend that you splash out on a grouse at least once every autumn, and make it one of your most memorable meals of the year. What follows is our guided tour of the grouse experience.

How to prepare grouse

To begin, a little bit about the shopping. You are highly unlikely to discover a grouse in your local supermarket. You will almost certainly have to approach a game supplier direct, or sweet talk your local butcher into finding you the best deal around. Make sure he or she knows you want a young, roasting bird, not an older, braising one. What's more (and squeamish types, look away now), it needs to come with all its guts intact, or at least the liver and heart.

Grouse, although slightly plumper than a partridge or pigeon, is essentially a portion-sized bird. The cocks are bigger than hens, and all the birds get fatter as the season progresses. Still, it's best to allow one bird per diner; most people can manage a whole one, and the leftovers are eminently useable (we'll come back to that later).

Here then, is the quintessential rendition of your grouse.

Traditionally, grouse is roasted then served on a slice of toast, spread with a pâté made from its offal. There may or may not be a side serving of game chips (see page 242) but bread sauce and watercress are compulsory! Grouse should be roasted whole, just like partridge, woodcock and snipe. Hence we have not included instructions for jointing or spatchcocking in this chapter.

For roasting, there is very little to do in the way of preparing grouse. If the bird has come long legged (meaning that the body has been plucked, but the head, wings and legs are intact and perhaps even feathered), simply cut off the head at the very base of the neck. Cut the legs off below the knee joint and remove the wings where the feathers stop (this happens at a sort of elbow joint, you can't miss it). Now carefully draw or gut the bird from the leg end of the cavity. The only way to do this is to put your hands in and tug very gently.

Sadly there is no little polybag with the giblets in for grouse fans, so you will have to sort the liver and heart from the other bits. The liver is unmissable: it looks like a chicken liver in a darker, miniature form. The heart will be nestling right next to it. The liver and heart are the only useful bits of grouse offal for eating, and we discard the rest.

Classic roast grouse for two

You will need
2 grouse (approximate weight 600g
    each), plus the livers and hearts kept
    separately
salt and freshly ground black pepper
3 tablespoons duck fat or lard
2 slices of bread (we prefer sourdough)
a good knob of butter
100ml brandy
1 bunch or 85g bag of watercress

Preheat your oven to 250°C / Gas Mark
9 (sometimes this is known as the max
setting on modern domestic ovens).

Generously season each grouse inside
and out with salt and pepper. Set the
birds aside. Heat two tablespoons of
the fat in the frying pan over a brisk
flame until the fat just starts to bubble.
Reduce the heat to medium and place
the birds in the pan, on one side, so that
you start to brown one of the legs.
Allow the leg to fry for about 2 minutes,
then turn the bird onto the other leg
and repeat the process. Turn the bird
around onto its breast so that the
backbone is facing you, and fry the
breast for a minute or so until it just
starts to brown. Then turn the bird all
the way over again so that it is now on
its back. Place it straight into the oven,
carefully, so that the bird does not roll
over onto a leg. Roast for 6 minutes.
(Just in case you have a really big grouse,
add a minute's cooking time per 100g
over 600g.) Test the grouse by pressing
your thumb and forefinger on the
fattest part of the breast just where it
meets the wing tips. When it is cooked it
will feel properly firm, but with a very
subtle 'give'. At this juncture, we should
point out that the grouse meat will be
pink or medium rare, like duck or
pigeon breast. If undercooked, grouse
meat is alarmingly dark and slightly
bitter near the breastbone. If overdone
it can be dry and lacking in that

heathery taste. If it feels underdone,
return it to the oven but test it again
every couple of minutes to avoid going
too far with it.

When the grouse feels ready, up end the
bird onto its breast and allow it to rest,
in a warm place out of the pan, facing
down like this for 10 minutes.

Meanwhile, you can make the toast and
the pâté. Return the pan to a very
gentle heat and add the final spoonful
of duck fat or lard. Add the bread slices
when the fat has melted and let them
fry in this rather lovely mix of fat and
grouse juices. Turn once, being careful
not to burn the toast (which, if we are
honest is a kind of gamey fried bread or
outsized crouton!).

In a separate, small pan, heat the butter
quite briskly until frothy. Add the livers
and hearts and lower the heat to
medium. Fry for 2–3 minutes, stirring
regularly, then add the brandy. At this
point it should gently flambé. If not,
you can encourage it to do so by
tipping the pan towards a gas flame.
If using an electric hob, you will have
to ignite it by hand. Use cooks' matches,
not a lighter, if you don't want a singed
knuckle. Remove the pan from the
heat. Take the hearts from the pan and
pop them next to the resting grouse.
Mash the livers into the butter and
brandy, in the pan, using the back of a
fork. Spread this mix onto the slices of
'toast'. You are now ready to present
the dish to the table. If this sounds a bit
grand, that's because it is. Park the
grouse on the slices of toast, breast-
side up. Give the watercress a turn
around the dish you used to rest the
birds, coating it in any juices they may
have produced (it won't be a lot). You
can either add a knot of watercress to
the plate as a garnish or, not to put too

fine a point on it, form it into two
small bunches, and ram the stalk ends
into the cavity of each bird, with the
leaves poking out of their derrières.
This sounds odd, but it is traditional!
Enjoy, with bread sauce, and a splash
of gravy (pages 238 and 245) or
optional extras game chips (page 242)
and pickled damsons (page 241).

2 Legs

Grouse broth

We think of grouse as Scottish birds even though they are shot all over England and Ireland. So our favourite thing to do with leftovers is to make a warming Scottish broth in the style of Cock a Leekie.

serves 4

the carcasses of 4 grouse
1 leek
1 medium onion
2 carrots
2 stalks of celery
100g pearl barley
½ small swede
2 tablespoons unsalted butter
salt and freshly ground black pepper
100g pitted prunes, sliced

With a heavy cook's knife, chop each of the grouse carcasses into 3 or 4 pieces. Trim the leek, onions and carrots and celery. Warm half of the butter in a heavy-based saucepan, gently sauté the vegetable trimmings and then add the grouse bones. Give it all a vigorous stir over a high heat then pour in water to cover. Bring to the boil, skimming any scum from the surface, then lower the heat and simmer for 45 minutes.

In the meantime, soak the barley in cold water, peel the swede and chop all of the vegetables into a fine dice. Once the stock is ready, pour into a bowl through a fine strainer.

Now melt the remaining butter in a heavy-based pot, add the diced vegetables with a pinch of salt and cook them over a low heat until they are slightly softened. Drain the barley, add to the stock and bring the broth to the boil. Lower the heat and simmer for 10 minutes, then add the prunes. Cook for another 10–15 minutes until the barley is done. If the soup looks as if it is getting too thick, just add a little water. Season to your liking with a tad more salt and black pepper. Serve immediately.

Grouse pie

A straight and full on grouse pie would be quite strong so we like to pad it out with braising steak. The result is a lovely autumn treat.

serves 4

2 large or 3 small grouse
6 juniper berries
1 bay leaf
12 sprigs of thyme
250g braising steak
150g smoked streaky bacon
150g sliced button mushrooms
50g duck fat or lard
50g flour
salt and freshly ground black pepper
1 egg, beaten

For the pastry
250g plain flour
125g unsalted butter, chilled and cubed
½ teaspoon salt
1 egg yolk

First make the pastry. Sift the flour and salt into a mixing bowl. Add the butter and, working quickly, rub it into the flour with your fingertips until the mixture resembles breadcrumbs. Add the egg yolk and stir in with a fork until it has been absorbed. If the mixture hasn't completely come together, add a teaspoon of water at a time until the dough begins to cohere. Knead the dough lightly on a floured surface for a minute then wrap it in clingfilm and refrigerate for 1 hour.

Joint the grouse into breast and legs, then fillet the breast meat and scrape the leg meat off the bones. Chop the carcass, put it in a pot along with the leg bones, juniper and herbs and cover with 500ml of water. Bring to the boil then simmer for 30 minutes to create a stock for the pie. Strain and set aside.

Preheat the oven to 180°C / Gas Mark 4.

Slice the grouse breasts into 2cm pieces and roll them in the flour, seasoned well with salt and pepper. Heat the fat in a wide pan and fry the grouse breast pieces until they have lightly browned. Remove and arrange them in a deep pie dish. Slice the beef into 1cm strips, roll them in the flour and fry them in the same pan until sealed and browned. Add them to the pie dish. Slice the bacon into 1cm strips and chop the leg meat and fry these together with the mushrooms until browned, then add these to the dish. If there is any flour left, add this to the fat and brown for half a minute, then pour over the stock. Bring to the boil, scraping the bottom and sides of the pan with a wooden spoon. Finally, season the sauce. Pour this into the dish and allow the mixture to cool slightly.

Roll out the pastry to make a lid for the pie. Brush the edges of the pie dish with the beaten egg then lay over the pastry. Brush the lid with the egg, make a little slit in the middle of the pastry to let the steam escape and place the pie onto the middle shelf of the oven. Bake for 10 minutes, then lower the heat to 150°C / Gas Mark 2 and continue cooking for a further 1¼ hours. If the pastry begins to brown too quickly, cover the lid with a piece of foil. However, you'll need to remove it for the last 15 minutes for a crisp, golden crust.

grouse

Woodcock and snipe

Woodcock and snipe are small waders: marsh-dwelling birds which use their distinctive, long beaks to snap up the worms and insect larvae which inhabit wetlands. Woodcock will also eat berries and seeds. Their diminutive size and natural shyness makes them hard to hunt. This is compounded by the fact that they are also mostly nocturnal, hiding in dense cover throughout the day.

Woodcock and snipe are a true delicacy. They have rich, quite dark, meat not unlike grouse, but without that in-your-face gaminess which some people find intimidating. Far less famous than their moor-dwelling cousins, they are probably the most elusive of game birds. Butchers and dealers are unlikely to carry them as a rule, and you will more than likely have to order them in advance. Be prepared: they can be expensive. But at the height of the season (December and January), there is the odd bargain to be had.

Like grouse, woodcock is a portion-sized bird: although it looks small, it is so flavoursome that one will be enough for most people. Snipe is smaller and you might find that serving two or even three birds per diner is not excessive.

How to prepare woodcock and snipe

This might just be the shortest chapter ever written on how to prepare a game bird. If you have bought either bird from a game dealer it will probably be long legged. This means the head, wings and legs will be untrimmed, and probably won't even have been plucked. You can remove the ends of the legs and wing tips if you like. The traditional way to cook and eat snipe and woodcock is almost the same and both birds are left otherwise intact: that is to say, with their heads on and their giblets in. This is not to everyone's taste and you can remove the giblets if you want, using them to make a pâté like the one served with grouse on page 68. A real die-hard gamer would wait until after the birds are cooked to remove the giblets, discard the intestines and mash the heart and livers onto the toast.

woodcock

Classic roast woodcock for two

You will need

2 woodcock (approximate weight 450g each)
3 tablespoons duck fat or lard
salt and fresh ground black pepper
2 slices of bread (we prefer sourdough)
1 lemon

Preheat your oven to 250°C / Gas Mark 9 (sometimes this is known as the max setting on modern domestic ovens).

Generously season each woodcock inside and out with salt and pepper. Now, this bit sounds macabre, but it is the most practical way to cook the bird. Press the legs and wings together with the thumb and forefinger of your left hand. Bring the woodcock's head around with your other hand, and tuck it in between one of the breasts and one of the wings, by piercing the meat there ever so slightly. Set the birds aside.

Heat 2 tablespoons of the fat in the frying pan over a brisk flame until the fat just starts to bubble. Reduce the heat to medium and place the birds in the pan, on one side, so that you start to brown one of the legs. Allow the leg to fry for about 2 minutes then turn the bird onto the other leg and repeat the process. Then turn the bird onto its breast so that the backbone is facing you, and fry the breast for a minute or so, until it just starts to brown. Then turn the bird all the way over again so that it is now on its back. Place it straight into the oven, carefully, so that the bird does not roll over onto a leg. Roast for 6 minutes.

Test the woodcock by pressing your thumb and forefinger on the fattest part of the breast just where it meets the wing tips. Once cooked it will feel properly firm, but with a very subtle 'give'. At this juncture, we should point out that woodcock is best eaten pink or medium rare, like duck or pigeon. If it feels underdone, return it to the oven but test it again after a couple of minutes to avoid going too far with it.

When the woodcock feels ready, remove from the pan, up end the bird onto its breast and allow it to rest on a separate dish, in a warm place, facing down like this for 10 minutes.

Return the pan to a very gentle heat and add the final spoonful of duck fat or lard. When the fat has melted, add the bread slices to the pan and let them fry in this mix of fat and woodcock juices. Turn once, being careful not to burn the toast.

Place the rested woodcock on a chopping board and pull the head free of its nestling position. Using a sharp knife split the head in half. This sounds awful, but the brain of a woodcock is very edible (its u.s.p. amongst true devotees). It has a very mild, nutty flavour, not unlike veal sweetbreads. Present the woodcocks, head and all, on the slices of toast, breast-side up. Halve the lemon and serve it as a garnish.

Classic roast snipe for two

You will need
6 snipe (each weighing approximately
    200g)
6 rashers dry cured smoked streaky
    bacon or pancetta
3 tablespoons duck fat or lard
salt and freshly ground black pepper
6 squares of bread, about 2cm across
    and down, each
2 skewers
2 lemons

Preheat your oven to 250°C / Gas Mark
9 (sometimes this is known as the max
setting on modern domestic ovens).

Generously season each snipe inside
and out with salt and pepper. As with
woodcock, you need to tuck the head
of each snipe under one of its wings.
Press the legs and wings together with
the thumb and forefinger of your left
hand. Bring the snipe's head around
with your other hand, and tuck it in
between one of the breasts and one of
the wings, by piercing the meat there
ever so slightly. Now tightly wrap each
bird with a bacon rasher and set it
aside. Melt the fat and use it to brush
each slice of bread. Now skewer the
first bird, through the shoulder, and
follow it with one square of bread.
Repeat the process until you have three
birds on each skewer with a slice of
bread between each one. Brush the
birds with any remaining fat and place
them on an oven tray, breast-sides up.

Place straight into the oven, carefully,
so that the skewers don't roll over.
Roast for 6 minutes. Test the snipes by
pressing your thumb and forefinger on
the fattest part of the breasts just
where they meet the wing tips. Once
cooked, each should feel properly firm,
but with a very subtle 'give'. At this
point, heat your grill to maximum and
place the tray underneath it, just to

crisp up the bacon. Don't go anywhere,
this won't take long and you want to
watch it like a hawk. Allow the birds to
rest for 10 minutes once grilled. Like
grouse and woodcock the meat should
be pink (medium rare) for optimum
tenderness and flavour.

Remove the rested birds from the
skewers, being careful not to break the
toasty bread bits. As with woodcocks,
you need to split the heads in half with
a sharp knife. Present the snipes, head
and all, on the little squares of toast,
breast-side up. Halve the lemon and
serve it as a garnish.

Trimmings and stuffings
Die-hard traditionalists would argue
that removing the giblets from snipe
and woodcock, only to replace them
with a contrived stuffing is akin to
madness. We wouldn't describe
ourselves as anything like die-hard, but,
even if you do decide to cook the birds
sans guts, it is probably best to leave
their insides be. This will allow you to
get the best of their delicious, natural
flavour. Getting hold of a woodcock is
hard-enough work. Make the cooking
as easy as possible.

2 Legs

Wild ducks

Just as today's farmed hens are descended from wild jungle fowl, nearly all domesticated ducks and geese are modern descendants of wild, migratory waterfowl. Huge numbers of these birds thrive in the UK; some winter here from the Arctic, and some have taken up permanent residence. When it comes to game, a few species are hunted as food, but not as enthusiastically as the galliforme birds such as partridge and pheasant.

One reason for this could be the fact that, as a rule, the Brits don't eat as much waterfowl meat as our friends on the continent. Until fairly recently duck was seen as a 'special occasion' meat: once eaten as part of a Chinese meal or in the form of duck in orange, that once ubiquitous staple of posh restaurants à la 1970s. Things are changing, however, and it is increasingly easy to buy farmed duck and goose meat in butchers' shops and supermarkets. Getting hold of their wild counterparts is still a bit more of an adventure but, if you are up for it, the rewards are many. Wild duck meat is fairly inexpensive and absolutely delicious. It is leaner than the farmed version, which can be notoriously fatty. As a result, it tends to be quicker and easier to cook. Wild goose meat is still almost entirely elusive to game enthusiasts in the UK, and for that reason we do not include it in this book.

There are many species of wild duck in the UK but the three types you are most likely to come across as game are mallard, widgeon and teal.

It's odd that Britain's most commonly sighted game bird is one of the least widely eaten. Wherever there is a park or pond, mallard ducks will be dabbling. All domestic ducks are descended from the mallard. It has an unmistakeable plumage. The head of the male is emerald green and the wings are blue-tipped. The female is more tawny, without the flashy colours. In the wild, mallards will live on a diet of grubs, seeds and berries but, as you will know if one has literally mugged you for a crust of stale bread, they can be voracious omnivores. We tend to be nervous about eating birds that are seen as scavengers. But, just as the wood pigeon (see pages 102 to 103) is a world away from its urban cousins, most mallards shot for the table are, in fact, only semi-feral. Their habitat around lakes and wetlands on estates is managed, and so is their diet which will be largely grain based. This puts just enough fat on them to give them a flavour not unlike a more full-on version of farmed duck, with leaner and darker meat.

Widgeon or teal

Slightly smaller, and more elusive to hunters and shoppers, is the widgeon. It has chestnut-coloured plumage around the head and neck, and is more commonly sighted in the winter, when it shelters in large numbers near our eastern coasts (often having migrated from Siberia and Scandinavia). The widgeon is mainly vegetarian, living on aquatic grasses and roots. This gives it a sweeter, gamier flavour than other waterfowl. Smaller and shyer still is the teal. Like the widgeon, it is often found wintering in the UK, on the run from the harsh, Siberian weather. It has a very pronounced, almost-concentrated duck flavour. This compensates for its diminutive size on the plate. What the teal lacks in bulk, it more than makes up for in flavour.

How to prepare wild ducks

If you have ever dealt with a whole farmed duck, mallard will look familiar to you. It is the only wild duck that is big enough to share. An average-sized specimen will easily feed two. Teal and widgeon are portion-sized birds. All the roasting recipes in this book require that you leave the ducks whole. However, some recipes require the breast meat only, so we will talk you through filleting the breasts in due course.

Jointing mallard

Place the bird on a chopping board with its breast facing up and its legs to the right. The duck has a unique, box like shape. The legs will be very firm, with markedly rounded thighs running close and parallel to the breast.

The easiest way to joint a duck is to start by removing the legs. Ease the leg nearest you gently away from the breast and, with a sharp boning knife, cut decisively between the thigh and breast. Now the leg falls naturally away from the breast. Hold it down on the board with the palm of your left hand, which will expose the socket, or joint. Work the tip of the knife delicately around this socket and the leg will come neatly away. You can now swing the other leg around to the front of your board and repeat the process.

Filleting wild duck breasts

To remove breast meat from either mallard or widgeon (teal is too small to fillet), here is how to take the breast meat off the bone. Keep the bird breast up. Take a small boning knife and gently run it along the bone, easing the flesh away as you go. What you are left with will resemble a smaller, gamier version of a duck breast with the stub of the wing attached. Leave this wing stub on the breast for cooking as it helps with flavour and is easily sliced away as you serve up later.

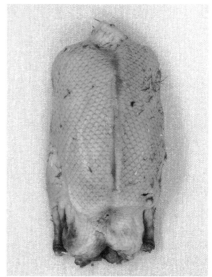

Classic roasts and suggested trimmings

The cooking method for all three types of wild duck will be the same, but the cooking times will vary according to their respective sizes. Classically roasted teal and widgeon would be served whole, whereas a mallard, to share between two people, will require carving at the table. Here is how to roast and serve a classic roast mallard for two people.

You will need
1 mallard (approximate weight 600g)
duck fat, lard or unsalted butter
salt and freshly ground black pepper

Preheat the oven to 200°C / Gas Mark 6. Generously season the mallard with salt and pepper inside and out. Warm the fat or butter in a large oven-proof pan and seal the bird, leg-side down first, for about 4 or 5 minutes over a low heat until the skin has browned. Turn the bird over and repeat the process on the other leg.

Now raise the heat to medium and seal the breasts, for about 3 minutes on either side of the central breastbone, until each side is nicely browned. Turn the bird onto its back and roast in the oven for 15 minutes. (Just in case you have a really big mallard, add a minute's cooking time per 100g over 600g.) Test by inserting a metal skewer or a small sharp knife into the plumpest part of the breast; the juices will run clear when it is ready.

Rest the birds in a warm place for 10 minutes. At this juncture, we should point out that the breast and leg meat, once cooked, will be pink or medium rare. You can enjoy wild duck meat fully cooked or brown, but it will be dryer than farmed duck meat cooked this way. If you want well-cooked wild duck, it is probably better to pot-roast

it, and you'll find a pot roast recipe on page 86.

Carving mallard
Carving a mallard at the table is best approached just as if you were jointing it before cooking. Start by removing the legs. Hold the tip of the leg away from

the breast meat and, with a swift cleave of the carving knife, cut through the thigh joint. You can now fillet the cooked breast meat away from the central breastbone and serve it intact or slice across the grain. Don't forget to keep the carcass for a delicious stock later.

Cooking times for widgeon and teal

If you follow the classic roasting method above for smaller wild ducks, with the same seasoning and oven temperature, here is our guide to their cooking times.

For widgeon (approximate weight 300g) allow 8 minutes cooking, plus 1 minute per 50g over this weight.

For teal (approximate weight 150g) allow 5 minutes cooking time plus 1 minute extra per 50g.

Stuffings and suggested trimmings
As with all the smaller game birds, we find that cooking and serving stuffings on the side of the roast (as opposed to putting them in the cavity) is much better for the meat. This is because the cooking time required for pink, succulent duck is too short to safely cook a stuffing to the required temperature.

However, and this is a pretty big however, a pot-roast wild duck stuffed with a faggot is a very fine thing indeed. You will find a recipe for faggots served next to pigeon on page 119.

Pickled and preserved fruits such as the damsons, quince, cherries and prunes on pages 241 are superb trimmings for any duck, wild or otherwise.

Pot-roast mallard, quince and star anise

There is some cheating involved in this recipe, since it is only the diminutive legs of the mallard that get a full-on, casserole treatment. You could add whole ducks to the pot, but the meat can take forever to cook, only to end up on the dry side. This recipe works well with mallards, but the other wild ducks are probably a little too small. If quinces elude you, either side of their late autumn season, you can swap in apples or pears.

serves 4

2 mallards
salt and freshly ground black pepper
2 quince (if using apples instead,
   Bramleys are best)
juice of a lemon
duck fat, lard or butter for cooking
50g dry-cured streaky bacon or
   pancetta, diced
4 cloves garlic, chopped
8 shallots or 4 red onions, peeled and
   halved
300ml cider
1 tablespoon tomato purée
3 pieces star anise
1 tablespoon runny honey
2 bay leaves

Joint the ducks following the instructions on page 83 Season the legs and breasts generously with salt and fresh ground black pepper and set aside. Peel, core and roughly dice the quinces or apples. Toss them in the lemon juice and set aside.

Heat 2 tablespoons of the fat in a pot large enough to hold all the ingredients and, when it is fizzing, add the duck legs. Let them brown all around, quite briskly, then remove them with a slotted spoon. Set them aside. Add the bacon to the pot and fry it for a minute or two, until it starts to colour. Add the garlic and shallots plus half a teaspoon of salt. Reduce the heat slightly but allow the vegetables to fry quite hard for a couple of minutes before adding the cider, tomato purée, honey, star anise and bay leaves. Let the mix come to a good simmer then return the duck legs to the pot. Cover them with water or a light stock and put the lid on the pan. Lower the heat dramatically. Allow the legs to cook on their own.

After an hour, add the quince pieces. Now add just enough extra stock or water to cover the fruit and simmer for another 30 minutes.

Meanwhile, heat the oven to 200°C / Gas Mark 6. Add 2 tablespoons of butter or duck fat to an ovenproof frying pan and, when hot, place the duck breasts in to the pan, skin-side down. Sear them until nicely browned then turn them over and transfer them to the oven for 15 minutes. Please note this will leave the meat pink, which will keep it nice and tender. For brown, fully cooked duck meat add another 5 minutes to the oven time. Once done to your liking, remove them from the pan and allow them to rest in a warm place for another 15 minutes, or until the quince in the pot is really tender. Remove the

casserole from the heat and check the seasoning.

You can now serve the duck breasts as they are, each with a leg and the shallot and quince mix, or you can whip the breasts off the bone and slice them crossways, before re-uniting them with the pot roast – easier to eat, but a bit fiddly for you!

Wild duck fricassée with sage and pumpkin

A fricassée is traditionally thickened with flour or egg yolks, but here that job is done by the naturally creamy nature of pumpkin. You can swap in butternut squash. The recipe will also work with guinea fowl and pheasant.

serves 4

2 mallards
4 shallots, diced
3 cloves garlic, chopped (keep the peelings of the shallots and garlic handy)
100ml milk
100g butter
½ small-ish pumpkin, or 1 medium butternut squash (approximate weight 600g), peeled and roughly diced
2 leaves sage
quarter of nutmeg, grated
4 tablespoons duck fat, butter or lard for frying
50g dry-cured streaky bacon or pancetta, diced
salt and freshly ground black pepper
1 tablespoon tomato purée
500ml game stock (you could make this from the mallard bones)
125ml (a wine glass full) rich red wine
a small bunch parsley

Fillet the mallard breasts from the bone following the instructions on page 83. You could now use the mallard carcasses to make a light game stock by roasting the bones in a hot oven until they are well browned, then simmering them with the peelings from the shallots and garlic for a couple of hours. If you don't fancy this, you can swap in chicken stock for this recipe.

Heat the milk and butter in a pot big enough for all the pumpkin pieces. When the butter has melted add the pumpkin to the pot with the sage leaves and nutmeg. Simmer gently until the pumpkin is very tender and on the edge of falling apart. Remove from the heat and purée it. Set the purée aside.

In another pot, heat half (2 tablespoons) of the duck fat, lard or butter over a gentle heat. Add the shallots and garlic, and the bacon with half a teaspoon of salt. Stir once, cover, lower the heat and allow this mix to sweat for 15–20 minutes or until it is really tender. Do not let it brown. Now add the tomato purée and stock, and then simmer for a further half-hour or so.

Meanwhile, season the duck breasts all over generously with salt and pepper. Heat the remaining fat in a frying pan and, when it is really hot, sear the duck breasts for 6 minutes on either side over a fairly brisk heat. This will leave them nice and pink. If you want them verging on well done, add another 3 minutes' cooking time on either side. Once they are cooked to your liking, set the breasts aside on a tray or plate to rest for a good 10 minutes. Deglaze the pan with the wine, allowing it to simmer briskly, until it has reduced by half. To finish the dish, add the winey juices to the pot of shallots, garlic and stock. Fold in the pumpkin purée and remove the sauce from the heat. Check the seasoning and adjust it to your liking.

Finally, slice the duck breasts and lay them on a serving plate. Pour or spoon the sauce over the duck breasts and serve immediately. This dish is lovely on a bed of rice, garnished with chopped parsley.

Indonesian-style roast wild duck

This recipe is very simple but effective, as the duck is marinated in a spice paste, then roasted slowly, wrapped in banana leaves. If you can't get hold of the leaves from an oriental supermarket (or, believe it or not, a friendly florist) you can wrap the duck in baking parchment. The recipe works well with wild or farmed duck.

serves 4

4 banana leaves or baking parchment
2 wooden skewers
6 shallots
6 cloves garlic
2 stalks lemon grass
5cm piece fresh ginger
2 red chillies
50g macadamia or cashew nuts
4 kaffir lime leaves, or the grated zest of half a lime
½ teaspoon turmeric
1 teaspoon black pepper
½ teaspoon salt
1 teaspoon coriander seeds
2 teaspoons fermented shrimp paste (sold as kapi or belachan) or 1 tablespoon Thai fish sauce (nam pla)
3 tablespoons mild vegetable oil
2 mallards

Soak the banana leaves and wooden skewers (if using) in plenty of hot water, straight from a just-boiled kettle. Leave them there for a good half-hour.

Chop the shallots, garlic, lemon grass, ginger and chillies roughly. Transfer them to a food processor or a pestle and mortar with the nuts and blitz or pound them to a paste. Add the seasonings and spices and blitz or pound again until you have a rough marinade. Stir in the oil.

Rub the paste well into the skins and the cavities of the ducks. Allow them to marinade for at least 2 hours (overnight is actually ideal).

Preheat the oven to 180°C / Gas Mark 4. Alternatively, you can cook this dish very successfully in a covered, Weber-type kettle barbecue. You will need the heat-diffuser rack if you have one.

Wrap the ducks in the banana leaves or baking parchment and secure them through the top with the skewers.

Roast the wrapped ducks for 45 minutes, and then test them. The duck can be medium-rare or cooked through for this recipe. Once cooked, allow it to rest, still wrapped, for a good 20 minutes before carving or chopping roughly to serve up. This dish is traditionally served over rice, but it is also really good with a fierce, peppery salad leaf such as watercress, and plenty of crusty bread.

Wild duck and green pepper stir-fry

Wild duck breasts are a fine addition to Chinese-style stir-fries. You could follow this recipe using farmed duck instead, and it also works with the breasts of pheasant and guinea fowl. If you do opt for a white meat like pheasant, you will need to change the method slightly; we will include instructions at the end of this recipe.

serves 4

2 mallards
2 tablespoons soy sauce
1 teaspoon cornflour
3 tablespoons water
1 tablespoon sherry vinegar
1 teaspoon runny honey
4 tablespoons mild vegetable oil for frying
2 garlic cloves, peeled and sliced finely
1 fresh red chilli, sliced finely
2 red onions, sliced roughly
2 green peppers, sliced roughly

Fillet the breast meat from the mallards following the instructions on page 83. Pop them in the fridge. You can use the carcasses to make a great stock later.

Mix the soy sauce, cornflour, water, vinegar and honey together to form a smooth sauce. Set this aside.

Heat 2 tablespoons of the oil in a sturdy frying pan over a brisk heat. Fry the duck breasts, skin-side down for 3 minutes, or until the skin is golden and some of the fat has rendered into the pan. Turn the breasts over, lower the heat to medium and cook the breasts on the other side for about 7 minutes, which should leave you with medium (pink) breast meat. Add another 4–5 minutes if you want the meat cooked through. Allow the duck breasts to rest on a plate whilst you cook the rest of the stir-fry.

Using another wide-bottomed frying pan or, ideally, a wok, heat the remaining oil until it is just beginning to send up wisps of smoke. Fry the garlic and chilli for half a minute, then throw in the onions and green peppers. After another minute or so, add the sauce. As soon as it thickens, remove the pan from the heat and check the seasoning of the stir-fry. You may wish to add more soy sauce. To serve, simply slice the duck breasts finely and toss them through the vegetables. Don't return the wok to the heat once you've added the duck. Serve immediately. You can accompany this dish with plenty of steamed rice or your favourite kind of noodles.

If you wish to swap in pheasant or guinea fowl for this recipe, then the method will be different. Simply fillet the breasts of either bird and then slice them uncooked. Heat the first 2 tablespoons of oil in the wok or pan and fry the cut breast meat for 3–4 minutes, or until fully cooked. Then set the pieces aside and return to the method above for cooking the vegetables and putting the finished parts of the dish together.

2 Legs

Warm widgeon breast salad

You can also use this recipe for pigeon, squab or rook breasts. Here, we have allowed for one breast per person, which makes this a light meal or starter. Increase the number of breasts if you want to make this a more substantial dish. If you do use pigeon or rook for this salad, you will definitely need at least two breasts per person. We have used curly endive for this recipe but if you are not a fan of bitter leaves, swap them for little gem, watercress or rocket.

serves 4

4 widgeon breasts
100ml mild olive oil for cooking
1 head of garlic
400g waxy potatoes (use new potatoes if you like)
salt and freshly ground pepper
1 curly endive frisèe or leaf of your choice
1 tablespoon red wine vinegar
a small sprig of tarragon
2 tablespoons duck fat or butter

Season the breasts generously on either side and place in the fridge.

Heat the oil in a small saucepan very gently. While it warms up divide the garlic head into cloves, but leave them unpeeled and whole. Immerse them in the warmed oil and simmer as gently as possible for roughly 20 minutes, by which time they should be soft and squidgy. Give them a little longer if they need it. Remove them with a slotted spoon. Keep the oil and allow both to cool.

Peel and dice the potatoes into cubes of about 1cm. Boil the potato in plenty of salted water until just cooked, but holding their shape well. Drain and allow to cool.

Wash and roughly shred the lettuces. Pick out any leggy or discoloured leaves around the outside of the crown (the best leaves on a whole frisèe are the palest ones near the heart). Combine the vinegar, 3 tablespoons of the garlicky oil and chopped tarragon to make a loose dressing. You can use more oil and more vinegar if you like.

Melt the duck fat or butter in a pan and sear the breasts for about 3 minutes on either side, which should leave them medium-rare (increase the time if you want them medium, but don't cook them through, as they can dry out). Remove the breasts from the pan and rest them. Now fry the potatoes in the same pan with 2 more spoonfuls of the garlic oil and, when the potatoes are nicely coloured, remove them and let them drain on kitchen paper. Now the dish is an assembly job. Combine the leaves and potatoes, plus the garlic cloves. Toss the dressing through this mix. Check the seasoning. Divide the salad between bowls or plates. Top each salad with the warm widgeon breasts and serve immediately.

game: a cookbook

Teal and olives

You can swap the teal for widgeon in this quick, but intensely flavoured casserole.

serves 4

4 teal
salt and freshly ground black pepper
50g unsalted butter
100g smoked bacon pieces, cut into
    1cm x 3cm lardons
1 medium onion, finely diced
150ml white wine
400ml good chicken stock
12 sage leaves
1 bay leaf
100g green olives, pitted

Preheat the oven to 160˚C / Gas Mark 3.

Season each teal inside and out with a little salt and black pepper. Heat the butter in a casserole that will hold all the teal comfortably, add the birds and gently seal them all over on a low heat for about 5 minutes. By this time they should be lovely and brown.

Transfer the birds to a plate then add the bacon to the pan. Let the lardons sizzle until lightly crisped then tip in the onion, cooking over a low heat until it has completely softened. Pour in the wine and let it bubble and reduce by half then add the stock and bring back to the boil.

Nestle the teal into the pot, tuck in the herbs, cover and place onto the middle shelf of the oven. Braise the birds for 10 minutes before adding the olives. Continue to cook for a further 5 minutes until the teal are tender. Remove the casserole from the oven and leave it to rest for 5 minutes before serving.

Wild duck ham

Known in its native Catalonia by the more romantic name *Jamon de pato*, this ham is a real joy to make and serve. A leg of *Jamon Serrano* takes the best part of a year to produce; this takes a matter of days and the results are spectacularly similar to the more famous pork hams. You can use either domestic or mallard ducks for this recipe.

serves 6–8

4 mallard or farmed duck breasts
    (if buying whole ducks follow our
    instructions for filleting the breast
    meat on page 83)
6 cloves garlic
6 juniper berries
1 teaspoon coriander seeds
2 cloves
2 bay leaves
a sprig of rosemary
a sprig of thyme
½ teaspoon black peppercorns
1 star anise
700g rough sea salt
700g golden caster sugar

The recipe is very straightforward: wash the duck breasts and make sure there are no dark patches of blood on the meat (this will only really apply to wild duck). Pat the breasts thoroughly dry.

In a food processor, blitz all the spices together with the salt and sugar to create the curing mixture. Place the duck breasts in a non-metallic container and completely cover them with the curing mixture. Refrigerate them in the cure for 3 days then wash and pat them dry once more. You can now use them immediately, or wrap them in a muslin cloth and keep them in the fridge. You could also hang each ham to dry it out further. Wrap the ham in muslin and suspend it in a cool dry place (a garage or shed is good for this). Once the ham has fully dried, which takes a week or so, it will feel like a very fresh salami.

To serve the duck, simply slice it as thinly as possible, across the grain, rather like smoked salmon. It is great as it is, or with a handful of cocktail gherkins (cornichons). You can also pair it with a relish such as Pickled Quince (see page 241) – one of our favourite ways to serve this ham.

2 Legs

Duck ham, figs and rocket

Unless you are lucky enough to have your own tree (and a very sheltered garden!), figs are always imported, and a bit of a gamble. In the British autumn those from southern Spain, Italy, Greece and Turkey are the best: you want them to be fat, soft and shot through with purple, whether they are the larger, green type or the small, black version. Don't buy them anywhere that won't allow you to test for ripeness.

If rocket isn't your thing, or if it eludes you, replace it with crunchy chicory leaves instead.

serves 4

2 breasts of wild duck ham (see page 96)
4 figs
a dozen or so fresh walnuts
1 tablespoon balsamic (or another posh wine) vinegar
3 tablespoons good extra-virgin olive oil
3 bunches or 1 x 85g packet rocket
salt

This recipe is really an assembly job. Slice the duck ham as finely as possible and set it aside. Quarter the figs down their length. Crack open and pick the walnuts. Mix together the vinegar and oil to make a very loose dressing. Combine all the ingredients and season to your liking with sea salt, remembering to go easy on it, as the ham is naturally salty. If you like, you could vary this salad by replacing the walnuts with shavings of very fresh Parmesan cheese.

Wild duck with sauce bigarade

Duck and oranges were made for each other. The classic sauce bigarade is made in those few short weeks when Seville oranges, or 'bigarades' as they are known in Provence, are in season. Any orange can be used; bloods are particularly good as they have the requisite bitterness. This sauce suits the deep richness of wild fowl but you can swap them for farmed duck.

serves 4

2 Seville oranges
1 lemon
3 tablespoons caster sugar
2 tablespoons white wine vinegar
400ml good chicken or duck stock
50g duck fat or butter with a small
2 mallards
salt and freshly ground black pepper

Peel the rind from the oranges and the lemon, easily done with a potato peeler, then slice the peel into long thin strips. Put the strips into a small saucepan and cover with cold water. Bring the pan to the boil then drain, cover again with water and boil one more time. This blanching will remove any excess bitterness. Rinse the strips, drain them and set aside. Bring the sugar and the vinegar to the boil in a saucepan, lower the heat to medium and cook until you have a light caramel. Add the stock and boil the sauce for 5 minutes until reduced by a third. Add the juice from the oranges and lemon along with the blanched rind and keep warm.

Preheat the oven to 200°C / Gas Mark 6. Generously season the mallards with salt and pepper inside and out. Warm the fat or butter in a large heavy-based pan and seal the birds, leg-side down first, for about 4 or 5 minutes over a low heat, until the skin has browned. Turn the birds over and repeat the process on the other legs. Now raise the heat to medium and seal the breasts for about 3 minutes, until they are nicely browned. Turn the birds onto their backs and roast in the oven for 12–15 minutes. Test by inserting a metal skewer or a small sharp knife into the plumpest part of the breast, the juices will run clear once the birds are cooked. Rest the birds in a warm place for 10 minutes.

Carve the mallards; place half a bird each on 4 warmed plates and spoon over the sauce.

Widgeon with shiitake mushroom and noodles

The Vietnamese eat a lot of duck; it's almost a countrywide staple. This is a wild duck and noodle dish with a Vietnamese feel. You can buy dried shiitake mushrooms in many oriental supermarkets and an increasing number of western ones. If dried shiitake elude you, opt for a mix of dried wild mushrooms, which is almost bound to contain some shiitake! Omit the chilli if you don't like its heat.

serves 4

2 widgeons, jointed (page 83)
70ml dark soy sauce
2 litres light chicken stock
1 bunch of spring onions
4 cloves of garlic
3cm piece of fresh ginger
100ml Thai fish sauce (nam pla)
1 star anise
½ cinnamon stick
12 dried shiitake mushrooms
100ml vegetable oil
2 teaspoons sugar
500g thin egg noodles
1 lemon, quartered
1 red chilli, sliced
a large handful of bean sprouts
a small bunch of coriander

Place the jointed widgeon into a bowl and pour over the soy sauce. Rub the sauce into the skin and leave to marinate for about an hour.

Preheat the oven to 180°C / Gas Mark 4.

Pour the chicken stock into a large stainless-steel pot and bring to the boil. Cut the spring onions in half, separating the white part from the green and set the green ends aside for later. Crush the white part of the onions with the back of a heavy knife and add to the stock. Bruise the garlic cloves and slice the ginger into 4, add them to the pot along with the mushrooms, fish sauce, star anise and cinnamon stick. Reduce the heat and simmer for 30 minutes.

Remove the duck from the soy sauce and wipe the skin dry with kitchen paper. Warm the oil in an ovenproof dish and seal the duck pieces over a medium heat until the skin is nicely browned. Turn the pieces over and roast on the middle shelf of the oven for 10 minutes. Rest the widgeon in a warm place for another 10 minutes. Strain the soup into another pan and discard the spices and vegetables but keep hold of the mushrooms. Season the soup with the sugar and a little more fish sauce should you want it a tad sharper.

To serve, cook the egg noodles as directed on their packet and divide them into 4 bowls. Top the noodles with a widgeon breast and leg each and 3 mushrooms, then pour over the boiling soup. Finely slice the spring onion greens and sprinkle them over the top of each bowl. Serve with lemon wedges, chilli, bean sprouts and coriander.

Pigeon, squab and rook

To generalise horribly, the game eaten in Britain falls into two distinct camps. In the first is that which is shot for sport as well as dinner. In the other is vermin. There, we've said the 'v' word. And as soon as most people see the word vermin, they think of rats and mice. This doesn't exactly get the digestive juices flowing, but the fact is that some of Britain's best wild foods are hunted out of necessity, to protect agriculture. Later on, in the 'four legs' part of this book we will deal with deer, rabbits and wild pigs, which are also hunted as pests. However, they don't seem to need nearly as much in the way of P.R. as their winged partners in crime. This is probably because, unless they live deep in the countryside, most people don't encounter rabbits and deer. Crows and pigeons are far less shy. They will thrive in an urban environment and, even though the type of pigeon that ends up on a plate will never have visited Trafalgar Square, it is not easy to totally distinguish the rustic bird from its brazen, filthy, streetwise counterpart.

More's the pity, because wood pigeon is a real delicacy, and a seriously cheap one at that. Pigeons are greedy for shoots and seedlings, especially those of peas and some brassica. As a result, vegetable farmers will pay people to shoot them. The biggest culls take place in the spring and early autumn when crops are at their most vulnerable, although pigeon has no closed season. It can be eaten all year. Pigeon has a flavoursome red meat, like grouse or wild duck in many ways. Squabs are domesticated pigeons, farmed for meat, and fed a rich diet to give them a layer of fat. They are dispatched at around four weeks' old, before they have had a chance to fly. This gives them paler and more tender meat than wood pigeon. It also

gives them a high price tag. Squab can be almost as expensive as grouse.

Is squab game? Some would argue that it can't be, since it is farmed. Because it is possible to buy farmed versions of many wild animals, we include squab in this book.

Although they belong to different bird families, pigeons and rooks (which are small crows) are quite alike in terms of their meat. Rooks favour a similar diet to pigeons: one of seeds, seedlings and shoots. They are gregarious animals and, unlike larger members of the crow family, live in huge flocks. These flocks can stay in one area for several generations. This means that young crops of cereals and vegetables close to established rookeries are very vulnerable if their populations are not kept down. Pigeons might be shot year round, but rooks tend to be culled in spring, when the young birds are leaving their nests. As the rooks take their first steps and ready themselves to fly, they are known as 'branchies'. Unfortunately for the branchy, he or she is easy to shoot and eminently edible. In fact, once it reaches maturity a rook is no good for food, so it has a very short season, centred on the last fortnight in May. You will probably need access to a specialised game dealer (see page 258) to get hold of young rooks, since we have never heard of a butcher stocking them.

How to prepare pigeons, squabs and rooks

The meat of pigeons and rooks resembles other darker-fleshed game birds such as wild ducks and grouse but, because a pigeon spends a lot more time in the air, its muscles work much harder. The legs and wings on a pigeon are pretty small and nearly all the meat is to be found on the breast. This breast muscle is a real powerhouse on pigeons and rooks. It is lean and dense and, as a result, it can be a little temperamental in the oven. Overcook a pigeon and you know it: just like a really lean steak, the meat can be dry and tough. On the plus side, this makes it one of the quickest cooking meats around. Game and fast food in one neat package!

Pigeons, squabs and rooks are portion-sized birds. One per person is usually enough if you are roasting them whole. Jointing a pigeon or rook will rarely be necessary (except for the Pigeon Pastilla recipe on page 118). However, some recipes call for the breast meat to be griddled or seared in its own right so we will talk you through filleting pigeon breasts. It is also possible to spatchcock and grill all three birds.

Spatchcocking pigeons and rooks

Hold the bird breast-side down, with one hand, with the neck cavity facing you. With the other hand using a pair of robust scissors (or even poultry shears) snip away at either side of the backbone from the neck downwards, finishing either side of the little legs, which are much tighter against the body than those on most poultry. The backbone will lift clean away. Ease the legs and wings apart and cut off the wing tips. Keep the backbones and wing tips for making an extremely flavoursome stock later. Place the bird on a chopping board, now breast-side up. Gently press the breast with the palm of your hand until the bird is flattened. You might hear a slight pop, as the wishbone breaks. This is normal. Now the spatchcocked bird is ready for seasoning or marinating.

Filleting pigeons and rooks

If a recipe requires that you sear the breast meat from pigeons and rooks, here is how to take the meat off the bone. Place the bird on a chopping board, breast up. Take a small boning knife and gently run it along the bone, easing the flesh away as you go. What you are left with will resemble a small version of a duck breast with the stub of the wing attached. Leave this wing stub on the breast for cooking as it helps with flavour and is easily sliced away as you serve up later.

Classic roasts and recommended trimmings

The three birds in this chapter are all roasted the same way; only the timings differ. Here is a classic roast pigeon or rook for two:

You will need
2 pigeons or rooks (approximate
  weight 300g each)
duck fat, lard or unsalted butter
salt and freshly ground black pepper

Preheat the oven to 200°C / Gas Mark 6. Warm the fat or butter in a small oven-proof pan and seal the birds, leg- side down first, for about 4 or 5 minutes over a low heat until the skin has browned. Turn the birds over and repeat the process on the other leg. Now raise the heat to medium and seal the breasts, for about 3 minutes on either side of the central breastbone, until each side is nicely browned. Turn the bird onto its back and roast in the oven for 7 minutes. Squabs, weighing around 350–400g, will take another minute's cooking time.

Test by pressing your thumb and forefinger on the fattest part of the breast just where it meets the wing tips. Once cooked, it will feel properly firm, but with a very subtle 'give'. Rest the birds in a warm place for 10 minutes.

At this juncture, we should point out that the breast and leg meat will still be deep red, i.e. medium-rare. This really is as far as you want to take pigeon or rook. The breast meat is terribly dry if cooked until it is brown. Moreover, the flavour can become bitter, almost like that of braised liver à la school dinners.

We never like to sound ardently didactic about cooking but if you don't like quite rare meat, pigeon and rook are probably not for you.

As if we haven't been bossy enough, we should also point out that we never pot roast or casserole wood pigeons and rooks. The meat simply won't tenderise, because of its near-total lack of fat. Squab, however, is a different matter and the subcutaneous fat helps it tenderise over a long, slow cooking time. You can swap squab pigeon for some of the pot-roast wild duck recipes in that chapter.

Stuffings and suggested trimmings
As with all the smaller game birds, we find that cooking and serving stuffings on the side of the roast (as opposed to putting them in the cavity) is much better for the meat. This is because the cooking time required for medium-rare pigeon or rook is too short to safely cook a stuffing to the required temperature. Our favourite adornment for simply roast pigeon is bread sauce (see page 238), with a knot of watercress on the side. Rook takes well to slightly sweet garnishes and pairs beautifully with Cumberland sauce (page 238).

2 Legs

Warm pigeon salad with runner beans and tapenade

Tapenade is a rough paste made from olives, anchovies and capers. It has an intensity that works well with seared pigeon breasts, but you could swap in squab or rooks. Rabbit tastes great with the olive paste, too. You could serve a confit of the legs in place of the pigeon breasts.

serves 4

2 rounds day-old bread (we prefer a sourdough)
mild vegetable or olive oil for frying
2 shallots, diced
4 cloves garlic, 2 chopped, 2 peeled and left whole
salt and freshly ground black pepper
125ml (a small glass) red wine
300g runner beans (dwarf or fine beans can be used in their place)
250g pitted black olives
3 anchovy fillets
1 tablespoon capers
leaves from a sprig of rosemary
juice of half a lemon
extra-virgin olive oil
4 wood pigeons
2 bunches or 1 x 85g bag rocket

Remove the crusts from the bread and cut it into rough dice. Toss the cubes with one or two tablespoons of the cooking oil and bake them in a low to moderate oven to make croûtons. Allow the croûtons to cool once cooked and set them aside.

Heat another two tablespoons of the cooking oil very gently in a wide bottomed frying pan and, when hot, add the shallots and garlic. Add a very scant pinch of salt and fry gently for 2 minutes. Add the wine and allow it to come to a simmer, and then braise the shallot mixture in the wine until all the liquid has evaporated and the shallots are soft and sticky. Set this reduction aside.

Top and tail the beans then cut them into sections similar in size to the croûtons. Steam or blanch them until tender but with a little crunch left (this will take about 3 minutes). Plunge the cooked beans into cold water to cool them, then drain them well and set aside.

Blitz or chop the olives, anchovies, capers and rosemary with the final 2 cloves of garlic until you have a paste. Loosen this with the lemon juice and about 3 tablespoons of the extra-virgin olive oil. Set the tapenade aside.

Finally, roast the wood pigeons whole, following the instructions on page 104. Then, once they have rested for 10 minutes after cooking, you can fillet the breasts by running a boning knife under the meat, to take it off the bone. Slice the breast meat and toss it with the beans, shallot reduction, tapenade, rocket and croûtons. Check the seasoning and serve immediately.

...geon breasts on toast

In a shallow, non-metallic dish combine the yoghurt, 1 tablespoon of the olive oil, the ginger, cumin, salt and paprika. Add the pigeon breasts to the dish, coat well in the yoghurty mixture and marinate for at least 2 hours, or preferably overnight.

Heat the oil in a wide-bottomed frying pan, remove the pigeon from the marinade and sear the breasts for about 2 minutes on each side. Take them out of the pan, place onto a separate dish, season generously with salt and pepper and set aside to rest for a good 5 minutes. Meanwhile, cut the bread into 4 rounds and toast it to your liking. Spread each slice of toast lightly with butter. Cut each pigeon breast into 3 and serve 2 breasts on each round of toast with a wedge of the lemon.

3 tablespoons ol...
½ teaspoon ground ginger
½ teaspoon ground cumin seeds
½ teaspoon salt
½ teaspoon hot paprika (smoked, if possible)
4 tablespoons mild olive oil for cooking
salt and freshly ground black pepper
bread (we prefer a sourdough loaf) and butter
1 lemon, cut into wedges

Squab and braised peas

Pigeons and peas are natural partners. The long, slow cooking time of the peas makes them very tender, although it does take away their bright, summery green-ness. Think of the classic braised petits pois 'à la Français'. You can use fresh or frozen peas for this recipe. If pigeon is not your thing, then this is great with duck.

You could add bacon to this dish. About 50g finely sliced dry-cured streaky bacon is ideal. Fry it with the onions or shallots. You could also copy the French habit of adding shredded lettuce to the peas just before taking them off the heat. Use a robust lettuce such as escarole, little gem or cos.

serves 4

1 tablespoon olive oil
2 tablespoons butter
2 onions or 4 shallots, diced finely
1 clove garlic, chopped to almost
    resemble a paste
1 small bunch of sage, picked and
    chopped
½ teaspoon salt
125ml (a small glass) red wine
1 teaspoon tomato purée
300g peas, thawed if using frozen
250ml fresh chicken or game stock
4 squab pigeons
salt and freshly ground black pepper
duck fat, lard or butter

Heat the oil and one tablespoon of the butter gently in a pan, add the onions or shallots, garlic and sage, then the salt, and stir a couple of times. Cover, lower the heat and leave the mixture to sweat for about 10 minutes. Don't let it brown. Add the wine and tomato purée, turn the heat back up and let the wine come to a simmer. Add the peas and wait for the sauce to simmer again. Add the stock and let it come to a simmer too. Now lower the heat and cook until the peas are murky and very tender, which will take a good 20 minutes. Adjust the seasoning and stir in the remaining tablespoon of butter.

Set the peas aside while you roast the squab pigeon following the instructions on page 104. Serve the whole pigeon on a bed of the braised peas, with plenty of crusty bread.

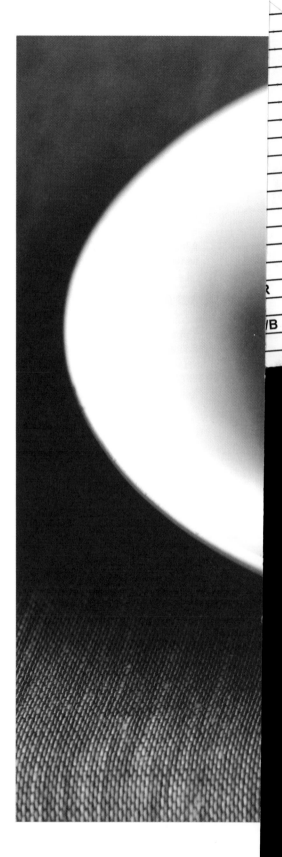

2 Legs

Pigeon and foie gras pasty

In truth this 'pasty' is a pithivier: a parcel of flaky or puff pastry containing an astonishingly rich filling of pigeon breast and duck or goose liver. It is a dish for special occasions and, although it takes some preparation, it is not hard to cook. This recipe came to us courtesy of Great Queen Street's head chef, Sam Hutchins, who, in turn, learned it whilst working with Richard Corrigan at the award-winning Lindsay House in London.

You don't need much of the liver for this recipe so, if you buy a whole one, there will be some leftovers (no bad thing if you are a foie fan). You can buy small lobes of fresh foie gras weighing as little as 400g from some suppliers. Caul fat is available from most good butchers, although you may need to phone ahead to arrange this.

serves 4

4 wood pigeons
1 tablespoon duck fat or lard
salt and freshly ground black pepper
200g foie gras
100g caul fat
1 Savoy cabbage
250g puff pastry
1 egg

Fillet the pigeon breasts following the instructions on page 103, then remove their skins. This is easily done by tugging them gently with thumb and forefinger. You can use the carcasses to make a stock, which can be reduced to a rich gravy – the perfect accompaniment to this recipe.

Remove the skin from the pigeon breasts by nicking them very gently with a small knife, before literally pulling the skin off them with thumb and forefinger. Season the fillets lightly with salt and pepper, then heat the duck fat or lard briskly in a wide bottomed frying pan, large enough to take all the breasts. Sear the breasts for just 30 seconds on either side and remove them from the pan. Note that this will leave the breasts rare, which is the ideal way to serve them. If you want them medium, double the searing time on each side. Don't cook them all the way through, as fully cooked pigeon meat is not tasty. Set the breasts aside and allow them to cool completely.

Meanwhile, soak the caul fat in plenty of cold, unsalted water and set it aside. Pull 8 leaves from the Savoy cabbage, avoiding the tougher, outer leaves. Heat a large saucepan of salted water and blanch the leaves for 2 minutes, or until they are tender, but not soggy. Plunge them into cold water to take the heat out of them then drain thoroughly. Now cut the stalk from the middle of each leaf, squeeze each one until totally dry and set aside.

Cut four pieces from the foie gras, to match the size of the pigeon breasts. Set them aside in the fridge.

Flour a worktop. Roll out the puff pastry until it is the thickness of a pound coin and cut eight discs out of the sheet. We use a saucer as a size guide. Keep the discs in a cool place (the fridge is ideal) until you are ready to use them.

Now you can assemble and cook the pasties. Preheat the oven to 220°C / Gas Mark 7.

Cut the caul fat into four pieces, each roughly twice the diameter of the pastry discs. Lay one of the cabbage leaves on each piece of the caul. Top each cabbage and caul base with a pigeon breast and top each breast with a piece of the foie gras. Now sandwich each piece of foie gras with another pigeon breast and top each breast with another cabbage leaf. Bring the caul fat up and round the pigeon, foie gras and cabbage sandwich and squish the parcel gently together so that you have 2 breasts of pigeon, with a foie gras filling and a wrap of cabbage and caul fat. Once you have this give it another squeeze to get rid of any excess moisture. Set these 4 parcels in the fridge and clean the worktop thoroughly.

Now line a roasting sheet big enough to take 4 discs of the pastry with baking parchment or silicone. Lay out 4 discs of the pastry on the sheet. Beat the egg with 2 tablespoons of water and lightly brush the pastry discs with the egg wash. Place the pigeon and foie gras parcels in the middle of each disc of pastry. Now lay the remaining discs of pastry on top of each parcel and press down the sides to seal the pasties. Egg wash the new lids of these pasties and transfer them to the preheated oven. Bake for 15 minutes, and check to see if the pastry is an even golden colour all over. Once cooked, rest the pasties for 10 minutes before serving with plenty of gravy which you have created by reducing the stock you made from the pigeon carcasses. One of the real thrills of this dish is the moment the diners cut through the pastry to reveal the pink breasts of pigeon and the 'only just' melting foie gras.

Rook pie

This is best eaten cold, like a raised pork pie. When rooks elude you, swap in pigeon or squab.

serves 4

4 rooks
300g minced veal or pork
200g smoked streaky bacon, diced
grated rind of ½ lemon
1 teaspoon juniper berries, lightly
   crushed
1 clove of garlic, crushed
10 sprigs of thyme, finely chopped
1 tablespoon unsalted butter
200g button mushrooms, finely sliced
salt and freshly ground black pepper
1 egg, beaten

For the pastry
250g plain flour
200g cold unsalted butter
100ml sour cream or crème fraîche

First start with the pastry. Cut the butter into 1cm dice and place it, along with the flour into the bowl of a food processor. Pulse in 1- or 2-second bursts until the mixture resembles breadcrumbs. Add the sour cream and pulse again until the mixture has just begun to come together. You need to be careful and work fast, this pastry is extremely short and you don't want to end up with a paste.

Tip the dough onto a lightly floured surface and gently pull it all together to form a ball. Wrap the dough in clingfilm and refrigerate for 30 minutes.

Now make the filling. Remove the legs from the rooks, peel off the skin, slice the meat off the bones and cut into fine dice. Cut the breast from the birds, remove the skin and chop into a 2cm dice. Put the rook meat into a bowl with the mince, bacon, lemon rind, juniper, garlic and thyme.

Melt the butter in a frying pan over a medium heat and sauté the mushrooms, with a pinch of salt, until they have softened. Remove from the heat and let them cool before adding them to the bowl with the rest of the ingredients. Season with a good pinch of salt and black pepper.

Lightly grease a 22cm pie dish with a little soft butter. Cut away a third of the pastry then roll out the larger piece into a circle just the right size to fit the pie dish. Lay the pastry into the base of the dish and then spoon in the filling. Roll out the remaining pastry into a disc for the lid. Brush the edges of the pastry base with the beaten egg, then lay over the pastry lid. Pinch all around the edges to seal, then brush the top of the pie with the egg wash and make a small hole in the lid. Chill in the fridge for 30 minutes.

Preheat the oven to 220°C / Gas Mark 7.

Place the pie onto the middle shelf of the oven and bake for 10 minutes before lowering the heat to 190°C / Gas Mark 5. Continue to cook for a further 20 minutes. Remove from the oven and rest in a warm place for at least 30 minutes before serving.

2 Legs

game: a cookbook

Pigeon terrine

A classic set terrine in the rustic, French style. You can add pigeon livers to the chicken ones if the birds come intact.

serves 10

1 small onion, finely diced
2 tablespoons duck fat or butter
200ml red wine
10 slices of smoked streaky bacon
750g pork belly, coarsely minced
150g chicken livers, trimmed
6 pigeon breasts
50g pistachio nuts, lightly roasted
1 clove of garlic, finely chopped
50ml brandy
1 teaspoon fresh thyme leaves
salt and freshly ground black pepper

Preheat the oven to 160°C / Gas Mark 3. Warm half of the duck fat or butter in a small saucepan and sauté the onion over a low heat until it has softened. Pour over the red wine and simmer over a low heat until all of the wine has been absorbed into the onions. Leave to cool. Meanwhile, heat the remaining duck fat in a pan and gently seal the breasts. 30 seconds a side will be enough to brown them, but also keep them quite undercooked. They will finish their cooking in the terrine. Leave the breasts to cool.

Line a 1-litre terrine or a loaf tin with the bacon strips crossways so that the edges are hanging over the sides. In a large bowl combine the pork belly, livers, nuts, garlic, brandy and thyme along with the cooled onions. Mix really well, the ideal method is to squish it all together with your hands – this slightly breaks up the livers, which tends to hold the finished terrine together a little better. Season with salt (don't be shy with this, it will take about 15g) and plenty of pepper.

Squash half of the mixture into the lined terrine. Season the pigeon breasts with a pinch of salt and a grinding of pepper then line them along the length of the terrine. Cover the breasts with the remaining mixture and then fold over the hanging ends of bacon.

Seal the top of the terrine with buttered foil, place it in a roasting pan and pour in boiling water to come halfway up the sides. Place the terrine in the oven and cook for 1¼ hours. To test and see if the terrine is cooked, pierce the terrine with a skewer, it should come out hot and the juices will be clear. Let the terrine cool for 30 minutes, then weigh it down, ideally with another loaf tin filled with food cans. Leave until the terrine has completely cooled down. Then remove the weights and refrigerate it overnight.

Serve sliced with sourdough toast, cornichons or fruit chutney.

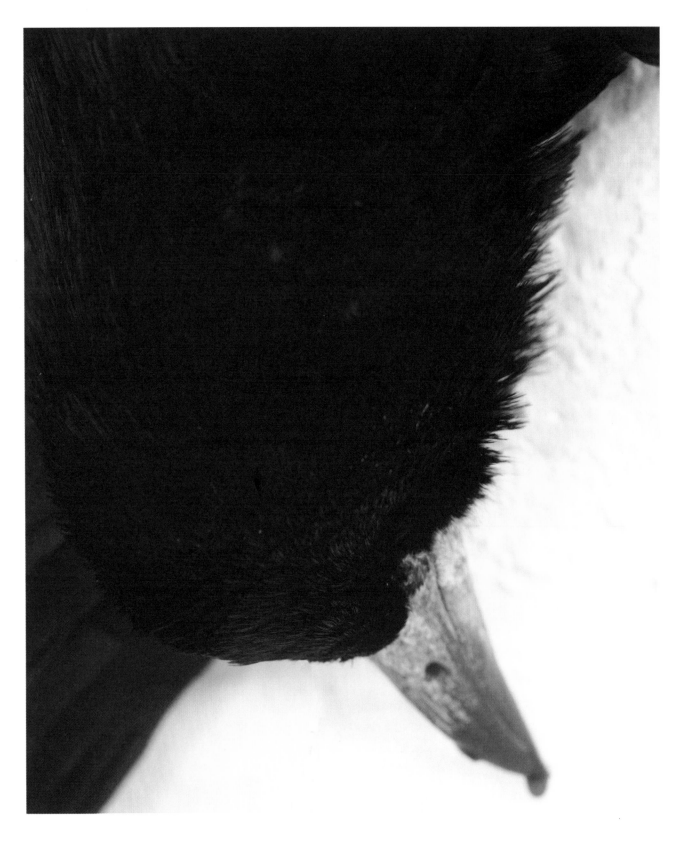

Grilled rook and Romesco sauce

Romesco sauce is a Catalan dish, the focus of which is sweet pepper (although sometimes chillies can be used as well). It can be thickened with stale bread or almonds. We prefer the almond version.

serves 4

3 red peppers, halved and deseeded
3 cloves of garlic
1 long red chilli
150ml extra-virgin olive oil
salt and freshly ground black pepper
150g whole blanched almonds
½ teaspoon sweet smoked paprika
1 tablespoon sherry vinegar
6 young rooks, spatchcocked
   (see page 103)
olive oil for grilling

Preheat the oven to 150°C / Gas Mark 2. Put the peppers, garlic and chilli into a baking dish, rub them with a touch of olive oil. Give them a sprinkle of salt and cover the dish with foil. Place the dish into the middle of the oven and bake for 30 minutes – by this time the vegetables will be soft and should have given off quite a lot of liquid. Remove from the oven, take off the foil lid and leave to cool.

Meanwhile, place the almonds on a baking tray and onto the top shelf of the oven. Roast them for between 10 and 15 minutes until they are golden brown. Remove and leave to cool. When the peppers are cool enough to handle, take them from the liquid, peel off the skins, discard the seeds, set them aside and reserve the juices. Slip the garlic cloves from their skin, carefully peel and seed the chilli and sit it with the peppers.

Pound the almonds with the peppers, garlic and chilli in a pestle and mortar, or pulse in the bowl of a food processor, until you have a thick but chunky paste. Add the paprika and vinegar then slowly pour in the olive oil, as if you were making mayonnaise. Season with salt and pepper and, if it seems a little too thick, let it down with some of the reserved pepper juice. The sauce is now complete.

Preheat a barbecue or griddle pan. Put the spatchcocked rooks breast-side down on a chopping board and with a large knife, cut through the centre of the breastbones, leaving you with 12 rook halves. Lightly oil the bird halves, season with salt and pepper and lay them on the grill skin-side down. Leave the birds to cook on their skins for 2 minutes before turning them onto the bone and cooking for a further 2 minutes. You'll need to repeat this process a few times

to avoid charring the skin. In all it should take 8–10 minutes to cook the birds until the meat is a rosy pink. Like quails, the flesh becomes quite tough if over cooked. Rest in a warm place for 10 minutes.

Serve 3 rook halves per person with a good spoonful of sauce.

Pigeon pastilla

A pastilla is a small parcel of pigeon meat, usually spiced and sweetened. It is not unlike an Indian samosa. The correct Moroccan name is 'b'stilla', though historically the dish is said to have originated in Andalusia.

serves 6–8

3 wood pigeons
200g unsalted butter
1 large onion, grated
½ teaspoon ground ginger
½ cinnamon stick
6 allspice berries
½ bunch of parsley
½ bunch of coriander
2 whole eggs
4 egg yolks
salt and freshly ground black pepper
10 sheets of filo pastry
200g flaked almonds
2 tablespoons icing sugar
½ teaspoon ground cinnamon

Spatchcock the pigeon following the instructions on page 103. Preheat the oven to 180°C / Gas Mark 4.

Place the pieces flesh-side down in a pan where they will fit snugly and add 40g of the butter, the onion, ginger, cinnamon stick, allspice and herbs along with a good pinch of salt and a grinding of pepper. Pour over enough water to cover and bring the pan slowly up to the boil. Cover and simmer over the lowest heat for 1 hour, adding a little more water if necessary.

Melt 30g of butter in a pan and when it starts to froth, gently fry the flaked almonds until they are golden. Drain the nuts on kitchen paper.

When the pigeon is cooked, drain off the stock and reserve the liquid in a jug. Leave the meat to cool, and then remove the skin from the birds and shred the flesh from the bones. You should now have 300ml of stock. If you have more, reduce the liquid; if not quite enough, then add a touch of water. Beat the eggs and the yolks together and add them to the stock. Pour into a small pan and stir over a low heat until the mixture is thick and creamy, kind of like a custard. This should take around 5 minutes. Check the seasoning.

Melt the remaining butter until it just starts to bubble and remove from the heat. Brush the base and sides of a 26cm pie tin with the warm butter. Fit a sheet of the pastry into the dish, letting the edges hang over the side, and brush it lightly with more butter. Lay over another sheet of pastry at a 45-degree angle, and again brush with butter. Repeat this with another 4 sheets of pastry until the dish is evenly covered. Cover the base of the pie with the shredded pigeon, then pour over the eggy sauce. Mix the almonds with the sugar and scatter over the top. Cover the top of the pie with a sheet of pastry and gently butter the surface. Repeat this again with the remaining pastry, again at the same angles, then tuck the top between the overlapping bottom sheets and the sides of the tin. Fold the overhanging pastry over the top and brush with the rest of the butter.

Bake in the oven for 30 minutes, then raise the temperature to 200°C / Gas Mark 6 and cook for a further 10 minutes until the pastry is crisp and golden. Serve sprinkled with a little more icing sugar and the ground cinnamon.

Wood pigeon and faggots

A faggot is essentially a strongly flavoured meatball, traditionally made with pork and its offal. If that doesn't sound like your thing, you could buy a coarse sausage and add it to the pot, rather than making the faggots.

serves 4

3 tablespoons duck fat or unsalted butter
2 onions, chopped
1 clove of garlic, chopped
300g pork belly, coarsely minced
150g livers of your choice; pig's, chicken or duck, finely chopped
6–8 sage leaves, finely sliced
1/4 teaspoon ground mace
1/4 teaspoon ground allspice
1 egg
60g fresh breadcrumbs
1 piece of caul fat, around 100g
1 onion, sliced
2 bay leaves
250ml dry cider
4 wood pigeons
salt and freshly ground black pepper

Preheat the oven to 180°C / Gas Mark 4. Heat 1 tablespoon of the duck fat or butter in a small saucepan and add the onion and garlic, along with a pinch of salt. Increase the heat to get a good sizzle going, then cover, turn the heat right down low and sweat the onion until it's translucent for around 5 or 6 minutes. You'll be left with soft onions and lovely sweet juices. Let it cool in the pan. In a bowl, combine the pork mince, livers, sage, spices, onion mixture and egg and give it a good mix, preferably scrunching it all together with your hands. Add the breadcrumbs, about 1/2 a teaspoon of salt and a good grind of pepper, then give it another mix. If you find the mixture is a bit loose add some extra breadcrumbs; the mix should be just firm enough to handle.

Soak the caul fat in a bowl of cold water to loosen it, then stretch the fat out into a sheet on a flat surface before cutting out 4 squares of around 20cm. Divide the meat into 4, roll into balls and place these balls in the middle of the squares of fat, then wrap the faggots, pulling the fat right around to cover them tightly.

Heat another tablespoon of duck fat or butter in a small ovenproof dish just large enough to hold the faggots, and sauté the sliced onions with a pinch of salt until softened and slightly browned. Place the faggots on top of the onions in the dish, tuck in the bay leaves, and then pour over the cider. Bring the liquid up to the boil, check the seasoning and transfer the dish to the oven. Bake for 30 minutes until the tops are nicely browned. Remove the faggots from the oven, cover the dish with a sheet of foil and leave them to sit in a warm place while you cook the pigeons.

Raise the oven temperature to 200°C / Gas Mark 6. Heat the remaining duck fat or butter in a roasting tray, season the pigeons all over and inside the cavity with salt and pepper. Seal the birds, starting on the legs over a medium heat. Once the skin has browned nicely, after about 2–3 minutes, turn the birds over and repeat the process on the other leg. Prop the pigeons onto one side of the breast and gently let the skin brown for a minute or so, then tilt the birds over onto the other side and brown gently. Pop the birds onto their backs and place the dish into the oven and cook for 12–15 minutes. You can test the birds by inserting a metal skewer or small sharp knife into the plumpest part of the breast by the leg. If the metal is warm to the touch when it comes out, the birds are done. If not, continue cooking for another 2–3 minutes and test again.

Once cooked, leave the birds to rest in a warm place, breast-side down, for 10 minutes. At this point you can turn the oven off and put the faggots back in where they will warm in the residual heat.

Serve one pigeon and one faggot on warmed plates and spoon over the oniony gravy.

Rabbit and squirrel

Nothing sums up Britain's curious relationship with its wild food better than our attitude to rabbit. It is the easiest game to come across. It is ridiculously cheap and, perhaps most importantly, it has a tender, pink and tasty meat that manages to be satisfying rather than challenging. Few would describe the flavour of rabbit as gamey, and many people think it tastes 'a bit like chicken'. We wish that more of the miserably raised and ultimately tasteless chickens that this country consumes tasted more like wild rabbit. Rabbit should outsell battery chicken by a million miles. It is leaner, more flavoursome and properly free range.

Quite why we don't eat a lot more rabbit in the UK is mystifying, if not exactly a mystery. A veritable jumble of reasons, some more logical than others, put many people off buying rabbits for the pot.

It would be too easy for a couple of cooks who grew up in the seventies to lay the blame at Richard Adams' door, but the huge popularity of *Watership Down* must take some of the blame. His wasn't the first work of shameless, bunny-related anthropomorphology. Beatrix Potter was at it decades earlier. There is no getting away from the fact that rabbits are cute, with fluffy tails, floppy ears and big brown eyes. Some people even consider them to be good pets. Once any predominantly wild animal is domesticated outside the arena of husbandry, the notion of eating it becomes taboo. An extreme example of this is the collective western distaste for eating dog or cat. People know it is considered normal in the Far East, but it's something they prefer not to think about.

On the other side of the coin, some people are put off eating rabbit because it is, to be frank, a rodent and, moreover, a pest. The same problem exists when it comes to selling the idea of wood pigeon as a tasty morsel (see page 102). We are nervous about eating vermin.

More fool us. Rabbit's unrivalled status as a farmyard pest makes it one of the cheapest wild meats on offer. The indefatigable breeding prowess of Britain's bunnies means that rabbit has no closed season. It can be caught and eaten all year round.

Not all the rabbit eaten in Britain, and indeed Europe, is wild. Farmed rabbit is actually more common on the continent (particularly in France), but there is an increasing amount of tame rabbit for sale in the UK. Some game dealers and aficionados will tell you that this is not game, and some people question the ethics of rabbit farming on the grounds that it is impossible to produce free-range meat this way. For a more detailed discussion on the anomaly that is 'farmed game', see page 12. Whilst we always recommend wild rabbit over farmed, we will include instructions for cooking farmed rabbit in this chapter simply because it is available.

Anyone who remembers the old nursery rhyme 'run, rabbit run' will be au fait with the idea of bunnies for dinner. Seeing squirrels on a menu will probably cause more than a few raised eyebrows and, until a couple of years ago, we had never been offered squirrel by any of the game dealers who supply our restaurants. That is beginning to change. The grey squirrel was introduced to Britain in the nineteenth century from North America and quickly established itself as a pest in this country, doing damage to forestry, thieving from young cereal and vegetable crops and, perhaps worst of all, becoming a threat to the survival of our native red squirrel, which has been unable to compete with its foreign cousins.

When it is not pillaging commercial crops, the grey squirrel enjoys a diet of wild nuts and berries, particularly acorns. In Spain, the highly prized Iberico pig is encouraged to forage for acorns, which gives its meat an intense, nutty flavour. Certainly, the grey squirrel's eating habits have a marked influence on the flavour of its meat: some fans even compare it to wild boar or pork. We have to say we find it overtly similar in character to wild rabbit. To that end, some recipes in this chapter can utilise squirrel in place of rabbit. We must point out that not all rabbit recipes will work with squirrel. Rabbit saddles, for example are much meatier than those on a squirrel. The leg is where you will find the bulk of a squirrel's meat. The other cuts are pretty rangey: they are best used for dishes like rillettes and confit.

4 Legs

How to prepare rabbits and squirrels

As mammals, rabbit, squirrel, hare and venison are essentially like lamb or pork carcasses. They won't look that way at a glance, but they offer up similar cuts of meat. There are two small front legs (sometimes known as arms or shoulders), a neck, a loin (or 'saddle'), plus two back legs. Unlike venison there is no shin or shank on the legs; you cook rabbit and squirrel legs, front or back, as one entity.

Lay the rabbit or squirrel on the chopping board with the rib cage facing upwards, and the small front legs to the left. First, using a small boning knife, cut off these legs. You do this by working the knife along the join between the leg and rib cage, until the joint comes clean away. In this book we call these small front legs 'shoulders'. Now cut off the two larger rear legs. You will find a small hip and thigh joint just below the rump. It is easy to tease the joints apart with the tip of your boning knife, while you very gently pull the leg away from the hip. You now have a very neat pair of legs. All that will be left is the saddle, with rib and neck attached. Because the rib bones are incredibly fiddly, we tend to remove them from the saddle with a good pair of household scissors, cutting them just where they meet the loin. Don't throw anything away! The ribs and necks make a great, blonde stock, not unlike the kind you would get from chicken bones. You can also render the ribs for a dish like rillettes (see page 143).

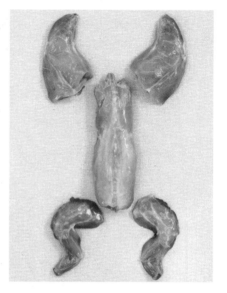

Roasts and trimmings

We only use the saddle of wild rabbit for roasting, in the true sense of the word. The other cuts fare much better in pot roasts and braises. When it comes to the farmed rabbit, which is marginally fattier, you can roast the saddle and back legs. We have never roasted squirrel. All that tree climbing means its muscles work so much harder. The most forgiving way to cook meat like this is slowly.

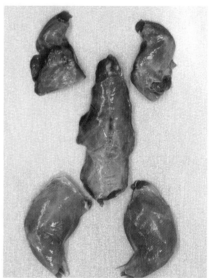

Roast wild rabbit saddle for two

You want to aim to serve about 250g of rabbit saddle as a portion. This is pretty much one whole saddle on most wild rabbits. If they come up very small, allow two saddles per person.

2 good-sized or 4 small saddles of wild rabbit
salt and freshly ground black pepper
3 tablespoons duck fat or butter

Preheat the oven to 220°C / Gas Mark 7. The first thing you need to do is remove any sinew from the saddle. This is easily done by slipping a sharp knife under the sinew by the rib cage, detaching it there and then running your knife over the fillet and detaching it from the spine. It's a little like trimming a fillet of lamb or beef. You will be left with a lean loin cut, with the two breasts clearly defined on either side. On lamb this would be the breast meat (a fatty, braising cut), on rabbit it is a good way to protect the lean meat on the true saddle.

Season the saddle with salt and pepper. Melt the duck fat or butter in an ovenproof frying pan and seal the saddles on all sides over a medium heat. To transfer them to the oven, make sure they are saddle-side up, which is to say, they are on their fronts (with the breast meat tucked underneath them). Roast for 5 minutes. If the saddles are bigger, add another minute per 50g. Check the saddles: once cooked, they will feel quite tight when you pinch them between thumb and forefinger. Remove the pan from the oven. Cover the saddles with a sheet of foil and leave them to rest in a warm place for 10 minutes before serving whole.

Roast, jointed farmed rabbit for two

This really only works with the pale, naturally tender meat on a farmed rabbit.

1 farmed rabbit
4 tablespoons extra-virgin olive oil
2 tablespoons Dijon mustard
salt and freshly ground black pepper
duck fat, lard or unsalted butter
125ml chicken stock (you could use rabbit stock if you have made any)

Joint the rabbit (see opposite).

Mix together the olive oil, Dijon mustard and a grind of black pepper in a bowl and toss the rabbit pieces through this marinade. Leave for a minimum of one hour; a couple is actually ideal.

Set the oven to 220°C / Gas Mark 7. Warm the duck fat, lard or butter in an ovenproof frying pan over a brisk heat and, when it is hot, brown the rabbit pieces all over. Transfer them to the oven and cook for 6–8 minutes, and then test them. Once cooked, the meat will feel firm to the touch. Drain the fat from the pan, put it back over a medium heat and pour in the stock. As soon as it comes to a simmer remove the pan from the heat and leave to rest in a warm place for 10 minutes.

Suggested trimmings and stuffings

Because it is such a lean meat we prefer to roast rabbit on the bone for flavour and to keep it moist. We only stuff rabbit for one recipe in this book, and it is on page 137, with instructions on how to bone and roll a rabbit saddle. However, when served on the bone, any stuffing you like to use with poultry suits rabbit, served on the side. Our personal favourites are prune and pistachio or wild mushroom (see pages 236–237).

Rabbit braised with prunes and beer

There are many fine, Flemish dishes consisting of game braised with dried fruit. This is easily the best. Something about the gamey notes in rabbit meat marries brilliantly with beer. This is definitely a dish for wild bunnies with stronger-tasting meat than their farmed counterparts.

serves 4

2 rabbits, jointed (see page 124 if you want to do this yourself)
2 tablespoons duck fat or lard
100g smoked streaky bacon cut into strips
2 cloves garlic, chopped
4 leaves sage (optional)
2 medium onions, finely chopped
salt and freshly ground pepper, to taste
330ml (about a bottle) of beer
1 tablespoon tomato purée
200g pitted prunes
100ml water or light chicken stock

Joint the rabbit. Heat the duck fat or lard over a low to medium flame and fry the bacon until it starts to render up some of its smoky fat. Remove it, keeping as much fat as possible in the pan and use this to brown the rabbit pieces. When they are done, remove them and set aside. Now add the garlic, sage and onions, plus about half a teaspoon of salt. Lower the heat to a whisper, cover the pan and let everything 'sweat' for about a quarter of an hour. Don't let the vegetables brown.

When everything has softened, add the beer, turn up the heat and allow it to bubble fiercely for a minute or so. Stir in the tomato purée and return all the meat to the pot, plus the prunes. Cover with water (you may need a little more than 100ml) and cook for about 45 minutes, or until the rabbit is tender.

Make sure, when cooking whole, jointed rabbit, that it is the legs you test for tenderness, as they can take slightly longer than the other sections. Season the stew to taste when the cooking is done.

Rabbit confit

You can confit rabbit legs and shoulders, a process which preserves them and makes the meat incredibly rich and tender.

serves 4

2 tablespoons of coarse sea salt
1 bay leaf
a handful of whole black peppercorns
a sliver of lemon or orange peel
4 rabbit legs or 8 shoulders
1 medium tin of duck or goose fat
  (approximately 340g)

Infuse the salt with the bay, peppercorns and zest for an hour or two before you plan to use it. If you are a serial confiteer it is well worth making yourself a large tub of fragrant confit salt. It keeps indefinitely. Lay the rabbit legs in a roasting tray or a box large enough for a single layer (make sure you can fit whatever it is in the fridge). Cover them completely with the salt and leave in the fridge for 2–6 hours.

When you return to the legs, drain them of any liquid that might have appeared. Wipe the excess salt from the legs.

Preheat the oven to 150°C / Gas Mark 2. Decant the duck or goose fat into a deep-ish baking tray or a casserole dish. Pop it in the oven to warm up and liquefy. Now submerge the legs or shoulders. Cover with a casserole lid or foil and cook for about 1½ hours. Check them after this time, they might be yielding but they could take a little longer. The meat should be very tender but not falling apart.

Now you can keep the legs, in the fat, until you want to use them. They will keep, refrigerated, for weeks.

Deep-fried, bread-crumbed rabbit

Once confited, the legs and shoulders of rabbit can be fried, which is delicious and very indulgent. A leg and a shoulder make up one good portion. All you need to serve this with is a fine salad and a wedge of lemon, but ketchup is great, too.

serves 4

4 shoulders and 4 legs of confited
    rabbit (see previous recipe)
4 tablespoons Dijon mustard
3 eggs
2 tablespoons milk
4 tablespoons plain flour
200g dry breadcrumbs
oil for deep-frying

Make sure you use cold confit rabbit for this; it won't work fresh from the cooker, as the meat will be too soft. Remove the rabbit confit from its preservative fat and wipe it totally dry. Then, using a pastry brush, generously anoint each leg and shoulder with the mustard. Set the meat aside.

Beat the eggs with the milk in a good-sized mixing bowl. Place the flour in another mixing bowl and the breadcrumbs in another. Toss the rabbit legs in the flour, then in the egg mix. Finally, coat them generously with the crumbs.

Heat the oil to 150°C if you have a deep-fryer. If you don't have a fryer, test the oil for readiness by dropping a small cube of bread into the oil. If it fizzes enthusiastically and browns within a minute the oil is hot enough to fry. Fry the rabbit pieces for 8 minutes, until the crumbs are golden and the meat very tender. Rest the fried rabbit on kitchen towel for a couple of minutes then serve immediately.

4 Legs

game: a cookbook

Bottled rabbit

Here is an oddity, adapted from Matthew Fort's book, *Eating up Italy*. The Italian name for the recipe is 'Tonno di coniglio' (rabbit like tuna) and the results are a little like the confited tuna in oil sold in cans or jars all around the Mediterranean. You can use the whole rabbit for this recipe.

serves 4

For one whole rabbit you will need
salt and freshly ground black pepper
a handful of sage, leaves left whole
1 litre extra-virgin olive oil, a mild one
is best here
2 bulbs garlic, cloves peeled but left
whole

Joint the rabbit following the instructions on page 124. The whole rabbit can be bottled, but you might want to leave out the neck and ribcage, as the bones can be very hard to pick. We prefer to use this part of the rabbit for stock. Pop the rest of the jointed rabbit into a pan of salted water, bring to a boil, then immediately lower the heat and simmer gently for about an hour. If you are using a farmed rabbit, this will probably be enough time. You want the meat to feel tender like poached chicken. If using a wild rabbit, you might need double the cooking time.

Once ready, drain the meat thoroughly, then allow it to cool until it is easy to handle. Pick all the meat from the bones, keeping the pieces as chunky as possible. Now start to layer the meat, garlic, oil and sage, into a non-metallic container, seasoning lightly as you go. Cover the whole thing with any remaining oil. This is best eaten at least a day later.

Rabbit niçoise

This recipe was inspired by the Italian name for bottled rabbit, which is 'rabbit like tuna'. Since rabbit replaces the tuna, we use charcuterie to complement it instead of anchovies. A niçoise salad without anchovies is probably sacrilege, but we love it. You can use any spicy, salami-type sausage, or even lardons of bacon.

serves 4

400g new potatoes (small ones such as
    Jersey Royals are best)
100g bobby (aka dwarf) beans
4 eggs
4 tomatoes
1 cos lettuce or 2 little gem lettuces
50g cured sausage or salami (our
    favourite is Italian finocchiata) or
    streaky bacon
1 bottled rabbit (see page 129)
100g black olives
a small bunch of basil
75ml extra-virgin olive oil
1 tablespoon lemon juice or wine vinegar
½ teaspoon freshly ground black pepper
salt
2 tablespoons capers

First of all, cook the potatoes until tender. Leave them to cool, and then break them up by hand, rather than slicing them. This creates little crumbs that fall into the dressing and emulsify it ever so slightly. Next, cook the beans: blanch or steam them for 2 minutes. Then drain and cool them instantly under a cold tap. If the beans are not too babyish, they look and taste fantastic when shucked. This means squishing them out of their skins. Using your thumb and forefinger, literally squeeze the membrane lightly at one end of the bean. Don't press too hard. It is a bit fiddly but worth it. Eggs next. For creamy yolks, bring a pan of water to the boil, carefully put in the eggs, then cover and cook for exactly 6 minutes. Cool immediately by plunging them into cold water. Peel them as soon as possible, as the shell comes off most easily just after they have been cooked. Cut them into quarters.

Deseed the tomatoes by cutting them open from top (stalk end) to bottom; place on a chopping board and scoop out the seeds with a spoon. Then cut each tomato half into 4. Shred the lettuce roughly. Slice or dice the salami or bacon. If using bacon fry it until crispy.

Pick the bottled rabbit, keeping the meat as chunky as possible; discard the bones. Stone the olives and pick the basil leaves. Leave them whole.

The rest of the work is assembly. Whisk up the oil and lemon juice or vinegar with the pepper and some salt, then dress the potatoes with some of this mixture. Then toss everything (except the eggs) in a large bowl with the remaining dressing. Check the seasoning. Garnish with the eggs, halved or quartered.

4 Legs

Jellied rabbit and chips

An intensely refreshing dish for a hot day. You can serve it with a really mustardy mayonnaise if you wish. If you don't fancy the idea of letting the rabbit set in its own stock you can serve the dish warm, as a very simple braise. Chervil is a superb herb for rabbit but, should it prove elusive, you can use tarragon instead.

A word about chips: these can be tricky to make in a domestic setting, unless you have a deep-fat fryer, or a really suitable pan and a probe thermometer that you can immerse in oil. Good chips need to be cooked twice: once on a low heat and again on a high heat, and the temperature control is important. If all this sounds like a palaver then do what we regularly do at home, and buy oven chips!

serves 4

2 whole rabbits
2 onions
2 carrots
3 cloves garlic
2 stalks celery
1 bay leaf
3 tablespoons red wine vinegar
½ teaspoon sugar
1 litre chicken stock
salt and freshly ground black pepper
1 small bunch chervil
1 small bunch parsley
800g floury potatoes
oil for deep-frying

Joint the rabbits following the instructions on page 124. Peel the onions, carrots and garlic, but leave them whole. Top and tail the celery. Place the jointed pieces in a suitable pot with the vegetables, the whole tomato, bay leaf, vinegar, sugar and stock. Add a level teaspoon of salt. Simmer the rabbit in this rough *court bouillon* until the meat is very tender. It could take about 2 hours. Allow the meat to cool completely in the stock. This is actually best done overnight, which enables you to skim any fat from the top of the stock. Now pull the meat from the stock and pick it, being careful to get rid of any bones. Strain the stock. Keep the carrots and onions, but discard the other bits and bobs. Now return the stock to a fairly brisk heat and reduce it by about a third, until it feels slightly silky between finger and thumb.

To put the jellied rabbit together, roughly chop the carrots and onions. Mix them in with the meat and add just enough of the stock to cover the ingredients. Chop the chervil and parsley. Stir them into the meaty mixture. Check the seasoning. You might want to add a little more salt, and another dash of vinegar is good for the overall flavour, too. Set the rabbit by chilling it in a terrine or a suitable serving dish. It will take another few hours. If you like, it could be pressed into individual ramekins.

To make the chips, peel and cut the potatoes into the desired shapes, about a centimetre thick is ideal. If you have a deep-fat fryer set it to 150°C. If not, you need plenty of oil in a large, high-sided saucepan, and a temperature probe.

'Blanch' the chips on this low setting for about 5 minutes. They need to be totally cooked through but still pale. Let them drain and turn the heat up to 190°C. Blanch them again for just 2 minutes, or until they are gold and crispy on the outside. Drain again, on kitchen towel for a minute or so before serving.

Rabbit pie

If you don't fancy the jellied rabbit and chips opposite, why not replace the cold rabbit with something as comforting as this pie? It is not unlike chicken pie, with soft flakes of tender white meat in a white sauce, spiked with a little mustard and tarragon.

serves 4

2 whole wild rabbits
2 carrots
1 bay leaf
3 onions, two left whole, one roughly diced
salt and freshly ground black pepper
1 tablespoon mild olive oil for frying
4 tablespoons butter
3 leeks, roughly sliced
2 stalks celery, roughly sliced
2 tablespoons plain flour
1 tablespoon Dijon or English mustard
a small bunch of tarragon, picked and chopped
250g puff pastry
1 egg
3 tablespoons milk

Joint the rabbits following the instructions on page 124. Place the jointed pieces in a suitable pot with the carrots, left whole, the bay leaf, and two of the onions, also left whole. Add a level teaspoon of salt and cover the meat and vegetables with about a litre of cold water. You don't want the meat swimming in a huge amount of liquid; it should just be covered. Simmer the rabbit in this rough *court bouillon* until the meat is very tender. It could take about 2 hours. Allow the meat to cool completely in the stock. This is actually best done overnight, which enables you to skim any fat from the top of the stock. Pull the cold rabbit from the stock and pick it clean off the bones. Make sure there are no bones left, as they can be very fiddly. Strain the stock and set both the meat and the liquid aside.

Heat the oil and 2 tablespoons of the butter in a wide-bottomed pan and very gently fry the diced onion, plus the leeks and celery for about 10 minutes, or until they are good and tender. Don't let them brown. If this looks like it is in danger of happening, add a couple of tablespoons of the rabbit stock to the pot.

Once the vegetables are tender set them aside in their cooking pot. Stir in the cooked rabbit meat.

Preheat the oven to 200°C / Gas Mark 6. In a saucepan, heat the remaining butter and once it has melted stir in the flour. Fry the butter and flour mixture very, very gently for 5 minutes, after which it will start to smell 'biscuity'. This sounds odd but you will know what we mean. Remove the mix from the heat and start to stir in the rabbit stock, stirring hard to avoid lumps. Reheat the mix slowly to form a *velouté* (a stocky version of white sauce,

really). Remove it from the heat once it is as thick as you want it. Stir in the rabbit and vegetables, the mustard and tarragon. Check the seasoning. This is the pie filling. Allow it to cool once more. Finally, transfer it to an ovenproof dish: the kind you might use for a crumble or shepherd's pie.

Flour a worktop and roll out the pastry until it is roughly half a centimetre thick. Beat the egg with the milk. Egg wash the rim of the baking dish and drape the pastry over the dish. Press it only to the rim of the dish. You don't need to trim it to fit the rim if there is any overhang, although you can if you wish. Egg wash the pastry lid and pierce it with a fork in 3 or 4 places, to allow some steam to escape when baking. Bake the pie for 20–25 minutes, or until the pastry is golden and the middle piping hot. Serve immediately, with a perky salad or steamed greens.

game: a cookbook

Rabbit stuffed with black pudding

Rabbit's tender white meat tastes delicious spiked with the richness of black pudding. Serve it up on a pile of mash with a good gravy, made from the rabbit bones if you have time. If this recipe seems a little involved, you could actually augment a simple roast saddle of rabbit with some fried black pudding on the side. That said, the stuffing part is easier than it sounds. This dish works well with wild and farmed rabbits. A farmed rabbit saddle might feed two people if large enough. You need a good, flavoursome black pudding and, if you have access to it, why not try the Spanish version, morcilla? It has an intense smoky flavour, not unlike chorizo.

You need caul fat for this recipe, so you might have to ask the butcher for it in advance.

serves 4

4 wild rabbit saddles or two, larger
  farmed saddles
250g caul fat
200g black pudding
1 egg
2 tablespoons milk
2 tablespoons butter
1 tablespoon mild olive oil for cooking
salt and freshly ground black pepper

First you need to bone the rabbit saddles. A very friendly butcher might be happy to do this for you but, if not, here's how. Place the saddle on a chopping board with the underside (where the ribs are) facing upwards. Run a sharp boning knife under and along the ribs, edging them away from the meat as carefully as possible. Finally you will come to the backbone, and you have to run the same knife carefully along its length, removing the meat as you go. Repeat the process on the other side. You should be left with the two sides of loin meat, without the central bone, and two flaps of breast or belly meat either side of the central, lean part. Don't worry if it doesn't all hold together totally, as this issue will be solved when you stuff and roll the meat. Remove the skin from the black pudding and mash it until fairly smooth. Set the black pudding aside.

Meanwhile soak the caul fat in plenty of cold, unsalted water and set it aside.

Beat the egg with the milk and brush the insides of the saddles with the egg wash. Divide the stuffing of black pudding between the saddles and carefully roll them up, keeping the black pudding well inside the rolls of rabbit meat. Don't over stuff the meat: you literally only need about a tablespoon's worth of black pudding inside each saddle. Season the outside of the stuffed saddles with salt and pepper and set them aside in the fridge.

Preheat the oven to 200°C / Gas Mark 6. On a clean chopping board, cut the caul fat into 4 pieces, each roughly twice the size of the rabbit saddles. Place a saddle in the middle of each piece of caul fat and wrap it carefully around the meat. Press the wrapped saddle gently to remove any excess moisture

from the caul fat. Now put the saddles aside in the fridge for at least an hour before cooking.

Heat the butter and oil in a wide-bottomed, ovenproof frying pan until it is just fizzing. Prick each saddle gently like a sausage, in a couple of places. Very gently brown the saddles on all sides and transfer them to the oven. Cook for 20 minutes, and then allow the saddles to rest in a warm place for 10 more minutes before serving. The saddles look great if you slice them into 3 or 4 discs and lay them across the plate, either on top of some mash or the celeriac and apple purée on page 243.

Rabbit, sherry and wild garlic

Rabbit is one of the few game meats that remains plentiful once wild garlic leaves start to carpet British woodland floors in spring. Wild garlic (aka ramsons) is a pungent allium, with a sweet-strong flavour, not unlike chives. It is possible to buy it from some farmers' markets and greengrocers. If you have trouble getting hold of it, you can substitute cloves of conventional garlic, by adding them to the initial *court bouillon*. Then you can wilt a light green, like watercress, in the finished dish in place of the wild leaves. Another alternative to wild garlic is the Chinese green 'garlic chive', sold at many oriental supermarkets. This recipe is adapted from one by Jonathon Jones, chef-patron at the Anchor and Hope in Waterloo.

serves 4

4 large farmed or 8 small wild rabbit legs
2 carrots
1 onion
2 leeks
2 stalks celery
salt and freshly ground black pepper
1 litre chicken stock (or rabbit stock)
125ml (a small glass) dry sherry plus
   extra to finish.
2 handfuls of wild garlic leaves
extra-virgin olive oil

Place the rabbit legs in a suitable pot with the carrots, onions, leeks and celery, all left whole. Add a level teaspoon of salt and cover the meat and vegetables with the stock and sherry. Simmer the rabbit in this rough *court bouillon* until the meat is very tender. It could take about 2 hours if the legs are wild, but might take only an hour if they are farmed.

Allow the meat to cool completely in the stock. This is actually best done overnight, which enables you to skim any fat from the top of the stock. Remove the cold rabbit legs and vegetables from the stock and discard the vegetables. Heat the stock and reduce it by half, skimming any froth or fat that comes to the surface. Season the finished stock, which should resemble a rabbity consommé.

Return the legs to the broth and reheat them gently until they are good and tender again. Check the seasoning, and add more salt if you need it.

Pick the wild garlic leaves from their stalks and divide them between four bowls. Add a sprinkling more of sherry to each bowl. You only need about a tablespoon's worth in each bowl. Place the rabbit legs on top of the leaves and divide the broth between the bowls to wilt them. Garnish with a small slug of olive oil in each bowl.

Rabbit, snails and Spanish rice

This dish is based, somewhat loosely, on one of the classic, Valencian paellas. Traditionally the rice, meat and vegetables would be cooked in a wide, two-handled paella pan, and the snails would be left in their shells. Other Spanish rice dishes are cooked in pots, similar to the way that Italians make risotto, and this is more like one of those. You can actually make this dish with risotto rice if the paella rice is hard to come by.

You can braise and pick a whole rabbit for this dish or, alternatively, use picked rabbit meat left over from another meal; it is a great way to use leftovers. It also works well with confited or bottled rabbit meat (see page 129 for instructions on how to make this).

You can buy snails ready-cooked, in cans or frozen, and they are fine for this dish. You can also leave them out if you're not a fan.

serves 4

1 litre of rabbit or chicken stock
mild olive oil for cooking
50g dry-cured, smoked bacon or pancetta, diced
50g cooking chorizo, cut into bite-sized slices
2 onions, roughly diced
4 cloves garlic, chopped
2 carrots, roughly diced
2 stalks celery, roughly diced
2 green peppers, roughly diced
salt
300g Spanish paella rice
125ml (a small glass) dry sherry or white wine
a pinch of saffron
1 tablespoon tomato purée
200g cooked rabbit meat, picked off the bones
100g cooked snails, out of the shell
100g peas or broad beans (thawed if using frozen)
a small bunch of parsley
extra-virgin olive oil

Bring the chicken or rabbit stock to a simmer in a small saucepan. Keep it ticking over on the hob.

Heat the cooking oil in a wide-bottomed, low-sided pan; a really large frying pan is fine, so is a large casserole dish. Once hot, add the bacon and chorizo and fry them fairly briskly until cooked through. Remove them with a slotted spoon and set aside. Add the onion, garlic, carrots, celery and peppers to the same pan with half a teaspoon of salt. Stir once, lower the heat and allow the vegetables to sweat very gently for at least 20 minutes. Stir them from time to time and don't let them brown. A little colour is okay for this dish, but really keep an eye on everything. If the vegetables look as if they are catching, add a few tablespoons of water to the pot.

Once the vegetables are very soft, stir in the rice, the cooked bacon and the chorizo. Ensure that the rice is coated with everything, then add the sherry, saffron and tomato purée. Add just enough of the hot stock to cover the rice. Simmer, stirring only occasionally, until all the stock has been absorbed. Now fold in the rabbit meat, snails and peas or broad beans, and cover everything with stock again. If you need more liquid, it is fine to top up the stock with water from a boiled kettle.

Now cook again, stirring only occasionally to stop the rice from sticking. You don't want to churn away at the pot, as this dish should not be creamy like a risotto. Check the seasoning once the rice is cooked through (it can be a little *al dente* if you like). Turn off the heat and let the dish rest for 5 minutes before serving. Chop the parsley finely and garnish each portion with a little as you serve up. You can also anoint each portion with a small slug of olive oil if you like.

4 Legs

Rabbit with Sichuan peppers and choi greens

Rabbit is a great swap for chicken meat in most Chinese stir-fries. The saddle meat is best for this dish. You need to bone it and dice it, so you could ask a friendly butcher to do this for you.

Sichuan peppers are increasingly common in supermarkets or speciality food stores. They are about as hot as black pepper, only slightly more aromatic. They also have a very mild and pleasant numbing effect on the lips! Should they elude you, try pounding a handful of black peppercorns in a pestle and mortar with one or two cloves.

'Choi' is the Cantonese word for vegetable, and usually implies a member of the brassica family. Pak choi is the most famous choi sold in the UK, closely followed by choi sum (a sort of broccoli). Calabrese or sprouting broccoli make fine substitutes.

serves 4

4 rabbit saddles
½ teaspoon salt
1 level teaspoon Sichuan peppers, roughly ground or pounded
1 level teaspoon cornflour
3 tablespoons water
4 tablespoon mild vegetable oil for frying
2 cloves garlic and 1cm cube (approximately) fresh ginger, chopped to almost resemble a paste
a bunch of spring onions, trimmed and sliced
2 big handfuls of choi greens, washed and chopped roughly
3 tablespoons soy sauce
2 tablespoons sherry or dry white wine
½ teaspoon sugar
125ml (a small glass) rabbit or chicken stock
a small bunch of coriander for garnish

The cooking takes hardly any time, so have all the parts of this dish ready to throw into the wok. Set them all out, TV chef style! Bone and dice the rabbit saddles into bite-size pieces (to bone them follow the instructions on page 124). Toss them with the salt and peppercorns. Set them aside in the fridge.

Mix the cornflour with the water in a very small bowl. Set aside.

Heat half the oil in a wok or frying pan over a brisk heat. Stir-fry the rabbit for 3 or 4 minutes, until it is cooked through. Remove it and set it aside. Wash the wok, and return it to the heat. Add the remaining cooking oil and heat it again, briskly. Add the garlic and ginger and stir-fry for half a minute. Add the spring onions and do the same. Add the greens, soy, sherry and sugar and, as soon as the greens start to wilt, add the stock and cornflour mixture. Add the rabbit and, once the greens have wilted and the sauce looks glossy, the stir-fry is ready.

Serve with boiled rice or noodles. Garnish with the coriander leaves, if you fancy them.

Rabbit rillettes

This is something that we do with the front section of a jointed rabbit if we're not braising the shoulders. You can use the same recipe for the back legs, but rillettes don't really work with the saddle, which is much better roasted.

serves 6–8

500g of pork belly, skin and bones
   removed
1kg rabbit legs
coarse sea salt
1 bay leaf
4 sprigs of thyme
2 sprigs of rosemary
3 cloves of garlic
100ml water
200g duck fat
freshly ground black pepper

Cut the pork belly into 3cm cubes; place these and the rabbit shoulders into a bowl. Rub the meat well with around 2 tablespoons of sea salt. Cover the bowl and refrigerate overnight.

Preheat the oven to 130°C / Gas Mark 2.

Quickly rinse the salt from the meat under a cold running tap. Then put it into an ovenproof dish along with the herbs and garlic, the water, duck fat and a grind of pepper.

Place the dish over a medium heat and slowly bring to a simmer. Cover the dish tightly; transfer it to the oven and cook for 2½–3 hours until the pork is soft and giving and the rabbit falling away from the bone. The meat should never become dry or dark, so keep an eye on it and add more water if necessary.

Remove the dish from the oven, uncover and allow to cool. Pour the meat into a colander over a bowl, reserving the fatty liquid, and discard the herbs. Remove the rabbit first and strip the meat from the bones and place it in a bowl. Now add the pork and, with the aid of 2 forks, shred the meats together. It should be soft and stringy. Pour over the fatty liquid to bind the meat together and season again to taste.

Spoon the rillettes into either a clean Kilner jar or into ramekins. Cover and refrigerate until set.

Perfect served with crusty bread and cornichons.

Rabbit saddle in ham with chicory

Wrapping a rabbit saddle with a richly flavoured ham protects the meat, which is naturally very lean. It also gives this dish an intense favour. If Serrano ham eludes you, Italian proscuitto makes a fine substitute.

serves 4

4 saddles of wild rabbit
salt and freshly ground black pepper
4 slices of Serrano ham
4 heads of chicory
3 tablespoons duck fat or butter
100ml white wine
½ teaspoon caster sugar
300ml chicken stock

Preheat the oven to 220°C / Gas Mark 7. First, remove the sinew from the saddle. This is easily done by slipping a sharp knife under the sinew by the rib cage, detaching it there and then running your knife over the fillet and detaching it now from the spine. It's a little like trimming a fillet of lamb or beef.

Season the saddle with a grind of black pepper then wrap each saddle in a slice of ham, securing the ham on the underside of the saddle with a toothpick. Set aside while you turn your attention to the chicory.

Slice each head of chicory in half lengthways and season the cut face with salt and pepper. Warm half of the duck fat or butter in a pan wide enough to fit the chicory snugly. Seal the chicory, face down, over a medium heat for around 5 minutes until the leaves have browned nicely, then turn over and seal the other side for another 2–3 minutes. Pour over the wine, let it bubble and reduce by half. Sprinkle over the sugar and then pour in 200ml of the chicken stock. Bring the pan to a simmer, cover and braise in the oven for 10 minutes until the chicory is soft and giving. Check the seasoning and keep warm.

Melt the rest of the duck fat or butter in a roasting tray and gently seal the saddles over a medium heat until the ham is crisp and golden. Make sure the saddles are resting bone-side down and roast in the oven for 5 minutes. Check the meat, once cooked it will feel quite tight when you pinch it between thumb and forefinger. Remove the pan from the oven and pour over the remaining warmed stock. Cover the saddles with a sheet of foil and leave them to rest in a warm place for 10 minutes.

To serve, warm the chicory, distribute it between 4 plates and top with a rabbit saddle. Spoon the stock over each saddle.

Rabbit cacciatore (hunter's rabbit)

'Cacciatore' means 'hunter' in Italian. This is rabbit, cooked in the 'hunter's style'. Although they are often made with chicken or rabbit, there are many permutations of 'cacciatore' sauces. They usually contain tomatoes, onions and wine. This is the recipe we've been using for years, it's Trish's mum's version.

serves 4

1 tablespoon unsalted butter
1 tablespoon extra-virgin olive oil
4 tame or 8 wild rabbit legs
salt and freshly ground black pepper
100g dry-cured smoked streaky bacon, cut into 50mm strips
1 large onion, finely sliced
100g button mushrooms, finely sliced
1 clove of garlic, crushed
200ml dry white wine
400g tin of good Italian tomatoes, chopped with their juice
4 sprigs of thyme
2 bay leaves

Choose a wide casserole dish that will accommodate all of the rabbit legs comfortably and warm the butter and olive oil over a medium-high heat. Season the rabbit legs with salt and pepper and return them to the pan once the fats have begun to bubble. Brown the legs, turning them frequently until they have an even golden colour and transfer them to a warm plate.

With the heat still on medium-high, add the bacon to the pan and sauté until nice and crisp, then introduce the onions. Reduce the heat a little and cook the onion until it has softened. Now raise the heat again to medium-high and add the sliced mushrooms. Fry for a good 3 minutes, stirring occasionally, until the mushrooms have given up their juices, then pop in the garlic. Give the pan one more good stir to mix the garlic through and then pour in the white wine. Simmer the wine for a minute, then add the tomatoes and herbs and return the rabbit legs to the pan. Check the seasoning, it may need a touch more at this stage. Cover the pan tightly and leave over the lowest heat to simmer for 45 minutes, or until the rabbit is tender. Depending on the size and age of the rabbit, this may take a little longer. If this is the case, keep checking the braise every 5 minutes.

When the rabbit is done, transfer the legs to a warm plate. If the sauce is looking thin, place the pan over a high heat and let it bubble briskly until it has reduced; you want to have a nice dense coating. Stir the legs back through the sauce and serve, ideally, with soft polenta.

Rabbit with mustard and bacon

This casserole is based on the classic French dish 'lapin à moutarde'. The mustard mellows as it cooks so, even if you don't relish the idea of cooking with such a spicy condiment, the smooth results make it worth taking a punt on this recipe.

serves 4

200ml chicken stock
12 round shallots
2 tablespoons unsalted butter or duck
    fat
200g piece of smoked streaky bacon,
    cut into 1cm lardons
4 tame or 8 wild rabbit legs
1 clove garlic, finely chopped
150ml dry white wine
300ml double cream
2 tablespoons Dijon mustard
salt and freshly ground black pepper

Preheat the oven to 150°C / Gas Mark 2.

Pour the chicken stock into a small saucepan and bring it to a brisk boil. Add the whole shallots, turn the heat underneath down to medium and poach for five minutes, until they are just tender. Scoop them out of the pan and set aside.

Heat the butter or duck fat in a heavy-based frying pan and, over a medium heat, gently sauté the bacon pieces until they are crisp and golden. Spoon the bacon from the pan into a casserole dish and return the pan to the heat. Brown the rabbit legs, in batches if needs be, until they are completely sealed and have a good, even colour, then add them to the casserole. Now turn the poached shallots around the fat in the pan, giving them a good coating, stir through the garlic and pour over the white wine. Give the wine a blast of

heat: let it bubble for a minute before adding the stock and the cream. Whisk in the Dijon mustard and check the seasoning (it may only need a small grind of pepper at this point) before pouring the sauce over the rabbit and bacon in the casserole. Cover the pan tightly, place onto the middle shelf of the oven and leave to braise for 45 minutes or until the rabbit is tender. Depending on the size and age of the rabbit, this may take a little longer. If this is the case, keep checking the meat every 5 minutes. When the rabbit is done, transfer the legs to a warm plate.

Place the casserole over a high heat and let it bubble briskly until it has reduced by about a third, the sauce wants to be a quite thick and creamy. You could also add a little more mustard at this stage if you feel that it has lost some of its piquancy during cooking. Stir the legs back through the sauce and serve. Our perfect accompaniment to this dish would be a big bowl of mash.

4 Legs

Rabbit in Thai yellow curry

Rabbit takes beautifully to Thai curry sauces and this dish, from the north of Thailand, is a great way to try it. Coconut milk is seldom used in northern Thai curries, which makes them taste cleaner and lighter than the famous southern versions. The paste in this recipe is adapted from David Thompson's definitive *Thai Food*. If you are pressed for time, a ready-made paste is fine. Our favourite brand is the peerless Mae Ploy.

serves 4

For the paste
1–2 tablespoons small red chillies
¼ teaspoon sea salt
2 tablespoons lemongrass, finely
    chopped
1 tablespoon coriander roots, chopped
1 teaspoon turmeric
2 tablespoons ginger, peeled and
    chopped
2 tablespoons round shallots, chopped
1 tablespoon garlic, chopped
1 tablespoon Thai fish sauce (nam pla)

600ml chicken stock
½ teaspoon caster sugar
2 tablespoons Thai fish sauce (nam pla)
12 rabbit shoulders
1 bunch of Chinese greens such as gai
    lan, choi sum or Chinese broccoli
    cut in half between the leaves and
    stalks
2 limes, halved

First make the paste. You could do this in a pestle and morter, crushing the chilli with the salt until you get a rough paste, before adding each further ingredient, one at a time, crushing each well before you add the next.

Alternatively you can make the paste in a blender. A food processor or hand blender won't do, with only 2 blades you will never get a smooth paste. Blend all the ingredients together with a tablespoon or 2 of water if necessary. You may need to scrape down the sides a few times until the purée has been achieved. Any curry paste left over from the recipe can be kept, tightly covered for 2 weeks in the fridge.

Bring the stock to the boil in a wide-based saucepan, large enough to hold all the legs comfortably, and add the sugar and the fish sauce. Stir in 2–3 tablespoons of the paste until it has dissolved and taste a little of the stock. Add a touch more paste at this point if you prefer a fiery curry.

Add the rabbit shoulders and bring the pan to a simmer. Cover the pan with a tight fitting lid and cook over a low heat for around 1½ hours, until the legs are tender. Now add the greens, stirring them through the curry, and simmer until they have wilted. Taste again and add a tablespoon more of fish sauce if you feel it's needed. It should taste hot and slightly salty.

Scatter each bowl of curry with coriander leaves and serve each with half a lime, which is squeezed into the bowl at the table.

rabbi

4 Legs

Venison and hare

Venison

Venison is the culinary term for deer meat, which is fast becoming Britain's most popular form of game. Of all our wild foods, this is the one you are most likely to find in supermarkets and restaurants.

In fact, not all venison is wild. There is a lot of farmed deer around. Most retailers don't differentiate between the two. It seems hard to tell the difference between tame and feral versions because the animal's lifestyle is similar, whether it is managed or completely free.

What is the reason for the huge surge in venison's popularity? It's not hard to see why people love eating deer. It is rich, sweet and deeply red meat, not unlike beef. Venison has been blessed with the 'good for you' tag, and successfully marketed as a healthy alternative to beef, with its lower saturated fat content. It is usually cheaper than beef, too, or at least cheaper than prized breeds of beef such as Angus and Hereford. Yet it has somehow retained the caché of being luxury meat, suitable for special occasions. This might be why restaurateurs love it!

The most common type of deer killed for meat in the UK is the largest, the red deer. This is also the only deer that is farmed on any significant level. Red deer are highland animals, found mainly in the north of England and Scotland. In southern England, particularly in the West Country, large populations of roe, fallow, sika and muntjak deer live in the plentiful moors and woodlands. Many of these deer are escapees from parks and estates. They eat the shoots of trees in forests and will boldly steal from vegetable patches and market gardens. Owing to a lack of natural predators these marauding deer have become pests, and they are regularly culled to keep a cap on their booming populations. This means that, unlike wild red deer, which is only in season from July to February, other breeds may be available almost all year round.

We are being offered more and more roe deer every year. It has a fantastic flavour. Although it tends to be slightly pricier than red deer (especially the farmed version), it does have its advantages for the domestic cook in that its joints are smaller, and easier to use in domestic ovens.

Hare

Putting venison and hare in the same chapter might seem like an odd choice on the face of it. You might be wondering why we didn't pair hare with rabbit. Although they are members of the same family of mammals and look a bit like each other, hares and rabbits are very different in almost every other aspect. Hares are much larger than rabbits. They live almost entirely above ground, in pairs rather than large groups, and they are far more active. In fact, hares are one of the fastest land animals in Europe, and can reach speeds of up to 40 miles per hour when evading predators. Their powerful limbs translate into meat that is far denser and darker than that on a rabbit. To look at, the meat has more in common with venison. Hare meat is the gamiest of all the furred animals. It has an intensity perhaps only matched by grouse.

Hare has a closed season and is hunted for food from the beginning of August until the end of March.

How to buy and prepare venison and hare

Buying venison

Unlike rabbit, venison is usually sold more like farmed meat, in cuts or joints. A whole venison carcass will be roughly the same size as that of a lamb, and you are unlikely to be buying it wholly intact. If you do buy a whole specimen direct from a game dealer, we recommend asking him or her to cut it into three sections: the fore quarter (shoulders and neck), the loin (or saddle) and the haunches, (or hind legs). The vast majority of us will buy venison by the joint, as we do with beef, lamb and pork. The cuts behave in a similar way to lamb. The haunch, or back leg, is mainly for roasting on or off the bone. It can also be barbecued like leg of lamb. The saddle is another roasting joint and is usually done on the bone, although the loin can be boned for steaks or noisettes. It can also be cut into chops. The neck and shoulders are strictly for braises and casseroles. These sections can be cooked whole, or diced for casseroles. It is possible to mince the braising sections for an excellent burger (see page 172), although it is usually necessary to add fat from another animal (back fat from pork or bone marrow from beef and veal) because of venison's natural tendency towards ultra-leanness.

Larding and marinades

Traditional recipes for cooking venison (and hare, for that matter) often call for larding the meat, which is to say, spiking it with the fat from bacon to counteract the meat's very lean nature. Many people are fearful of cooking game because they think it will taste dry. We haven't included any instructions for larding in the following roasts. We believe that if the meat is cooked simply and swiftly, in a moderately hot oven to begin with, and is then properly rested, it will be tender and juicy. More importantly, it won't taste of bacon! Game and bacon are good partners, but we prefer to include it in the garnishes or side dishes, letting the flavour of the roast shine rather than be dominated.

We do not recommend marinating venison or hare with wine either. Many older recipes call for this as a way of tenderising what was once regarded as a dense and therefore potentially tough meat. We believe that this was probably due to the somewhat erratic temperatures of old ovens, which made it hard for early cookery writers to give readers the requisite cooking times for guaranteed tenderness. Dousing meat in alcohol actually encourages it to lose moisture, so we don't do it.

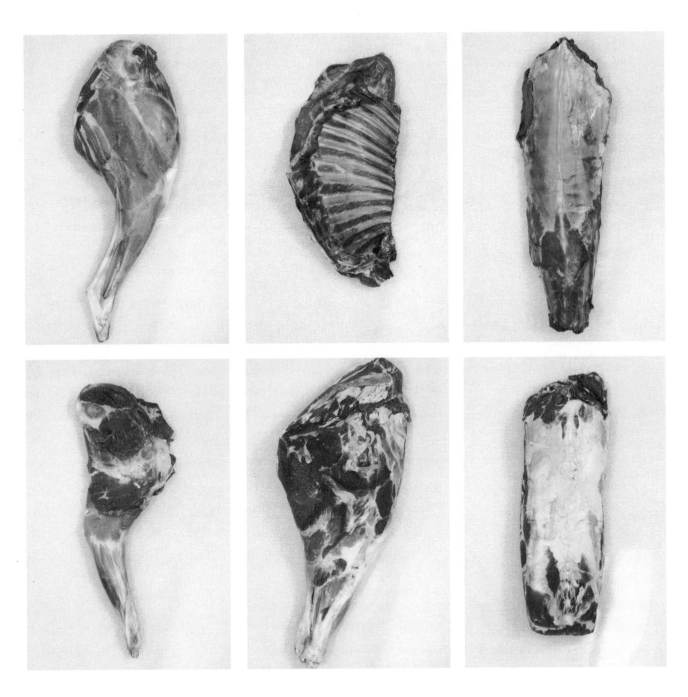

4 Legs

Classic roasts and suggested trimmings for venison

The two cuts of venison we favour for roasting are saddle (loin) and haunch (back legs). Both are best cooked on the bone for flavour and succulence. When it comes to roasting these joints, you might want to consider roe deer over red, simply because its smaller size is more user-friendly in a domestic setting. With all roasting recipes for larger animals, we highly recommend talking to your butcher and allowing him or her to choose the joint that best suits your needs, depending on how many are coming for dinner.

Saddle of venison for four or six

When it comes to successfully roasting any joint of meat make sure that you get the correct weight. Our cooking times depend on a couple of very simple sums, depending on the weight of the meat. You want to aim to serve about 250g of meat as a portion. The average saddle on a young roe deer is around 2 kilos which, once you have taken into account the weight of the bones, is ideal for four to six people. Leftover venison meat is delicious cold, sliced thinly, or it can be chopped up and used to make a gamey version of shepherd's pie (hunter's pie perhaps?).

You will need
1 saddle of venison
5 tablespoons duck fat or butter
125ml (a small glass) of red wine
salt and freshly ground black pepper

Preheat the oven to 220°C / Gas Mark 7. Season the saddle generously with salt and pepper.

Melt the duck fat or butter in a roasting tray and seal the saddle on all sides over a medium heat. To transfer it to the oven, make sure the saddle is rib side down, which is to say, resting on the short rib bones. Roast at 220°C / Gas Mark 7 for 20 minutes then lower the heat to 150°C / Gas Mark 2, pull out the joint and pour the wine into the roasting tray. Return the saddle to the tray and pop it back into the oven. Now allow another ten minutes per 500g. This will give you medium-rare (i.e. pretty pink) meat. If you prefer medium to well-done meat allow 15 minutes per 500g. Remove the saddle from the oven. Wrap the joint loosely with a sheet of foil and leave to rest in a warm place for 20 minutes before carving. Use the juices and remnants of wine in the roasting tray as the basis for delicious game gravy.

Roast haunch of venison for 6–8

A haunch of adult roe deer will weigh 2–2.5kg which, taking into account the weight of the bones, is ideal for six to eight people. If you want to feed more, a red deer haunch will weigh about twice as much. It should be possible to get smaller roasting joints cut from the haunch of red deer, like the top and silver side that you find on a leg of beef. Ask your butcher about these (it might even be possible to get them boned and rolled).

You will need
1 haunch of venison
salt and freshly ground black pepper
duck fat, lard or butter

Preheat the oven to 220°C / Gas Mark 7. Rub the haunch of venison generously with about half a tablespoon of salt and then augment this with a twist of black pepper. Heat the fat in a roasting tray and when it is hot, brown the haunch briskly on all sides. Transfer it to the oven, on a rack over the roasting tray. Cook the haunch at 220°C / Gas Mark 7 for 20 minutes, then lower the heat to 150°C / Gas Mark 2. Cook it for 10 minutes per 500g if you want the meat to be vividly pink (medium-rare). Cook it for 15 minutes per 500g if you prefer it medium to well-done. If you want it cooked through, stop right there! You want a different joint. Pot-roast a shoulder instead (see page 158).

Once you remove it from the oven, wrap the haunch loosely in foil and rest it in a warm place for 20–30 minutes before carving.

Recommended trimmings

Venison is incredibly versatile when it comes to the accompaniments because it will take all the traditional, fruity, and slightly sweet embellishments that go so well with most game. It is excellent with quince (see the compôte on page 239) and Cumberland sauce (page 238). However, like beef, venison loves horseradish, although this is not such a well-known fact. Try serving it with nothing more than a watercress salad and a dollop of Horseradish Sauce (page 238).

Jointing hare

Hare offers up very similar cooking cuts to venison even though it might not seem that way at a glance. There are two, small front legs (sometimes known as arms or shoulders), a neck, a loin (or 'saddle'), plus two back legs. Unlike venison there is no shin or shank on the legs; you cook hare legs, front or back, as one entity.

Lay the hare on the chopping board with the rib cage facing upwards, and the smaller, front legs to the left. First, using a small boning knife, cut off the front legs. You do this by working the knife along the join between the leg and rib cage, until the joint comes clean away. You now have two shoulders of hare, which are great for braising; a pair of shoulders can be one portion of meat. Now cut off the two larger, rear legs. You will find a small hip and thigh joint just below the rump. It is easy to tease the joints apart with the tip of your boning knife, while you pull the leg very gently away from the hip. Set these aside. Each is a good, portion-sized braising cut. Now you are left with the saddle, with ribs and neck attached. Be warned: the rib cage, above the saddle, is likely to be very bloody, and will often contain the 'pluck' (liver, heart and lungs). It is best to cut the rib cage away from the saddle, using scissors. Do this over a bowl, which you can use to catch any blood left in the cavity. This blood is a much-prized ingredient for jugged hare along with the heart and liver (see page 181). Once the rib cage is off you can see that the saddle is quite long and meaty; this is the only roasting joint on a hare. The kidneys are sometimes left on it, and you can leave them on, as they are delicious when served with the roasted saddle.

Once you have got all the blood out of the ribs, remove the pluck and give the ribcage a good wash. You can use the cleaned rib cage to make a deeply gamey stock, which can be reduced for gravy (see page 245). There is some meat on the neck and in amongst the ribs, but the bones here are perhaps the most fiddly and hazardous of any meat we know and we don't like trying to pick them out of braises.

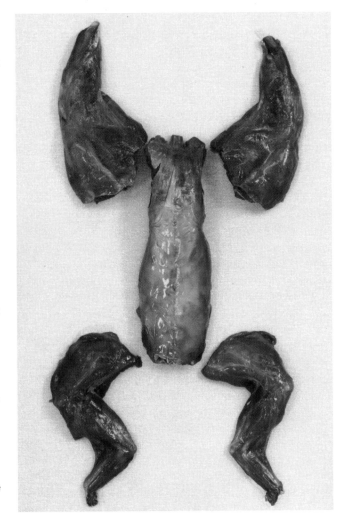

Classic roasts and recommended trimmings for hare

The saddle is a perfect dinner for two. We ought to say that, as with wood pigeon, grouse and wild ducks, hare saddle must be left rare to be enjoyed. If you don't like red, rare and pretty robustly flavoured meat, then it is better to try one of the braises in this chapter, for which the saddle is also suitable.

Roast hare saddle for two

A hare saddle weighing about 700g is ideal for two. It sounds like a lot of meat but once you take the bones into account, it really isn't too hefty.

1 hare saddle
salt and freshly ground black pepper
3 tablespoons duck fat or butter

Preheat the oven to 220°C / Gas Mark 7. The first thing you need to do is to remove any sinew from the saddle. This is easily done by slipping a sharp knife under the sinew by the rib cage, detaching it there and then running your knife over the fillet and detaching it from the spine. You will be left with a lean loin cut, with the two breasts clearly defined on either side. These will protect the lean meat on the true saddle while you roast the hare. Season the saddle with salt and pepper.

Melt the duck fat or butter in an ovenproof frying pan and seal the saddle on all sides over a medium heat. To transfer it to the oven, make sure it is loin-side up, which is to say, lying on its front, ribs facing downwards. The breast flaps should be tucked underneath the meat, protecting the kidneys (if they remained attached). Roast for 7 minutes. If the saddle is bigger than 700g, add another minute per 50g. Check the meat to see if it is cooked; it will feel quite tight when you pinch it between thumb and forefinger. Remove the pan from the oven. Cover the saddle with a sheet of foil and leave it to rest in a warm place for 10 minutes before carving.

Recommended trimmings

Like venison, hare pairs well with both Cumberland and horseradish sauces (page 238) but it is also wonderful with more continental accompaniments. You could swap it for the rabbit saddle wrapped in ham and served with Braised Chicory (on page 148). Hare and polenta are natural partners and you could serve this roast saddle with the polenta on page 170. Just don't forget to add gravy!

Seven-hour shoulder of venison and gratin dauphinoise

This is best done through the day to be served that evening, or overnight if you want it for lunch. By cooking the meat so slowly, surrounded by vegetables and aromatic herbs, you get an incredibly rich and comforting meal. Everything you need is there in the roasting tray. You could serve it with the gratin dauphinoise but, sometimes, we think a loaf of crusty bread and a peppery salad is just as fine. The shoulder is an excellent braising cut on most meat and, if venison eludes you, this method works well with wild boar, veal, lamb and mutton.

We call this seven-hour shoulder, but you can cook it faster. If done at 180°C / Gas Mark 4 it could be ready in 3–4 hours, but you must check it every couple of hours to make sure that the stock is not evaporating.

serves 4–6

2 large carrots
2 large onions
4 cloves garlic
2 stalks celery
3 tablespoons olive oil
1 shoulder of venison, on the bone
1 tablespoon red wine vinegar
250ml (two glasses) red wine
1 teaspoon salt
1 teaspoon sugar
1 tablespoon tomato purée
575ml water or a game stock if you
    have it
2 bay leaves
a handful of juniper berries (don't use
    these with lamb or mutton – rather,
    swap in thyme or rosemary)

Preheat the oven to 200°C / Gas Mark 6. Peel and halve each carrot, onion, garlic clove and celery stick. Set them aside. Heat the olive oil gently in a large pot or casserole and add the shoulder, browning it slowly and generously all over. Give it at least 10–15 minutes on each side. Once this is done, remove the shoulder. Brown the vegetables in the same pot. Increase the heat and let them caramelise slightly. Then return the meat to the pot. Mix the vinegar, wine, salt, sugar, tomato purée and water into a slightly unpromising and cloudy-looking sauce. Pour it all over the meat and bring it to a simmer. Throw in the bay leaves and juniper berries. Cover and transfer to the oven. Let the pot cook at 200°C / Gas Mark 6 for roughly half an hour then lower the heat to 100°C / Gas Mark ¼. Now you can let the meat tick over very slowly, for roughly 7 hours, or until the shoulder is so tender you can cut (or portion it) with a spoon. The juices should be slightly opaque and glossy.

Ideally, rest it away from the heat for a good 20 minutes, once cooked, so that it is extra tender. This dish can be rested overnight, too, but you must reheat it slowly for at least 45 minutes to ensure that it comes back up to the right temperature all the way through, without drying out or catching.

Gratin dauphinoise

This is the perfect side dish for shoulder of venison or, indeed, most roasts. Here we give you instructions on how to cook the gratin to serve with the shoulder, as if you were cooking them together. You can cook the gratin harder and faster, too, starting it at 180°C / Gas Mark 4 instead of the low oven we have prescribed for the meat. If you do this, it will take roughly half the time to cook.

serves 4–6

500g yellow-fleshed potatoes (Desirée are our favourite)
2 cloves garlic
a small bunch of thyme or rosemary
2 tablespoons soft butter
1 tablespoon light olive oil for cooking
200ml whole milk
200ml double cream
salt and freshly ground black pepper

Peel and slice the potatoes as finely as possible. Pop them in a bowl of cold water and give them a good rinse to remove any excess starch. Drain and pat dry, then set aside. Peel and slice the garlic and chop the thyme or rosemary. Heat the butter and oil gently in a large pan and add the milk and cream. Bring the cream to a simmer and add the garlic and herbs. Lay the potatoes in a lightly greased baking dish, seasoning each layer with salt and pepper. Then pour the hot cream and milk mix over the top of the gratin. Nudge the potatoes here and there to make sure the cream gets between them all. Cover the gratin with foil and add it to the oven, about an hour before the venison is finished.

Then, as you take the venison out, remove the foil and raise the oven heat back up to 200°C / Gas Mark 6. Cook the gratin, uncovered, for another half hour. By this time the potatoes should be tender and the top should be starting to brown. You should check the potatoes before serving. A fork should meet no resistance if you give them a gentle probing. If they are al dente, continue to cook them while you continue to rest the venison. The meat will not suffer, so keep the faith!

Braised venison shanks and carrots

The sweetness of carrots is a perfect foil for the rich, dark meat on a venison shank. This dish would also work with lamb, mutton or shin of beef. All meat as rich in connective tissue as the lower legs can take longer to cook than you think. It is incredibly hard to tell you, in writing, when such a dish will be ready, so be prepared to check this dish a few times as it cooks. It is ideal for making the day before serving, and is one of those stews that works really well in a counter-top slow cooker.

serves 4

4 venison shanks
2 tablespoons plain flour
½ teaspoon salt
½ teaspoon freshly ground black pepper
duck fat, lard or mild vegetable oil for
    cooking
4 onions, sliced finely
6 carrots, sliced roughly (as chunky as
    you like them)
2 bay leaves
2 tablespoons Worcestershire sauce
1 tablespoon tomato purée
2 litres water or game stock if you
    have it
2 tablespoons unsalted butter

Toss the shanks with the flour, salt and pepper and set them aside. Heat the fat in a casserole or large pot and, when it is hot, add the shanks and brown them, fairly briskly, all over. Remove them and set aside. Add the onions and carrots to the pot with half a teaspoon more of salt. Stir them once, lower the heat and allow them to sweat for 10–15 minutes. Don't let them brown. If this looks like it is in danger of happening, add about 3 tablespoons of water or stock to the pot.

Once the vegetables have softened, return the shanks to the pot. Add the bay leaves. Combine the Worcestershire sauce, tomato purée and water or stock, so that you get a rather murky and unpromising-looking liquid. Pour this all over the meat and vegetables and bring it to a good simmer. Now cover the pot and, either transfer it to an oven set at 180°C / Gas Mark 4 OR cook it on the hob with the lowest heat possible underneath it. The stock should just blip rather than bubble. Shanks of lamb and venison are hard to time, so we are not going to promise you that they will be ready in two hours. Give them at least two hours and then check them periodically. They will yield, and when they do they might give up their hold on the shank bone. This is perfectly fine.

Check the seasoning once the shanks are done and just before serving, stir the butter into the cooking pot.

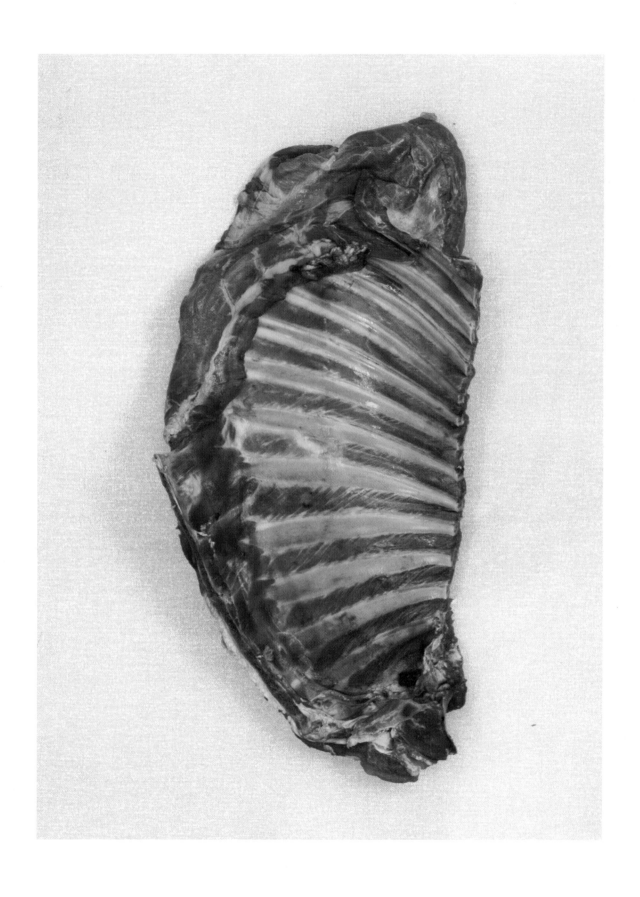

4 Legs

Venison rendang

'Rendang' is a popular dish in south-east Asia, originating in Indonesia, where it is usually made with beef or buffalo. Venison is an excellent riff on this tradition. You want the shoulder or neck meat, with all its connective tissue, as this is a slow-cooking dish.

A rendang is sort of a curry. Sort of! With a rendang, you take the received currying wisdom of frying meat with spices, then braising it in a sauce, and turn it on its head. First the meat is boiled, in spiced coconut milk. Then, as the cooking juices evaporate, the fat from the meat and coconut 'fries' the finished dish. The result is hard to describe: delicious, slightly shredded and very soft meat in a nearly dry marinade. We serve rendang with rice and a garnish of hard-boiled eggs and cucumber. If this doesn't grab you, a good alternative is to pair rendang with the bitterest greens you can get your mitts on. Steamed spring greens are excellent.

serves 4

4 cloves garlic
8 small shallots
a 2cm-ish piece of ginger
1 stalk of lemongrass (or use a sliver of lemon peel)
2 red chillies
2 cloves
quarter of nutmeg
800g diced venison meat
1 level teaspoon salt
½ teaspoon chilli powder
½ teaspoon turmeric
½ teaspoon ground cinnamon
2 x 400ml tins coconut milk
300ml water
2 bay leaves

To garnish
½ cucumber
pinch of sea salt
2 hard-boiled eggs

Peel the garlic and shallots. Pound or finely chop the ginger, lemongrass, chillies, shallots and garlic to a near paste. Smash or grind the cloves and grate the nutmeg. Combine them with the wet garlic and chilli paste. Toss the venison meat with the salt, chilli powder, turmeric and cinnamon, and then combine it with the spice paste. Pour the coconut milk and water into a pot large enough for everything then add the meat mix. Bring the mix to a healthy simmer and allow it to cook very gently, stirring occasionally, until the meat is tender and the liquid is reducing. It is hard to give precise cooking times as the meat can take a while to truly tenderise. You must keep checking it, and it will take at least 2 hours. Once the meat is really soft, check the seasoning to see if you require a little more salt. At this stage you can actually serve this more like a conventional curry, with a rich coconut sauce. Or you can transfer the curry to a wider-bottomed pan or wok and start to fry, gently, until the coconut milk reduces to a richer, darker sauce around the meat.

Allow the finished dish to rest for at least half an hour before serving. Traditionally it would not be served hot, but lukewarm. As the meat rests, you can steam some rice (if you wish to serve it) and assemble the garnish. Slice the cucumber as finely or as roughly as you like, and toss it with a pinch of salt. Soft boil, cool, peel and halve the eggs. Serve the rendang with a pile of rice, a little of the cucumber and half a soft-boiled egg. A further garnish of picked coriander leaves is also good here.

4 Legs

Venison ragu and flatbread

The flatbread in this dish is Sardinian *pane carasau*, also known as *carta musica* ('manuscript bread'). It is crisp baked and paper-thin. The bread can be eaten as it is with cheeses or charcuterie, but it really comes into its own when it is wilted under the hot juices of a good soup or stew. Then it behaves like pasta as it softens. This dish resembles lasagne, with its alternate layers of rich ragu and silky sheets of bread. Should *pane carasau* elude you, you can split open pitta or naan bread, Melba toast style, and crisp it up in a very slow oven. If you don't fancy the flatbread idea at all, this ragu is great served with some pasta. This recipe works just as well with hare, wild boar and lamb.

serves 4–6

1 shoulder venison
½ teaspoon salt
½ teaspoon ground cinnamon
¼ teaspoon grated nutmeg
¼ teaspoon dried chilli (optional)
2 tablespoons lard or duck fat or mild olive oil for cooking
50g smoked, streaky bacon or pancetta, diced very finely
3 onions, diced as finely as possible
2 cloves garlic, chopped to almost resemble a paste
1 bay leaf
125g (a glass) red wine
800g (two average-sized tins) plum tomatoes
500ml game or chicken stock (or water)
1 tablespoon butter
8 sheets *pane carasau* or similar
50g fresh grated hard ewe's milk cheese (we use Italian Pecorino or Spanish Manchego; good UK alternatives are Spenwood or Berkswell)
a small bunch of flat-leaf parsley, for garnish

This dish is best cooked on the bone and then picked, which really helps with the flavour and juiciness of the meat. If the whole shoulder looks too big for any of your casserole dishes, get the butcher to separate the shank from the wide part of the shoulder. Rub the shoulder all over with the salt, cinnamon, nutmeg and chilli powder. Heat the fat very gently in a large roasting dish or casserole and brown the shoulder on all sides. Meanwhile, dice the bacon, onions and garlic as finely as possible. Remove the browned meat from the fat and throw in the bacon. Fry it gently for 2 or 3 minutes then add the garlic and onions. Fry them for another 5 minutes, as gently as possible then add the bay leaf and wine. Simmer for 5 minutes. Finally, tip the tinned tomatoes into the pot. Bring the mix to a simmer then return the venison shoulder to the pot. Make sure it is covered with the juices, add as much stock or water as you need to do this. You can adjust the seasoning later. Cover the pot and cook the shoulder for at least 2 hours, or for as long as it takes to become very tender. It is hard to give exact cooking times for shoulder meat, so keep checking it. When done, the meat will be very soft and can be pulled from the bone with a spoon.

Allow the meat to cool until it is easy to handle, pull it from the bone and shred it roughly. Mix the shredded meat back into all the dark, smoky cooking liquor. Check the seasoning. The ragu is now ready to use but you can keep it for up to three days in the fridge. It also freezes well.

To serve the ragu with flatbread, warm it thoroughly and stir in the butter. Heat a pan of water to boiling point then remove it from the heat. Add a small ladle or serving spoonful of the ragu to each bowl. Dip sheets of the flatbread into the water, one by one, for just 5 seconds and top each serving of ragu with a sheet of the bread. Repeat the process and, finally, spoon any further meat and juices over the top sheet of bread. Garnish the ragu with grated cheese, chopped parsley and, if you fancy it, a slug of extra-virgin olive oil.

Hare ragu and pappardelle

This is a classic ragu from the north of Italy. 'Pappardelle' is wide, flat egg pasta that goes well with rich gamey sauces like this one. You could use fettuccine or tagliatelle in its place. The hare in this recipe benefits from an overnight marinade, which deepens the flavour. You don't need to do this, but at least a couple of hours with the aromatics will intensify the finished sauce.

serves 4

1 hare (approximately weight 1.5kg)

For the marinade
1 bay leaf, shredded
leaves from 1 small sprig thyme
6 juniper berries, crushed
4 cloves garlic, chopped to almost
    resemble a paste
1 onion, finely diced
2 carrots, finely diced
2 stalks celery, finely diced
2 leeks, finely diced
2 tablespoons extra-virgin olive oil
mild olive oil for cooking

100g smoked streaky bacon, finely
    diced
500ml red wine
1 tablespoon tomato purée
25g (1 level teaspoon, really) cocoa
    powder
salt and freshly ground black pepper
300g pappardelle or similar pasta
2 tablespoons butter
50g Parmesan cheese

Joint the hare following the instructions on page 155. Reserve any blood.

Combine the hare, vegetables and aromatics with the extra-virgin olive oil and any of the hare's blood. Transfer to a mixing bowl or a tub that can fit in the fridge and marinate the hare overnight.

The next day, strain the meat through a colander, reserving any juices from the marinade. Pick the meat from the vegetables and pat it dry. Reserve the vegetables.

Heat the cooking oil in a large, wide-bottomed pot and brown the hare pieces all over. Remove them with a slotted spoon and fry the bacon until it starts to crisp up. At this point add the vegetables and any marinade juices. Allow the juices to evaporate and then add the wine. Allow it to evaporate too, and then stir in the tomato purée and cocoa powder. Return the hare to the pot and cover it with water. Season generously and bring the pot to a gentle simmer. Let the hare cook for at least 2 hours. You want the meat to be very tender, almost falling away from the bones, and the time this takes will depend on the hare, really. Once the hare is cooked, let it cool until it is easy to handle. At this point pull the meat from the bones. This can be fiddly, especially near the ribs. Make sure all the bones are gone. Mix the shredded meat back into the cooking liquor and check the seasoning.

To serve, boil the pasta in plenty of salty water until it is cooked *al dente*. Meanwhile bring the hare ragu back to a good simmer and stir in the butter. Drain the cooked pasta very briefly, leaving it damp, rather than fully dry. Toss the pasta with the ragu to serve, check the seasoning once more and garnish with freshly grated Parmesan.

4 Legs

game: a cookbook

Hare stovie

If you ever find that you have more hare ragu than you bargained for, here is a delicious way of utilising the leftovers. Stovies are fried potato cakes, usually made with salted or corned beef. In fact, if you are not Scottish, you might have eaten something almost identical under the name of hash.

serves 2

2 medium floury potatoes
    (approximately 400g)
1 small onion
roughly 200g of leftover hare ragu
salt and freshly ground black pepper
duck fat or butter
200ml double cream
1 tablespoon Dijon mustard
2 good hen or duck eggs

Peel the potatoes and cut them into rough dice. Peel and finely slice the onion. Bring the potatoes and onion to the boil in plenty of salted water, lower the heat to medium and simmer gently until the potatoes are just done. Drain thoroughly and tip the potato and onion mix into a bowl. Meanwhile, strain the ragu in a colander, or simply pick the hare and bacon from the sauce. Once the potato and onion mix is ready, combine it with the meat and check the seasoning. You might want a touch of salt and pepper.

Preheat the oven to 200°C / Gas Mark 5. Melt 2 tablespoons of the fat into a small, heavy-based frying pan and pour in the stovie mixture. Shake the pan over the heat to prevent the stovie from sticking. Once you have a light crust forming on the underside, transfer the stovie to the oven and bake for 10–15 minutes, or until browned nicely on top.

Meanwhile, heat the cream and mustard together in a milk pan over a very gentle heat, until you have a smooth mustard sauce. Keep it warm while the stovie cooks.

Once the stovie is ready, melt another tablespoon of the fat in a frying pan and, when it is hot, break in the eggs. Fry them to your liking (we are soft yolk people, since this mingles brilliantly with the sauce). Serve the stovie topped with the fried eggs and spoon the sauce all around the sides.

Braised leg of hare and polenta

The richness of hare meat is possibly one of the best foils for polenta that we know of, but it isn't everyone's cup of tea. If you don't fancy it, try this casserole with a pile of mash instead.

serves 4

2 tablespoons mixed dried mushrooms
1 litre of hot water, straight from a
    kettle
6 shallots or 2 red onions
4 cloves garlic
2 carrots
3 stalks celery
6 large flat field mushrooms
    (aka Portobello)
2 tablespoons mild olive oil for cooking
4 tablespoons butter
4 hare legs
salt and freshly ground black pepper
250ml red wine
1 tablespoon tomato purée
1 small bunch of flat-leaf parsley
1 small bunch tarragon

Soak the mushrooms in the water for a good half hour or so. Peel and dice the shallots, garlic, carrots and celery as finely as possible. Dice or slice the Portobello mushrooms roughly. Set them aside. Heat the oil and half the butter in a casserole or similar pan, large enough for all the ingredients. When it is hot, brown the hare legs all over briskly. Remove them from the pan with a slotted spoon. Now add the shallots, garlic, carrots and celery to the same pot. Stir in half a teaspoon of salt, lower the heat, cover the pot and allow the vegetables to sweat for 10–15 minutes. Don't let them brown. Once the vegetables are soft, add the wine, tomato purée and mushrooms to the pot. Bring them to a simmer until most of the wine has evaporated. Strain the dried-mushroom water and add it to the vegetables. Return the hare legs to the pot and, if the mushroom stock has not covered them, top it up with just enough hot water to submerge the hare. Don't add too much.

Simmer the casserole until the hare legs are tender, but not falling off the bone. The time this takes will depend on the hare, but it should take at least 2 hours.

If you like, you can add soaked dried mushrooms to this stew. Give them a good rinse, because they can sometimes harbour grit. Then chop them to almost resemble a paste before adding them to the other ingredients. Just before the casserole is ready to serve, fold in the remaining butter. Check the seasoning. Chop the parsley and tarragon together to use as a garnish.

4 Legs

A good venison burger

Venison burgers are delicious but, in our experience, you need to add some fat to them to stop the incredibly lean meat from drying out. Our favourite tools for this are bone marrow or pork back fat, which a good butcher should be happy to get for you. Most butchers can mince meat for you too, but in an ideal world you want to grind the meat at home; you get a vastly superior mince.

If you do mince at home, try and chill both the meat and the mincer before you begin. This sounds odd, but it keeps the ground meat and fat fairly separate and you only really want to pull the meat together lightly, not compact it. This will give you a properly crumbly burger.

serves 4

700g venison loin, minced
200g venison shoulder, minced
100g veal bone marrow or pork back
    fat, minced or finely chopped
salt and freshly ground black pepper
2 banana shallots
1 tablespoon red wine vinegar
1 tablespoon tiny capers
a small bunch of flat-leaf parsley
2 tablespoons extra-virgin olive oil
sourdough bread
duck fat
4 pickled walnuts

Place both of the meats and the marrow in a wide bowl and season with a scant teaspoon of salt and pepper.

Mix everything together lightly with your fingertips until the meats are combined. Now separate the mix into four and just gather together into four patties, don't press together too hard.

Heat the barbecue or a griddle pan to a medium-high heat and grill the burgers for 4–5 minutes before flipping over for a further 4 minutes to achieve a medium-rare burger. Don't be tempted to flatten the burger on the grill: you will loose precious juices. You can keep them cooking for a further 2 minutes either side for medium but we wouldn't take them any further than that; they would be too dry.

Rest the burgers for 3–4 minutes while you get the salad together. Peel, halve lengthways then finely slice the shallots. Tip them into a bowl then add a pinch of sea salt and the vinegar. Rub the salt and vinegar through the shallots until they are completely coated, then introduce the capers. Pick the parsley, leaving a small length of the stalk attached, and then toss the leaves through the shallot mixture. Dress with the olive oil and toss again.

Now for the toast. Cut 4 slices off a loaf of good sourdough bread, at least a finger thick, and then spread them with duck fat, as you would do butter. Place the slices onto a tray, then under a medium grill. Toast the bread until it is crisp, golden and bubbling with the fat, then turn them over to grill the other side.

Divide the toast between 4 plates and top each with a burger. Drizzle the resting juices over each burger, then garnish with the parsley salad and a pickled walnut.

4 Legs

Venison liver, sage and bacon

Venison liver is not widely eaten in the UK, since it isn't easy to get hold of. A good game dealer or butcher will be able to secure it for you. The liver of smaller roe deer is finer and sweeter than the larger varieties. As with any offal, the fresher it is, the better.

serves 4

100g unsalted butter
3 large onions, finely sliced
a pinch of sugar
salt and freshly ground black pepper
1 tablespoon sherry vinegar
8 slices of dry-cured smoked streaky
 bacon
4 slices of venison liver, weighing
 around 150g each
extra-virgin olive oil
1 tablespoon finely chopped sage
 leaves

Melt half the butter in a heavy-based saucepan and sauté the onions with the sugar and a pinch of salt over a medium heat for around 10 minutes, stirring occasionally. Cover the pan with a tight fitting lid and let the onions stew over a low heat for 20 minutes until they are soft and lightly caramelised. Remove the lid and turn up the heat, then pour in the sherry vinegar. Let the pan bubble for half a minute. Take the pan from the heat, season with a little more salt and pepper and keep warm.

Preheat a griddle pan to medium heat and grill the bacon rashers until they are browned and crisp, transfer them to a plate and keep them in a warm place.

Preheat a large frying pan over medium heat. Melt the remaining butter in the frying pan and as it starts to bubble, raise the heat to high. Brush the liver slices with olive oil and evenly cover them with the chopped sage, pressing it lightly into the flesh. Lay the liver slices onto the pan, cook for 2 minutes until crisp and brown before turning over to cook for 1 minute more. This will give you a lovely browned outside with a juicy pink middle: the ideal slice of liver. Season the slices with salt and pepper.

To serve, lay the liver onto warmed plates, topped with the bacon slices and a dollop of braised onion on the side.

Venison bresaola

If you fancy the idea of making your own charcuterie, bresaola is an easy way to start. You only need small pieces and the results can be on the table within a fortnight. Bresaola is generally made from beef, and topside is the cut most often used. You can swap the venison meat in the recipe below for a cut of beef; one of the smaller joints from the leg is ideal.

1 piece of venison rump, weighing
    around 1kg
750ml red wine
200g coarse sea salt
100g Demerara sugar
4 bay leaves
2 sprigs of rosemary
2 cloves of garlic, bruised
1 teaspoon clove
1 teaspoon black peppercorns
1 whole red chilli, split
4 strips of orange peel
4 strips of lemon peel

Trim the venison of any fat and sinew.

For the brine, place all of the other ingredients into a stainless-steel pot and bring to the boil. Once it has reached boiling point, give it a good stir until the salt and sugar has dissolved, and leave to cool completely.

Put the venison into a plastic bowl or tub and pour over the cold marinade. Weigh the meat down with a small plate or saucer, cover the bowl and refrigerate for 4 days. Turn the meat once a day before removing it from the brine. Pat the meat dry with a cloth then wrap it in muslin. Don't exceed 2 layers of muslin, the bresaola needs to breathe easily.

Leave the bresaola to hang in a cool, dry place or in a corner of the fridge with plenty of room around it for around 7–10 days. At this point it should feel quite firm.

To serve, trim the harder edges off the meat, around half a centimetre, and slice as thinly as possible. A meat slicer is the perfect tool for the job, but a good, sharp knife will suffice.

Cover a platter with the slices and drizzle them with good olive oil. Serve with a wedge of lemon. Your bresaola will keep well in the fridge for 2–3 weeks wrapped in clingfilm or baking parchment.

Venison Wellington

Beef Wellington is a classic, rich dish, also known in France as *boeuf en croûte*. Venison is the perfect meat to use in place of beef fillet, especially for a smaller group of diners (beef fillets can be a hefty weight, not to mention price!). It's definitely a special occasion meal, but don't be put off if you have never done a 'welly' before – they really aren't hard to put together. The key to success is in the advance preparation. The pâté and the mushroom duxelles are best made the day before to set properly. Then the actual assembly takes about 20 minutes. This is a seriously rich dish, so your accompaniment should, ideally, be light. Steamed spring greens or a watercress salad would both be perfect.

serves 4–6

1 length of boned loin or saddle meat
    of venison, weighing around 1kg,
    trimmed of any fat or sinew
olive oil
salt and freshly ground black pepper

For the duxelles
600g large black field mushrooms
2 round shallots
2 tablespoons of unsalted butter
salt and freshly ground black pepper
a small bunch of tarragon

For the pâté
2½ tablespoons duck fat or soft butter
2 shallots, finely diced
1 clove of garlic, crushed
sea salt and freshly ground black pepper
100ml Madeira wine
1kg free-range chicken livers
2 tablespoons brandy
1 egg yolk
150g cold unsalted butter, chopped into
    1cm pieces

500g good butter puff pastry
1 egg, beaten

Mushroom duxelles

Slice the mushrooms as finely as possible, then turn your knife and chop them until you have a fine dice. Dice the shallots as finely as possible, too. Warm the butter in a wide pan. Add the mushrooms and shallots with a good pinch of salt and sauté over a high-ish heat until the mushrooms give off their liquid. Finely chop the tarragon and stir it into the pan. Reduce the heat to a low flame and continue to cook, stirring occasionally, until all of the moisture from the mushrooms has evaporated. This should take around 20 minutes. Cool the mixture to room temperature, then pop it into a container, covering the mix with clingfilm and then into the fridge to set.

Chicken liver pâté
Melt a tablespoon of the fat in a small pan. Add the shallots and garlic with a pinch of sea salt. Sauté until they have become soft and translucent, about 3 minutes, then pour over the Madeira. Simmer until the liquid has reduced by half. Tip the mixture into the bowl of a food processor.

Trim the livers of any sinew and season them with a good pinch of sea salt and pepper. You will probably need to cook the livers in two batches so melt half of the fat or butter in a wide pan over a high heat and, when it starts to bubble, add half of the livers. Fry the livers for 1 minute on either side until they are sealed, and tip them from the pan into the food processor. Repeat with the remaining livers but, after you've cooked the second lot of livers, add them to the food processor and deglaze the pan with the brandy. Let it bubble and then pour the juices into the food processor with the livers. Add the egg yolk, then give everything a good blitz. Feed the butter into the processor one piece at a time while the motor is running and keep

going until the mixture is smooth. Check the seasoning: you might want a touch more salt. Then, scrape the pâté into a container, cover and refrigerate.

The venison
This needs to be done a good couple of hours or so before you put the dish together. Rub the venison all over with the olive oil and season with salt and pepper. Heat a heavy-based pan over a high heat and when it is smoking, add the meat. Sear it on all sides for no more than a minute each side. Place the meat onto a cooling rack and let it get completely cold.

Assembly
Preheat the oven to 200°C / Gas Mark 6. Cut a piece of baking parchment to fit the tray you'll be baking the Wellington on. Halve the pastry and roll out both pieces into rectangles, a good 3cm longer and wider than the venison fillet. Keep all of the trimmings. Place one of the pastry sheets onto the parchment, then brush the edges with some of the beaten egg. Now spread a third of the pâté onto the middle of the pastry and top that with a third of the mushroom mixture. Sit the venison on the middle of the pastry and smear the top and sides of the fillet with the pâté. Finally, press the mushroom duxelles onto the pâté. Drape the second piece of pastry over the top and crimp the edges, trimming again if necessary.

Roll out the pastry trimmings to create a lattice over the top of the Wellington, like an old-fashioned pie, and brush the pastry with the remaining egg wash. Bake the Wellington for about 20 minutes, turning the tray 180 degrees half way. It's ready when the pastry is golden and crisp – if not, it might need 5–10 minutes more in the oven. Allow the Wellington to rest for 10 minutes before carving (at the table, of course, where it will wow everyone).

4 Legs

Venison osso bucco

Venison shanks take a long time to cook but, once tender, they are delicious. This recipe is a slightly deeper and darker version of an Italian braise, ordinarily made with veal. Italians would insist that only the back leg shank is used, but if this isn't possible to come by, front shanks will suffice.

serves 4

4 venison shanks cut into 4–5cm discs
50g unsalted butter
2 tablespoons olive oil
salt and freshly ground black pepper
plain flour for dusting
1 onion, finely diced
2 stalks of celery, finely diced
4 cloves of garlic, crushed
175ml dry white wine
250ml chicken stock
400g tin of good Italian tomatoes, chopped
4 sprigs of thyme
2 bay leaves

For the gremolata
1 small bunch of flat-leaf parsley, finely chopped
1 clove of garlic, finely chopped
finely grated zest of 1 lemon

Preheat the oven to 160°C / Gas Mark 3. Choose a casserole dish large enough to hold all the shanks comfortably, preferably in a single layer. However, they can slightly overlap if need be. Warm the butter and oil over a medium heat. Season the flour generously with salt and pepper and lightly dust the shanks, shaking off any excess flour. Slip the meat into the foaming fats and gently brown the discs all over. This should take around 5 minutes. Transfer the meat to a plate and, in the remaining fat, sauté the onion, celery and garlic with a pinch of salt for 2–3 minutes until they have softened. Add the wine, letting it bubble and reduce by a quarter then add the chicken stock, tomatoes and herbs. Now tuck in the shanks, bring the pot to a simmer and check for seasoning. The liquid in the pot should just cover the meat. If it hasn't reached this level, add a little more stock or water. Cover the pot tightly and place it onto the middle shelf of the oven. Braise for 2–2½ hours or until the meat feels very tender and is coming away from the bone.

While the meat is cooking, make the gremolata. Lightly mix all of the ingredients together with the tips of your fingers. It's important not to chop it all together; you want it to be a light sprinkling garnish, rather than a wet mess.

When the osso bucco is ready, carefully transfer the shanks to a warmed platter. If your sauce is looking a little thin, place the pot over a brisk flame and boil it down to a thicker consistency. Pour the sauce over the shanks and scatter over the gremolata.

Jugged hare

Don't be put off by the following statement. There's no getting round it. The main ingredient for an authentic jugged hare is blood.

Still hungry? Good. You'll need to acquire the freshest hare possible. Even if the animal has been gutted, you'll find the blood in a cavity behind the lights, or lungs. As it's quite a gruesome job, a butcher or game dealer will do it for you, but remember to ask for the blood. Add a teaspoon of vinegar to the blood to keep it fresh while you marinate the hare. One hare will comfortably feed 4 people.

serves 4

1 hare jointed (page 155), blood
    reserved
½ teaspoon juniper berries
2 cloves
500ml red wine
2 bay leaves
4 sprigs of thyme
3 tablespoons of duck fat
plain flour, for dusting
salt and freshly ground black pepper
1 large onion, chopped
2 carrots, chopped
2 stalks of celery, chopped
2 leeks, chopped
3 cloves of garlic, chopped
1 litre chicken stock

Take your jointed hare and place it in a non-metallic bowl. Lightly crush the juniper berries and the cloves and add them to the bowl, then pour over the red wine. Tuck in the herbs, cover the bowl and refrigerate for 12 hours or overnight.

Drain the hare in a colander over a bowl, reserving the marinade. Pat the meat dry with kitchen paper.

Preheat the oven to 160°C / Gas Mark 3. Warm 2 tablespoons of the duck fat in a heavy-based frying pan over a medium heat until it begins to bubble. Season the flour generously with salt and pepper and lightly dust the hare pieces. Shake off any excess flour and slip the hare into the pan. Brown the hare gently all over, taking care not to go too dark, or you may singe the flour. Remove the pieces to a plate, pour the reserved marinade into the frying pan and bring it to a simmer.

Meanwhile, in a casserole dish, heat the remaining duck fat and sauté the onion, carrots, celery, leeks and garlic until the vegetables have softened. This should take around 5 minutes over a medium heat.

Add the hare and the marinade to the casserole dish and pour in the chicken stock. Gently bring to the boil, then add the herbs and spices. Check the seasoning and cover the dish with a tight-fitting lid. Braise the hare on the middle shelf of the oven for 2–2½ hours until the meat is tender and just coming away from the bone.

When the meat is done, remove the pieces to a warm place and set the casserole again over a low heat. Stir in the reserved blood and let the sauce gently reduce and thicken. Return the hare to the sauce to let it warm through. Adjust the seasoning again and serve with mashed potato.

Wild Boar

Wild boar is an unusual and slightly contentious addition to the canon of British game. Once upon a time, the densely forested British Isles supported a large population of truly wild pigs. But the boar lived in direct competition with humans who demanded ever-increasing amounts of land for agriculture and towns. By the Middle Ages the boar had lost the fight. It was hunted to extinction. This is astonishing, really, considering that wild boar is an incredibly adaptable animal that can thrive in several climactic zones, from tropical Asia to sub-Arctic Scandinavia. On the European continent, its survival has never been under threat. An attempt was made to reintroduce wild boar to the UK in the 17th century but it failed. Then in the late 20th century a few entrepreneurial Brits started farming wild boar for meat. Some escapees from these farms have bred in the wild. There are established colonies of wild boar in Kent, Dorset, the Forest of Dean and Gloucestershire.

These wild pigs are once again in direct competition with their biggest predator: us. Farmers hate wild boar because they will rob crops and churn fields of pasture into mud baths, if left unchecked. At the moment, our wild population of boar is small enough not to be seen as a pest like deer and rabbit. This might change. On the Continent, and in the Americas, wild boar has natural predators such as wolves. This is not the case in Britain and boar culling may one day be a feature of our countryside.

In Europe, where the population is significantly bigger than in the UK, wild boar is hunted for food on a large scale. The meat is highly prized by our near neighbours France, Germany and Italy. In the UK the meat is gaining in popularity, but there is, as yet, no commercialised hunting of wild boar here. If you encounter British wild boar in the shops it is almost certainly farmed. This is where the definition of wild boar as game can get tricky. How wild is a wild boar if it lives on a farm? And how gamey is game if it is farmed and not hunted?

We will leave the answers to those questions in your hands. You can buy truly wild, wild boar from butchers who are happy to source it from overseas. Lest you think we are copping out, we should say here and now that, currently, we actually prefer to source 'wild' boar from these pioneering, British farms. As with venison, we find that farmed wild boar is an excellent product to cook with. British pork is some of the best on the planet, and wild boar is as good as some of our more traditional, rare breeds of domestic pig. If you like pork, but prefer it on the leaner side, farmed wild boar is an excellent choice for you.

Buying and preparing wild boar

Some caveats are needed when it comes to buying British wild boar. A good farmer will allow the pigs to roam fairly freely, with plenty of shelter from trees and scrub. Wild boar takes one year to 18 months to reach maturity, and this should be allowed to take place naturally, without growth hormones or, in fact, any other intervention. Boars are omnivores, like domestic pigs. In the wild they will forage for roots and wild nuts like acorns. Very hungry wild boar will eat grubs, insects and carrion. A well-farmed boar will be acorn fed, and some farmers might supplement the diet with root vegetables. Pig pellets needn't and shouldn't feature in the feed. Lastly, you might want to check up on how pure the breed is. Some wild boar have been crossed with larger, fattier domestic pigs like the Tamworth. When bred with domestic pigs, wild boar produce bigger litters, which mature faster. You might want to ask whether this has been done for the benefit of the customer or the farmer. We have eaten and enjoyed hybrid pork, but it isn't wild boar.

Wild boar is usually sold cut into joints like domestic pork. A whole carcass would be roughly the same size as that of a small breed of pig (like Middlewhite, for example) and you are unlikely to be buying it wholly intact. If you do buy a whole specimen direct from a wild boar farm, it will have been split down the length. We recommend asking your supplier to further divide it into three sections: the fore quarter (shoulder and neck), the loin and the leg. The vast majority of us will buy wild boar by the joint, as we would with pork. The cuts behave in a similar way to pork, although they will have much less fat covering the meat. The fattiest cut on a wild boar is the neck. This is definitely a braising joint, although it can be minced to produce excellent sausages. Wild boar sausages are also made from the shoulder and belly. The shoulder is a good roasting cut, as is the loin, which can also be cut into chops. The leg on wild boar is also great for roasting. However, it is much leaner than domestic pork leg and, as a result, can be dryer. Our favourite thing to do with wild boar leg is to cure it: either in a brine, for gammon, or with a dry salt cure à la Parma ham. Recipes for both methods can be found on pages 192–193.

Marinades

Traditional recipes for cooking wild boar often call for a marinade, with aromatics, to mask the gamey quality of the meat, and alcohol to tenderise it.

We do not recommend marinating wild boar meat with wine or any other alcohol. Once, when it was always truly wild, guessing the age (and therefore tenderness) of the pig would have been tricky. The animal's diet, which affects the taste of all game, would be another unknown quantity. Farmed wild boar from the UK is bound to be butchered young, and its diet will have been carefully managed. There will be no need to disguise the gaminess, which is mild at best. Dousing meat in alcoholic marinades also encourages it to lose moisture, so we don't do it.

Classic roasts and suggested trimmings

A word about crackling

The crackle (i.e. the skin) on a wild boar joint can look hairy and unappetising. You can shave the crackling with a disposable razor (we keep a stash in our kitchen for preparing pig trotters and brawn anyway). There is something about wild boar skin that takes a lot longer to turn into crackling than the skin on fattier domestic pigs. Whilst waiting for the crackle, you can overcook the meat underneath. Some recipes, therefore, call for removing the skin. The easiest way to do this is to work your way carefully along the underside with a sharp boning knife. Keep the knife as close to the actual skin as you can, as you want to leave as much fat around the meat as possible. The skin can either be roasted alongside the joint or discarded. It's up to you.

Roast loin of wild boar, for 4 or so

The loin is the leanest cut on wild boar and, if you roast it the same way you would a domestic pig, it might compare unfavourably. This method, which we picked up from an Italian recipe some years back, works brilliantly.

1 loin of wild boar (approxi. weight 2kg)
mild olive oil for cooking
1 level teaspoon salt
1 level teaspoon freshly ground black pepper
2 carrots
1 potato
1 onion
125ml dry white wine

Ask the butcher to chine the loin for you and remove the crackling. Chining the loin means removing the backbone, whilst leaving the ribs under the meat. Rub the loin all over with about 3 tablespoons of the oil. Then rub it with the salt and pepper.

Preheat the oven to 180°C / Gas Mark 4. Wash but don't peel the carrots and potato. Cut them in half, lengthways. Peel the onion and cut it into 3 discs. This motley collection of veg is going to be your trivet or roasting rack, protecting the meat from direct heat whilst in the roasting tray. Arrange them into a sort of platform, in the middle of your designated roasting dish. Lay the pork, fat-side up, on the platform of vegetables. Pour the wine around but not over the meat. Roast it for 45 minutes to start, and then test it, using a skewer, pressed briefly to the top lip or, even better, a probe thermometer. Pork is good to go at 64°C. Don't forget to follow our instructions to rest the meat once it reaches the right temperature, as the meat finishes its cooking processes during this time. Undercooked pork (i.e. that which is less than medium), is not really a good idea. If the meat is not ready after 45 minutes give it blasts of 5 minutes at a time until you are happy with it. Rest the cooked loin in a warm (but not hot) place for 20 minutes before serving.

If you want to cook the crackling alongside the meat, this is best done over a dry roasting tray, on a roasting rack. Rub the skin with salt on both sides. It should take around the same time to cook as the meat, but check on it halfway through.

By the way, the vegetable 'trivet' that you parked the meat on top of is absolutely delicious, having gone very sticky and Marmitey. You can use it to start gravy, along with the roasting juices, but prise the potato and at least one carrot out first, and eat them (cook's treat).

Roast leg of wild boar, for 6–8

1 leg of wild boar (approx. weight 4kg)
mild olive oil for cooking
salt and freshly ground black pepper
4 carrots
2 potatoes
2 onions
250ml dry white wine

Score the crackling on the leg at intervals of roughly 2cm, using a sharp Stanley knife or paper cutter (you can ask the butcher to do this for you). Rub the leg all over with the oil, then season it generously with salt and pepper. Preheat the oven to 220°C / Gas Mark 7.

Wash but don't peel the carrots and potatoes. Cut them in half, lengthways. Peel the onions and cut them into 3 discs. Arrange the vegetables into a platform in the middle of your designated roasting tray; they will act as a rack or trivet for the meat. Lay the leg on the vegetables, on the flattest side. Place it on the middle shelf of the oven, with any shelves above it removed. Cook the leg for 30 minutes at 220°C / Gas Mark 7 then lower the heat to 180°C / Gas Mark 4. At this point pour the glass of wine into the roasting tray, around but not over the meat. Cook the meat for 2 hours then check it. Leg of pork and boar should be 70°C in the middle. Ideally, use a probe thermometer, inserted into the thickest part of the leg (not against the bone). If the meat needs longer, give it sessions of 10 minutes until you are happy. Once it is cooked, rest the leg for half an hour. You want to rest pork on the bone in a fairly warm environment; turning off the oven and leaving the door ajar is ideal.

Roast, stuffed wild boar

We often refer to this version of roast boar, somewhat erroneously, as a 'porchetta'. In fact, a true porchetta is made from an entire suckling pig: boned, stuffed and roasted (traditionally over wood). If you can get hold of a suckling wild boar, this recipe is easy to adapt. For cooking in most domestic ovens, this cut of loin, with the belly still attached, is a more manageable option.

Porchetta can be served hot and cold. In fact, we almost prefer it cold. If you plan to serve it this way, removing the crackling then tying it back on for roasting makes the meat easier to carve once it has cooled. We'll talk you through how to do just that in the method.

Half a wild boar mid-section (approximate weight without stuffing will be 3kg); you want the loin to be boned, but with the belly still attached. Ask the butcher to give you the tenderloin and the chined bones.
2 kidneys of either pork or wild boar
1 liver of the same
3 cloves garlic
1 small bunch of rosemary
1 small bunch of parsley
1 level tablespoon fennel seeds
mild olive oil for cooking
salt and freshly ground black pepper
butcher's string

Trim the bones of any spare meat and cut the tenderloin into small dice, free of any sinew. Do the same to the liver and kidneys. Set them aside.

Skin the loin and belly, taking care not to separate them. You could ask the butcher to do this for you when he bones the meat.

Peel and chop the garlic roughly with the rosemary and parsley. Then add them to the offal and trimmed tenderloin with the fennel seeds. Add about a teaspoon full of salt and half a teaspoon of fresh ground black pepper. You can pound or blitz this stuffing to a near-paste using a food processor or mincer.

Lay the wild boar skin on a chopping board, with the inside facing upwards. Lay the loin and belly out flat on top of it, as if you were putting the meat and the skin back together. Obviously the meat should be fat-side down. Lay the stuffing along the seam where belly meets loin, as if it were a really rough sausage shape. Fold the belly right over the top of the loin then carefully turn the meat over so that the loin and its back fat are on top. Now tie the joint together, quite tightly. Tie either end first, then work your way towards the middle. How many times you tie it is up to you; but we reckon that if the ties are roughly two finger-widths apart from each other, the joint is nice and securely fastened.

Preheat the oven to 220°C / Gas Mark 7. Lay the pork on a rack over your designated roasting tray, and cook for 30 minutes, then lower the heat to 180°C / Gas Mark 4 and roast for a further one and a half to 2 hours. At this point check it; ideally with a probe thermometer. The meat is ready when the temperature in the middle is 70°C. If it needs more time, give the meat sessions of 10 minutes until you are happy with it. Once it is cooked, allow the meat to rest for 30 minutes before serving. We allow our porchetta to rest until it reaches an ambient temperature, and it is really good served cold, too. If carving proves tricky, you can easily remove the crackling, which is only tied on remember. If you remove the crackling, it can be great tossed through a bitter leaf salad like watercress or rocket, rather like porky croûtons.

Suggested trimmings

As it is a piggy meat, wild boar sits happily with all the goodies you would expect to find next to roast pork. Apple sauce and Cumberland sauce (see page 238) work well here, but so do all good mustards and, surprisingly, Horseradish Sauce (page 238), which is not uncommon in Eastern Europe. Our Pickled Quince recipe on page 239 is a superb pairing for wild boar, especially if you serve it near Christmas time.

Wild boar shoulder in milk

This Italianate recipe can also be made using domestic pork. Traditionally, the loin is used, but on a wild pig this cut can be a little dry for pot-roasting. Pork shoulder is an undervalued cut anyway, and is definitely the best part of a wild boar for braising.

Don't be alarmed by the finished look of this dish: the milk will separate into curds during the cooking process. This is meant to happen and, aside from tenderising the meat, the juices taste fantastic...even if they don't look pretty.

serves 4–6

1 wild boar or small pork shoulder
    (approximately 1–1.5kg)
salt and freshly ground black pepper
4 cloves garlic
6 shallots
1 lemon
1 small bunch sage
125ml white wine vinegar
3 tablespoons extra-virgin olive oil
2 tablespoons lard
300ml whole milk

Get the butcher to bone the shoulder and remove the crackling or skin, but ask him to leave the meat protected by any fat underneath the crackling. Rub the meat generously all over with salt and pepper. Place it in a nice deep dish for marinating. Peel and bruise the garlic cloves with the side of a knife. Peel the shallots and slice them finely. Peel the zest of the lemon and squeeze the juice. Pick the sage leaves and leave them whole. Pop all these ingredients into the dish with the meat. Combine the vinegar and oil and pour it over the meat. Mix everything together and leave the dish to marinate for several hours (ideally, overnight).

Preheat the oven to 200°C / Gas Mark 6. Melt the lard in a casserole or deep-sided roasting dish and, when it is hot, brown the meat all over fairly briskly. Transfer it to the oven, covered with a lid or foil, and cook it at 200°C / Gas Mark 6 for 20 minutes. Then lower the heat to 150°C / Gas Mark 2 and remove the meat from the oven. Add the marinade and all its ingredients to the roasting tray, then pour the milk over everything. Cover the dish and return it to the oven. Cook the joint for at least an hour and a half. Check it after this time. The meat, when ready, will be tender enough to cut with a spoon. It could take a while, and don't forget that the milk will curdle. This is fine. Once the meat is done to your liking, take it out of the juices and rest it for 20 minutes before serving. Check the seasoning of the juices and pour them back over the meat on the serving dish. We like to serve pork in milk with a rocket or similarly bitter-leafed salad. It is also good with new potatoes, left undressed, and thrown around the milky cooking juices.

Wild boar 'vindaloo'

Forget about those nonsensical versions in late-night curry houses. The real vindaloo is a surprisingly light dish from Goa in southwest India. Like many recipes from this region, it was inspired by the Portuguese love of marinating meat in wine (or vinegar) and garlic, hence the name – a colloquial version of 'vinho ahlo'. Wild boar is the best meat for making a (sort of) authentic version of vindaloo because it is not unlike the semi-wild pigs that roam Goa's beaches and palm plantations. This recipe was inspired by one from Madhur Jaffrey. You can easily swap the wild boar for pork.

serves 4

1kg diced wild boar (shoulder meat is best)
1½ teaspoons salt
½ teaspoon freshly ground black pepper
125ml red wine vinegar
4 tablespoons mild olive or vegetable oil
½ cinnamon stick
8 cloves
6 cardamom pods
1 level teaspoon crushed dried chillies (use less if you don't want heat)
½ teaspoon fennel seeds
½ teaspoon ground turmeric
¼ of a nutmeg, grated
3 onions, diced
8 cloves garlic, chopped roughly
1 x 400g tin peeled plum tomatoes
1 teaspoon sugar
6 green chillies (optional)

Season the boar with half the salt and the black pepper. Add the vinegar and half the oil and stir them through the meat. Set the meat aside.

Next prepare the spices. Grind the cinnamon, cloves and cardamom. Combine them with the dried chillies, turmeric and nutmeg. Heat a dry frying pan over a gentle flame and roast the spice mix very gently for about a minute. You will smell the flavours 'unlocking'. As soon as they do this tip the spices over the meat and stir them through.

Heat the remaining oil in a casserole or large saucepan. Add the onions and garlic with the remaining salt and fry them in the oil gently, until they just start to brown. Remove them and set aside.

Now turn up the heat a little and fry the meat all over. Once it is done, return the onions to the pan. Add any marinating juices left from the meat bowl. Squish the tomatoes using your hands, in a colander, so that the juice has gone and only a pulp remains. Add this pulp (not the juice) and the sugar to the pan. Bring the mix to a simmer, and the meat will start to let go of more of its juices. If it looks at all dry add just enough water to loosen the ingredients (but not enough to make it look like a stew). Cover the pot and cook the vindaloo as gently as possible for at least two hours, or until the meat is tender enough to cut with a spoon.

Finally, if you want the heat they will bring, add the green chillies, sliced, to the finished dish. If not, scatter them over the pot as a garnish.

This dish is great with piles of rice, but it is just as good with bread or potatoes, and you can make it up to 3 days in advance of eating. The vinegar was originally added as a preservative and, once upon a time, it was said a vindaloo could be kept for 10 days without refrigeration. We've never tested this theory!

4 Legs

Wild boar and bean casserole

The best beans for this dish are butter beans, which are fat and creamy. Canellini beans or haricots would be worthy substitutes. We prefer to soak then cook dried beans, as the cooking liquor from the beans makes an excellent stock. You can use tinned beans, of course.

serves 4

200g dried butter beans or 1 x 400g tin
3 cloves garlic
2 bay leaves
extra-virgin olive oil
2 onions
2 carrots
2 stalks celery
100g dry-cured smoked bacon
50g chorizo or similar coarse cured
   sausage
2 tablespoons mild olive oil for cooking
800g diced wild boar meat (from the
   shoulder and belly)
¼ teaspoon crushed, dried red chilli
   (optional)
salt and freshly ground black pepper
125ml red wine
1 level tablespoon tomato purée

If you are using dried beans soak them in plenty of cold water for several hours (overnight is ideal). Then, change their water and put them in a large pot, with 2 litres of fresh, unsalted water. Bring the beans to a vigorous boil and cook them hard for 10 minutes. Skim off any froth that gathers at the top of the water. After 10 minutes, drain the beans and cover them in 2 more litres of fresh cold water. Do not add salt. Peel the garlic and add it to the beans, whole. Add the bay leaves and 2 tablespoons of olive oil. Bring the water to a gentle simmer and cook it, without boiling, until the beans are soft and creamy. How long this takes depends on the shelf life of the beans, so it is important to check them a few times. Most beans take just over an hour, but some can need twice as long.

While the beans cook, prepare the meat and vegetables. Peel and roughly dice the onion, carrots and celery. Dice the bacon in a similar fashion. Slice the chorizo roughly. Heat the oil in a large pot or casserole and, when it is hot, fry the bacon and chorizo, briskly, until they are cooked and slightly crispy. Remove them with a slotted spoon and brown the wild boar meat all over. Remove it and set aside with the bacon. Now add the vegetables to the remaining fat and juices. Lower the heat, add about half a teaspoon of salt, stir once or twice, cover and let them sweat for 10 minutes, until they start to go tender. Don't let them brown. Add the wine and tomato purée and stir through the vegetables. Add the meat and bacon. Add the cooked beans and all their liquor. Bring everything to a slow simmer and cook the stew until the meat is tender enough to cut with a spoon. Check the seasoning once the meat is cooked.

You can serve this dish with a swirl of extra-virgin olive oil and the flaked dried chillies as a garnish.

Wild boar cider ham

Making your own gammon in a brine is surprisingly easy. You can use this recipe with either wild boar or domestic pork. If you have room in a cold place, like a garage or shed, then it's well worth a go. The brine can be made with cider, wine or beer. Just swap in whichever of the three you fancy.

serves 6–8

1 leg or shoulder of wild boar (approximate weight 2kg). Ask the butcher to take off the hock and trotter. You can brine these parts of the leg too, but everything fits into a smaller container if they have been separated.
6 litres water
1.5 litres cider
2kg salt
500g brown sugar
6 cloves
1 bay leaf
a small handful juniper berries

To make the brine, simply place the water, cider, salt, sugar and aromatics into a large saucepan (we use a stock pot). Simmer the brine until the salt and sugar have dissolved. Allow the brine to cool completely. Once it has, choose a suitable container and immerse the leg or shoulder in it. Use something weighty like a pan lid to hold all the meat underneath the surface. The trotter and hock will be ready to use in one week. Use them to make a delicious soup with split peas. You need to give the main section of the leg a minimum of 2 weeks to cure, but 3 weeks is ideal. After this time, remove it from the brine (which you should now discard). You can now keep the ham wrapped in cheesecloth or muslin in the fridge, until you want to cook it. The curing time in the brine will have preserved it, and it should be fine for a week or so.

To poach the ham and give it the traditional glaze you will need
2 onions, peeled but left whole
1 carrot, peeled but left whole
2 bay leaves
200g (an average-sized jar) of Dijon mustard
2 tablespoons soft brown sugar

Place the ham in a large cooking pot with the onions, carrot, and bay leaves. Cover everything with cold water. Just as you did when brining the ham, hold it under the surface with something weighty. Bring the pot to a fairly brisk simmer, skimming any froth that comes to the surface.

After 20–30 minutes, lower the heat, cover the pot and simmer for 2 hours. If the leg weighs more than 2kg add an extra half hour per 500g (i.e. an hour per kilo). After this time turn off the heat and remove the ham carefully from the liquor. Allow it to cool until

you can handle the surface easily. Carefully remove the skin of the ham (what would have been crackling on a roast). Combine the mustard and sugar and spread them evenly (but not neatly) over the surface of the meat.

Preheat the oven to 180°C / Gas Mark 4. Lay the glazed ham on a roasting dish lined with foil or silicone and bake it for half an hour, or until the glaze has gone slightly crispy and bubbly. Let the ham rest for at least 10 minutes before carving. Of course, you can now allow it to cool completely for serving cold. Wild boar ham is particularly good with Horseradish Sauce (see page 238).

Italian-style, dry-cured wild boar

On a visit to Sienna we were fed proscuitto made from the much prized, local 'cingale' (wild boar). We cannot pretend that this recipe will emulate such an artisanal bit of charcuterie but, even more so than with gammon, making your own dry-cured ham is incredibly rewarding.

Please note, this is a lengthy process. You also need some cool, dry space to hang ham. A chilly shed or loft is ideal. A garage is good, as long as you don't actually use it for keeping an active car! The ham will take between six to eight months to make. The plus side of course, is that, during that time, there is little or no work involved. We make hams for Christmas, starting our curing time in the early summer. The best cut of pork for hamming is the leg, but there are good shoulder hams about. They are fattier, but just as flavoursome. On wild boar the shoulder meat is leaner than that of a domestic pig. You could try curing one of each. It goes without saying that this recipe will work with pork, as well as wild boar.

A note about the flavouring of the cure: we love fennel seeds with wild boar, but you can swap in a preferred spice if you like. Juniper is good, as is rosemary.

1 leg or shoulder of wild boar
3kg salt
1kg sugar
a small handful fennel seeds
a small handful black peppercorns
a non-metal container large enough for
   the meat and the cure (wooden wine
   boxes are ideal)
a silicone sheet
a bottle of white wine vinegar
muslin cloth
a meat hook

First up, ask the butcher to tunnel bone the meat for you. This makes the process of curing it easier and slightly faster. It also makes the meat easier to slice once cured. When the meat is boned, weigh it, and make a written note of the weight. This is vital.

Mix all the ingredients for the cure together. Rub a handful of them into the cavity created by boning the meat. Make a bed of the cure about a centimetre thick on the base of your chosen container. Place the joint on to this base. You now need to cover the meat with the remaining cure. Literally bury it. Cover the meat with a sheet of silicone and lay a weight on top of it to press it. If the meat weighs around 2kg the weight should be roughly half that. Now the meat needs to rest in the cure, under the weight, for 5 days per kilo (this is why you must weigh it before beginning). After that time remove it from the salt, which you now discard. Wash the meat and pat it dry, then rub it all over with the vinegar. Wrap the meat in muslin and tie it securely. You now hang it in the muslin, in a cool, draughty place for one month. After a month, remove the cloth and hang it exposed to the air for a further 4–6 months. The longer you hang the ham, the more intense its flavour will be.

The ham is ready to eat when it feels firm and dry (but not rock hard). Do not be alarmed by any mould on the skin of the ham. This is perfectly normal. Slice away this 'bloom' if there is any, plus the outermost, hard layer of fat (the crackling) before you cut the ham meat, across the grain, as thinly as you can. You should reward yourself with the driest glass of wine or sherry you can get, as you cut and eat the first slices of your own proscuitto!

Larp of wild boar

We are both fanatical about Thai food, and wild boar is an excellent meat for this dish from the Northeast, or Issan region. 'Larp' is a salad of minced pork; quite powerfully flavoured with lime, fish sauce, mint and coriander. It is best eaten with crisp raw vegetables and steamed rice. If you can get hold of the famous sticky (or glutinous) rice of eastern Thailand, so much the better.

serves 2

2 tablespoons jasmine or basmati rice
300g minced wild boar
salt and freshly ground black pepper
sugar
1 tablespoon Thai fish sauce (nam pla)
1 small red chilli, deseeded and finely
    sliced
3 tablespoons lime juice
2 round shallots, finely sliced
a small handful of mint leaves
a small handful of coriander leaves

First, put the rice in a dry frying pan and roast it over a low heat, stirring as you go. It should take about 3 minutes before it becomes golden brown and gives off a nutty aroma. Leave the rice to cool then grind it in a pestle and mortar or spice grinder to a fine powder. The ground rice gives the salad a bit of body.

In a medium saucepan, simmer the minced boar in 4 tablespoons of water with a pinch each of salt and sugar for 3–4 minutes, or until just cooked. Try not to overcook the mince, it can easily become tough. Take the pan from the heat and stir in the fish sauce, chilli and lime juice. Mix in the shallot, herbs and ground rice and check the seasoning. The salad should be hot, salty and sour, so add more lime or fish sauce as necessary. Serve with lettuce, cucumber and spring onions on the side, plus a bowl of steamed rice.

Wild boar sausage and rigatoni

A good boar sausage will have all the robust flavour that you need for this very Tuscan recipe. Many different pastas work here, but short tubular types like rigatoni, penne or fusili are best.

serves 4–6

50g unsalted butter
1 tablespoon olive oil
1 medium red onion, finely chopped
6 good-quality wild boar sausages, around 600g or so
150ml dry white wine
1 bay leaf
400g tin of good Italian tomatoes, chopped
salt and freshly ground black pepper
500g rigatoni
6 tablespoons freshly grated Parmesan

Place the butter in a heavy-based saucepan over a medium heat and add the olive oil. When the butter has completely melted, add the onion and sauté for 10 minutes, stirring occasionally until it has softened. Meanwhile, remove the skins from the sausages and break the meat into pieces. Add the sausage meat to the pan and sauté for 10 minutes more, breaking the meat down with a wooden spoon as you go, until it is evenly minced and well browned. Pour in the wine, add the bay leaf and leave the pan to simmer for 5 minutes until all the wine has evaporated. Now add the tomatoes and season with a little salt and pepper. Cover the pan and leave to simmer over a low heat for 20 minutes, stirring every so often.

Bring a large pot of salted water to a rolling boil. Add the pasta. Cook for 8–11 minutes, depending on your chosen brand. When the pasta is cooked al dente, drain it in a colander, reserving a couple of tablespoons of the cooking water, and toss the pasta in the pan with the sauce. Add the reserved cooking water and half the Parmesan, and give the pan a good stir; the sauce should be quite loose and shiny. Serve immediately with the rest of the Parmesan sprinkled over the top.

Wild boar rissoles

The leftovers from just about any roasted joint could be used in this recipe. Try serving these rissoles with the Horseradish Sauce on page 238.

serves 2

250g cold roast wild boar
1 small onion
50g fresh breadcrumbs
a couple of pinches of freshly grated nutmeg
½ teaspoon finely grated lemon rind
1 small clove of garlic, crushed
1 tablespoon chopped parsley
1 egg
salt and freshly ground black pepper
plain flour
oil for frying, preferably a light olive oil

Chop the cold roast meat into 2cm cubes and finely chop the onion. If you have a food processor with a mincer attachment, mince the meat and onion using the finest blade or, alternatively, pulse them finely in a food processor. Tip the mixture into a bowl and add the breadcrumbs, nutmeg, lemon rind, garlic, parsley and egg.

Season with a good pinch of salt and a twist of pepper and mix together until thoroughly blended. Divide the mixture into 8 small balls, and then press the balls into patties. Season the flour with a touch of salt and pepper and coat the patties, shaking off any excess flour.

Choose a heavy-based frying pan that will fit all of the rissoles comfortably and heat just enough oil to cover the base. Cook the patties over a medium-high heat for around 4–5 minutes, either side, until lovely and brown.

Salmon, trout, sea trout, charr and pike

Salmon, river trout and sea trout will be familiar to all keen cooks and diners. However, it might come as a surprise to know that they all belong to the same aquatic family: the *Salmonidae*. There are many subtle differences between the various members of this family. What unites them all is their birth, for all *Salmonidae* are spawned and born in freshwater. Most trout will remain in lakes and rivers, but salmon are famous for their migratory habits.

In one of nature's most spectacular shows of willpower and guile, a young salmon heads out to sea, sometimes for as long as five years, then returns to the river it was born in to spawn. This return journey from sea to riverbed is the stuff of legend. You might have witnessed it first-hand or seen documentaries featuring spectacular displays of fishy athleticism, as not even rapids or waterfalls are allowed to impede the salmon's progress upstream. No one really knows how or why the salmon is so determined to return to its birthplace, but the journey is as perilous as it is photogenic, usually resulting in the fish's demise shortly after it has reproduced.

At this point we ought to mention sea trout. Whilst most species of trout remain in rivers and lakes, some, for reasons no one is entirely sure about, copy the behaviour of salmon, and head out to sea. Both of Britain's most common species of trout have been known to do this. When you come across sea trout in fishmongers or restaurants, the name refers to the fish's behaviour and not its genus.

Whilst at sea, salmon and sea trout undergo immense physical changes, partly to cope with life in salt water and partly due to their diet, which is rich in crustacea. This diet turns their meat from a pale pink to a deeper, almost coral colour. This is the point in their life cycle at which their predators, ourselves included, find them most delicious. Traditionally, as they entered river estuaries, the adult fish were netted just as they began the journey up stream to spawn. Nowadays, however, lots of salmon is fished at sea. Indeed, if you buy, rather than catch your own salmon, it is most likely to have been caught offshore. Unless, of course, it is farmed. Most salmon eaten in the UK these days is not remotely wild.

Salmon farming is a controversial subject. Once, salmon were hugely plentiful in the British Isles but, after the Industrial Revolution, man's impact on rivers caused stocks to decline sharply. By the latter part of the 20th century wild salmon was extremely hard to come by and carried a hefty price tag. When we were children, eating fresh salmon was almost unheard of; it was right up there with caviar and fillet steak. Salmon farms flourished in the 1980s, bringing the now-familiar fillets and steaks to an almost-uninitiated population at large. The rise of this farmed salmon was originally due to an increase in dietary awareness. Salmon is one of the so-called 'oily' fish, rich in omega-3 fats, and these types of fish have become a staple of the 'healthy eater'. So far so good. The trouble is that some salmon producers have been accused of the same kind of intensive farming that makes people uneasy about, say, caged chickens. You don't need to look far in any media to find aficionados of wild salmon denigrating the farmed version. The meat, they say, is a poor imitation of the real thing. Wild salmon, as you might expect from such a highly active fish, is lean and flavoursome, whereas the idle, farmed version is fatty and bland. If that were

the only objection anyone had to farmed salmon, deciding whether you approve of it or not might be easier. Salmon farming has come in for a lot more stick than mere culinary snobbery. The diet of farmed salmon has come under close scrutiny in recent years. We said earlier that the fish's natural diet makes its meat pink. Some salmon farms have used additives instead of crustacea to literally dye the flesh of farmed animals through their feed. When packed together in confined spaces, the fish also need inoculation and drugs to fight disease. The diet, the drugs and the huge mass of incarcerated fish involved have undoubtedly had an impact on our already-beleaguered aquatic environments. Salmon farmers have been accused of polluting rivers and estuaries, and of depleting stocks of wild sea fish in order to feed their quarry. Just as worryingly, escapees from salmon farms have been blamed for carrying diseases and parasites that their wild cousins have no immunity to. It might just be the case that, in their desire to bring this cheap salmon to the masses, salmon farmers have been responsible for yet more decline in the wild population.

As you can see, we are merely touching upon a hugely complex subject. It would be easy to say that everyone should avoid farmed salmon and go back to lusting after the wild stuff, which is still rare and pricey. However, some non-governmental organisations insist that wild salmon, particularly the Atlantic version, is now an endangered species. This might lead you to thinking that it is best avoided altogether.

However, it is possible, with some vigilance, to buy salmon with a relatively clear conscience. There is no doubt that by far the best (and least environmentally challenging) salmon is wild; fished using traditional methods, on a small scale. It will cost a bomb, but it will be worth every penny. Look on it as an occasional, strictly seasonal treat like grouse. Remember that the season here runs from early summer to early autumn. If you see wild salmon on a fishmonger's slab at any other time, it will probably have come from Alaska, Canada or the southern hemisphere. Possibly by air. Outside of the wild season, there are some very well reared versions of the farmed stuff. If the notion of organically farmed salmon reassures you, there are increasing numbers of these types of operation, especially off the coasts of Scotland and Ireland. Salmon ranching is still in its infancy, and involves hand rearing, then releasing young fish into rivers and lochs, in much the same way as birds like pheasant and partridge are managed on estates (see pages 20 and 44). This might be the most environmentally friendly way forward for the entire salmon industry.

Rainbow trout, brown trout and sea trout, as we touched upon earlier, are the salmon's close cousins, although most of these fish will not migrate to sea. As a result, they tend to remain smaller (although even river trout can grow to quite a size). Their flesh is a delicate pink colour, with a milder flavour than salmon. This mildness can work against them, and some people even say that trout can taste 'muddy'. This is usually a result of the fish's habitat. If it lives in clear, fast-flowing water, this muddiness will be negligible. Trout fishing is very popular in the UK and it is a controlled activity. Rivers and lakes are often stocked with rainbow trout for the benefit of anglers. The rainbow trout is not native to Britain, it was introduced from the Americas and, because it tends to outbreed our native brown trout, many of these stocked fish are bred to be sterile. There is some controversy over this practice as you might imagine. If you buy, rather than fish for trout, it will be farmed, and will almost certainly be rainbow trout. It may well be the same, sexless variety used to stock rivers for the pleasure of anglers. This is because sexless (or triploid) trout grow faster than the undoctored versions.

The trout-farming industry has, thus far, escaped the scrutiny and large-scale criticism visited upon the salmon industry but, if intensive farming concerns you, it pays to be just as vigilant when buying trout as salmon. The best fish are reared in running water, where they get to swim against the current. They should enjoy as natural a diet as possible and waste from the farm should not affect local waterways. There are organic trout farms around. Notably, organic trout cannot be bred as triploids. River trout are fished year round, but sea trout has the same season as salmon, and is best caught as it returns to river estuaries from open water. There is a growing sea trout farming industry in the UK and Ireland. If you wish to buy farmed sea-trout you should be just as cautious as you would over salmon.

Charr

Salmon and trout have an enigmatic and slightly misunderstood relation, less known to diners in the UK, but just as tasty. Charr (sometimes spelled char) is often wrongly identified as a type of trout. Although it is a member of the *Salmonidae* family, it comes from its own distinct lineage. A very ancient one at that. Charr is believed to have been amongst the first fish to swim into Arctic waters after the Ice Age, hence their other name, Arctic charr. Once they developed a taste for these glacial waters, the habit stuck. Modern charr favour glacial and alpine lakes. As a result, they are not common in the British Isles, save for parts of Scotland and Ireland. Like trout, they can, but don't always, switch between fresh and salt water. Like salmon and trout they can be farmed successfully and, if you buy charr in this country, it will almost certainly have been farmed in fresh water. The meat is very pale pink, which is probably why people often think the charr is a slightly oversized river trout. You could be forgiven for this when looking at the raw fish. On cooking, however, the texture and flavour of this fish is quite unique. Once cooked, the meat becomes markedly paler than trout or salmon. We think it is rather like a cross between trout and mullet; quite delicate, but very tasty nonetheless.

...and pike

The pike is Britain's largest freshwater fish. It is a ferocious, greedy beast that will eat just about anything from other fish to ducklings and water rats. This makes it quite easy to fish, as it is easily lured, by bait or by anything that remotely resembles something edible. For this reason, and due to the fact that it can put up a good fight once lured, it is popular among anglers. The meat on pike is pale, off-white and has a taste not wholly unlike freshwater eel.

Once upon a time, like the eel, pike was more widely eaten in the UK, but it has three things going against it for many modern diners. Firstly, people have a plethora of sea fish, including salmon, to choose from these days. Once this choice was only available to people who lived near the coast. The second is pike's flavour, which, if it lives in lakes, ponds or slow-flowing water, can be muddy. The third is its boniness. Pike bones are fiddly and plentiful, and this is why many traditional recipes come in the form of mousses and terrines, using the pounded meat, rather than fillets or steaks.

You are highly unlikely to find pike in a fishmonger's, unless you ask him or her to order one in advance. In short, getting hold of and cooking this magnificent animal is a challenge all round. Don't let it deter you! We have a list of people who might be able to source pike for you in our suppliers' section at the back of this book (page 258).

How to prepare river fish

Trout, charr, salmon and pike can all be prepared in a similar way. The main difference between them, in terms of filleting, is their size, but you can actually use the same tools and methods for all of them. Cleaning and preparing fish from scratch is not for the squeamish. It tends to be messier than jointing your own meat, mainly because there are scales to deal with, before you even start to think about all the fiddly bones and slippery fillets. We always recommend buying fish whole from a fishmonger (as opposed to the cling-wrapped versions in a supermarket), because that way you will know how fresh the fish is. But we also recommend asking the fishmonger to do the really messy work for you! However, if you do find yourself with a whole fish, here is how to deal with it as cleanly and simply as possible.

Scaling

The first job is scaling. If you eat a lot of fish and like to deal with it whole, we highly recommend buying a fish scaler. It looks like a sturdy, metal toothbrush, with little studs in place of bristles. It literally sweeps the scales from the skin and doesn't carry the small risk of tearing the fish in the process. If you don't have a scaler, the next best thing is a well-worn butter or steak knife: go for the oldest one in your cutlery drawer!

Another vital part of your scaling gear is a bin liner. When you scale fish there is a good chance that the scales will fly all over the kitchen. Those that don't cling to your arms, forehead and hair, will attach themselves, limpet-like, to worktops, sinks and other places where they have no business being. So, before you get to work, prise open a bin bag and use it like a baggy 'envelope' to loosely surround the fish, your hands, and your scaling tool. Wrap your left hand with a piece of kitchen towel or a cloth and use this to grasp the fish by the tail. Push the scales off, working from tail to head and they should end up in the bag. Now give the fish a wash and dry it thoroughly.

If the fish has not been gutted, the best place to do this is over the sink. Take the sharpest small knife you have. Near the fish's tail, on the underside, is a small hole (its bottom!). Run the knife, in one decisive movement, from this handy start point, up to the gills. Now you can literally tug the innards from the cavity. On larger fish, like salmon and sea trout, you might have to snip the head end of the entrails from the fish's body right up against the gills. Wash out the cavity of the fish and dry it again.

Filleting

To fillet the fish, lay it on its side on a chopping board, with the tail to your left. Use a boning knife and make your first incision directly beneath the head. You can actually cut the head off if you prefer, but it is easier to leave it on. Turn the knife clockwise, 90 degrees so that the side of the knife is flat against the fish's backbone and the blade faces the tail. Run the knife flat along the backbone, cutting towards the tail. If you place a gentle downwards pressure with your palm you will literally feel the knife edging along the backbone as the blade cuts through the flesh. When you get to the tail turn the blade up 45 degrees to cut the tail meat from the tail fin.

You can now turn the fish over and repeat the same action. Or you could try this method, which is slightly less wasteful. Keep the fish as it was when you took off the first fillet: that is to say with the backbone now facing you, tail still to the left. Cut carefully through the backbone as close to the tail as possible. Turn the knife 90 degrees again, with the flat side underneath the backbone and the blade facing the head end. This time apply the pressure upwards, so that the flat side of the knife runs along the underside of the backbone, with the blade cutting through the meat from tail to head. Finally you simply lift the backbones from the fillet underneath them.

Lay the fillets flat on the board, skin-side down, with the wider, head ends to the right (i.e. tail is still to the left). You can clearly see a flank on each fillet, which was the narrow strip of bony and fatty meat on the fish's belly. It is glossy, rather than meaty looking and, on salmon in particular, has a fair amount of creamy-looking fat. There are also a number of bones where this flank attaches itself to the meaty part of the fillet. You can either tweak these bones out with tweezers or you can run the knife underneath them, taking off the flank as you go. Now you have a clean fish fillet.

A word about pike here: if you fillet a pike this way, there are a number of small 'y'- shaped bones running through the middle of the fillet. Run your finger along the middle of the fillet and you can feel them. Using a small boning knife again, you need to cut a 'v'-shape either side of these bones, which will enable you to pull a ribbon of bones away from the flesh. This job is pretty fiddly and, if you buy a pike, it really is worth asking the fishmonger to fillet and 'v-pin' the fish for you.

You can now portion the fillets or leave them whole, depending on the recipe you are following.

Oven-poached salmon or trout

This way of cooking salmon was inspired by a method from Alice Waters' *Chez Panisse* cookbook, one of our favourite recipe collections of all time.

We always struggle to come up with a name to describe this treatment of the fish; 'oven poached' sounds like an oxymoron. You are really roasting, in a humidified oven, which results in very tender, moist meat. It works with sea trout, too. You can also use the method on fillets of salmon or trout, rather than the whole fish. We'll give you the tweaked times in the method, should you choose to do this.

serves 4–6

1 salmon or sea trout (approximately 1.5kg)
mild olive oil for cooking
salt and freshly ground black pepper
2–3 slices of lemon
baking parchment

Preheat the oven to 180°C / Gas Mark 4 and boil a kettle. Place a casserole or small roasting tray on the lower shelf of the oven and fill it two-thirds full with the hot water from the kettle. Line a second roasting tray with a sheet of silicone or baking paper at least twice the width of the tray. Rub it with a little oil. Generously season the salmon all over with salt and black pepper and slot the lemon slices into the cavity. Place it on the parchment-lined roasting tray. Bring up the excess paper to make a tent around the salmon (we use damp wooden clothes pegs to secure this). Cook the salmon in this tray-tent, above the water for 30 minutes, then let it rest for another 10 minutes before serving, as the fish settles and becomes even more tender that way. If you can wait even longer, the fish is at its ultimate best once it has cooled to room temperature.

For smaller river trout (approximate weight 300–400g), follow the same method, but reduce the cooking time to 15 minutes.

For fillets of sea trout or salmon (approximate weight 150–200g each), follow the same method, but cook the fish, skin-side down, for 10 minutes.

game: a cookbook

A handful of great side dishes for oven-poached salmon or trout

Roast beetroot and horseradish

serves 4–6

6 medium-sized beetroots
mild olive oil for cooking
salt and freshly ground black pepper
baking foil
2 shallots, finely sliced
2 tablespoons extra-virgin olive oil
1 tablespoon red wine vinegar
1 tablespoon capers
2 tablespoons Horseradish Sauce
(either bought in or made with the recipe on page 238)

Wash the beetroots, but keep them whole. Rub them with a little of the cooking oil, and some salt and pepper. Wrap each beetroot in the foil. Preheat the oven to 200°C / Gas Mark 6 and place the beetroots onto a roasting tray or baking sheet. Cook them for 30 minutes, checking them after this time by poking them with a sharp knife or skewer. They should feel tender right through to the middle, like jacket spuds. Allow them to cool in the foil and then you can rub the skins off with finger and thumb. Dice the beetroots as finely as you like. Toss the shallots with the olive oil, vinegar and capers. Allow this salad to sit together for at least half an hour before serving. You can now toss the salad with the horseradish sauce to season it further still, or serve the cream dolloped on the side. If you have never had salmon and horseradish before, it is a revelation. This dish also goes well with smoked salmon or trout.

Purple sprouting broccoli and brown shrimps

This is not so much a recipe as a suggested marriage of fine ingredients. All greens are wonderful dressed with brown shrimps. If broccoli leaves you cold, try spring greens or your favourite cabbage. The brown shrimps in question here are the potted variety for which Morecambe Bay in Lancashire is famous. It is probably easier to buy the shrimps ready potted in butter, than in their undressed state. However you get them, they will have been cooked, usually at sea before being taken ashore. Should the naked variety be available, we will tell you how to season them. Make sure you peel whole shrimps before potting them.

serves 4–6

200g potted shrimps
400g purple sprouting broccoli, picked into bite-sized florets
salt and freshly ground black pepper
juice of half a lemon

Melt the shrimps in all their dressing while you boil or steam the broccoli until it is done to your liking. Drain the broccoli thoroughly and toss it through the hot shrimps. Season (be wary, the shrimps are salty), then squeeze in the lemon juice. Serve immediately.

To pot your own shrimps (or indeed any crustacea of your choosing) you will need

250g boiled, peeled brown shrimps (or similar)
250g unsalted butter
⅓ teaspoon of mace
¼ of a nutmeg
2 shakes Tabasco sauce

Heat the butter in a saucepan until it has only just melted and carefully pour off the top half of it into a mixing bowl. Don't let the milky part run into this bowl.

To the other half of the butter add the spices and let them fry gently for 5 minutes or so. Then add the shrimps and heat them through gently, but thoroughly. Transfer to small pots or ramekins.

Use the remaining butter as a topping to seal the shrimps before refrigerating them until required.

Samphire, pear and hazelnut salad

Samphire is a marsh grass that grows by the sea and comes into its own just as the season for salmon and sea trout is at its height. Fishmongers usually sell it when it is available, and you can make this salad with the pickled version, should the fresh stuff prove tricky to find. If samphire eludes you completely, the salad works well with mange tout or sugar-snap peas. This recipe was inspired by one from *Wild garlic, gooseberries and me*, by the cook and author Dennis Cotter, owner of Café Paradiso in Eire. We recommend it with salmon or trout, but it is also wonderful on its own.

serves 4–6

100g shelled hazelnuts
150g samphire
1 pear, as crunchy as possible
2 Little Gem lettuces
3 tablespoons extra-virgin olive oil
1 tablespoon red wine vinegar
1 tablespoon Dijon mustard
salt and freshly ground black pepper

Roast the hazelnuts in a moderate oven for 20 minutes, or until they are golden and crunchy. Set them aside to cool completely, then either pulse them very briefly in a food processor or bash them with a pestle and mortar. You want rough pieces, not ground nuts. Wash and pick the samphire. You just need to snip off any discoloured, slightly woody parts at the base of the stems: they are very obvious. Boil the picked samphire in plenty of unsalted water for just half a minute, then cool and drain it immediately. Put it in a large mixing bowl. Core and slice the pear as thinly as you can. Add it to the samphire. Shred the lettuce leaves roughly (you can leave Little Gem leaves whole if you prefer). Dress the salad with the oil, vinegar and mustard and season it to your liking, then garnish it with the hazelnut pieces.

Braised peas, lettuce and bacon

Just like samphire, peas are everywhere when the wild salmon season is in full swing.

serves 4

2 banana shallots
80g smoked streaky bacon
100g unsalted butter
salt and freshly ground black pepper
500g freshly podded peas
1 head of lettuce, escarole, Little Gem
  or iceberg
200ml light chicken stock
sugar

Dice the shallots finely and cut the bacon into thin strips (lardons). First melt 50g of the butter in a heavy-based saucepan. Add the shallots and bacon with a pinch of salt. Cover the pan and stew over a low heat for around 10 minutes, until the shallots are soft and translucent. Stir in the peas, tossing them around in the butter to coat, then add the chicken stock, which should barely cover the contents of the pan. Bring the pan to a simmer over a medium heat, then lower, cover and cook the peas until they have just a tiny bite left to them. This should take anywhere between 5–15 minutes, depending on the size and the age of the peas. You could also add a pinch of sugar at this point if the peas are not as sweet as you'd like. Shred the lettuce and then stir it through the peas, let it wilt, then season with a tad more salt and a good grinding of pepper.

Fishcakes

We're putting this recipe right next to our suggestions for oven-poached salmon because, you never know, there may be leftovers to contend with. Here is the best thing to do with them. The following amounts should produce a good-sized fishcake feast for two.

serves 2

200g floury potatoes, peeled and cut
  into 4cm chunks
200g poached sea trout or wild salmon,
  skinned and boned
1 tablespoon finely chopped parsley
2 eggs, beaten
salt and freshly ground black pepper
30g plain flour
100g fresh breadcrumbs
sunflower oil
1 tablespoon unsalted butter
1 lemon

Cook the potatoes in plenty of salted, boiling water until tender and then drain well. Mash the spuds until smooth and then flake in the fish.
Add the parsley and half of the egg mixture, and give it a good stir to combine. Season to taste with a touch more salt and a good grind of pepper. Divide the mixture into 8 balls and, with a little flour on your hands, shape the balls into flattish cakes. Cover and refrigerate for an hour to let them set.

Now you need 3 bowls. One will hold the remaining beaten egg, in the second, season the flour with some salt and pepper. Have the breadcrumbs in the third. Dust them with the flour, dip them in the egg then finally roll them in the breadcrumbs, pressing the crumbs on so they stick well.

Add enough oil to a frying pan to just cover the base. Warm it briskly and add the butter. Once the butter is fizzing add the fishcakes and cook them over a medium heat until crisp and golden on the underside; this should take between 3–4 minutes. Carefully turn the cakes over and fry the other side until done. Drain on kitchen paper and serve immediately with a wedge of lemon.

Salmon or sea trout 'tartare'

A marine version of the famous steak dish, without the egg, but with a twist of its own.

serves 4

300g very fresh salmon – ask the
   fishmonger to skin and pin-bone it
   for you
1 lemon
a small bunch of parsley
2 tablespoons capers
2 tablespoons cornichons
1 shallot
salt and freshly ground black pepper

Chop the salmon as finely as you can. Steak tartare is sometimes minced, but you shouldn't do this to such a fine fish. Grate the zest of roughly half the lemon and chop the parsley as finely as possible. Combine the two. Set the mix aside.

Chop the capers and cornichons as finely as possible, too, and set them aside. Slice the shallot, again as finely as possible. Set it aside. Divide the fish between plates and garnish the portions with little piles of the parsley and lemon mix, the cornichon and caper mix and the shallot slices. You can also give everyone a wedge of lemon. Allow each diner to season the fish with salt and pepper, him or herself. Sometimes the capers are salty enough.

Anglicised gravadlax, with salmon or sea trout

Gravadlax is traditionally made with salmon. Sea trout tend to be smaller, thus less troublesome to cure and store in a domestic fridge. We got the idea of including mustard powder in the cure from chef Richard Corrigan, owner of Bentley's fish restaurant just by London's Piccadilly Circus and now the eponymous Corrigan's in Mayfair. You can freeze cured salmon and sea trout, once treated this way.

serves 6–8

A side of sea trout or salmon (tell the
   fishmonger you want it pin boned
   and scaled)
3 level tablespoons sea salt
1 level tablespoon sugar
1 tablespoon fresh dill
1 tablespoon fresh parsley
1 level teaspoon English mustard
   powder

Run your forefinger over the fillet to check for any bones that got away from the fishmonger. You'll feel them easily enough. Remove them with tweezers or nail scissors.

Combine the salt and sugar in a small bowl. Wash and pat dry the fish before laying it in a tray skin-side down. Rub the salt and sugar mix all over the fish. Wrap it in clingfilm. Weigh it down lightly (2 plates on top of each other is fine) and refrigerate for about 24 hours.

The next day, drain away any liquid, then wash and dry the fillet again. Chop the dill and parsley very finely and combine them with the mustard powder. Press the herb mix onto the cured salmon flesh (not the skin side). You can now keep the fish in the fridge for 3 or 4 days before using.

To serve cured salmon or trout, here is the best way to portion it: slice the fish as thinly as possible, in straight cross sections, stopping just shy of the skin. Work from the tail end toward the top of the fillet where the head was. The dish is best served with a dollop of sour cream and / or wedges of lemon.

No Legs

Quick-cured charr

This cure also works well with trout and small fillets of salmon. Giving the fish a few hours, rather than a whole day in the cure and then cooking it, as opposed to enjoying it raw, gives the charr a slightly sweet-salty intensity, not unlike kippers or smoked haddock.

serves 4

3 level tablespoons sea salt
1 level tablespoon sugar
4 fillets charr (approximately 300g each) – ask the fishmonger to scale and pin bone them for you
1 teapoon lightly crushed black pepper
50g unsalted butter
300ml double cream
a small bunch of chives

Combine the salt and sugar in a small bowl. Wash and pat dry the fish fillets before laying them in a tray skin-side down. Rub the salt and sugar mix all over the fillets. Sprinkle them all with the black pepper. Wrap them in clingfilm. Weigh them down lightly (2 plates on top of each other is fine) and refrigerate for at least 2 hours, but no more than 4.

To cook, rub a baking tray with the butter. Heat an overhead grill to its highest setting. Lay the fillets on the tray, skin-side down and cover them with the cream. Grill the fish for roughly 5 minutes, or until just cooked through. You might want to baste them with the cream once during the cooking time. It will bubble up and some might caramelise slightly, which is what you want.

Once the fillets are cooked, chop the chives roughly and scatter them over the fish just before serving. If you don't like chives, dill is a good substitute.

Steamed pike, beurre blanc and cucumber

The sweet-sour crunch of pickled cucumber complements most river fish perfectly. Here, it works as an essential foil to the rich pike meat and the butter sauce (beurre blanc).

serves 4

1 cucumber
100ml white wine vinegar
100g caster sugar
1 banana shallot, very finely diced
200ml dry white wine
200g of cold unsalted butter cut into
    1cm dice
juice of ½ lemon
salt and freshly ground black pepper
4 fillets of pike, weighing around 180g
    each

Pickle the cucumber first. Top and tail the cucumber and finely slice into discs. If you have a Japanese mandoline, then you have the perfect tool, if not, just go carefully with a very sharp knife. Place the discs into a colander over a bowl and season with a pinch of salt. Rub the salt through and leave the cucumber to sit for 30 minutes. Meanwhile, put the vinegar and sugar into a stainless-steel pan, place the pan over a medium heat and bring slowly to the boil. Simmer for 1 minute, until the sugar has dissolved, then leave to cool. Once the liquid is cold, pop the cucumber into a small bowl and pour over the pickling liquid.

Now for the beurre blanc. Place the shallot and wine into a heavy-based saucepan, bring to a simmer over a medium heat and leave to reduce. You'll want to have about a third of the wine left. Turn the heat down to a low flame, so the liquid is barely simmering, then start to whisk in the cold butter, a piece at a time. Once all of the butter is incorporated, your sauce will be thick and emulsified. Remove from the heat and season with a few drops of lemon juice, a good pinch of salt and a grinding of black pepper. You could now strain the sauce into a jug and discard the shallots; however, it's perfectly acceptable to leave them in. You can now leave the sauce in a warm place for 1–2 hours without the fear of it separating.

To steam the fish you'll, quite obviously, need to set up a steamer. Take your widest shallow pot or a deep saucepan, pour in boiling water to around 3cm and set in there a metal Chinese steamer or, failing that, upend a saucer and place a dinner plate on top. Go carefully, at no point should the fish fillets come into contact with the boiling water. Smear a light film of butter onto a dinner plate and lay the pike fillets on the plate. Season the fish with salt and pepper, place the plate into the steamer and bring the water to a simmer. Cover the pan with a tight fitting lid and steam for 6–7 minutes over a medium heat. The fillets will be done when they are firm and opaque.

To serve, carefully remove the pike fillets to 4 warmed plates, spoon a good quantity of butter sauce over each fillet, then add a small pile of pickled cucumber.

No Legs

game: a cookbook

Pike with red wine and bacon

If pike eludes you, try this dish with a robust alternative such as eel or monkfish. It also works with squid or cuttlefish.

serves 4

salt and freshly ground black pepper
12 round shallots, peeled
200ml red wine
300ml of light chicken stock
50g unsalted butter
100g piece of smoked streaky bacon, cut into 1cm lardons
4 fillets of pike, each weighing around 180g
2 tablespoons freshly chopped parsley
1 clove of garlic, finely chopped

First bring a small pot of water to the boil, add a pinch of salt, and then drop in your whole shallots. Bring the pot back up to the boil, turn the heat down to a medium flame and simmer the shallots for 3–4 minutes or until they have softened. Drain them and set aside.

Pour the red wine into another pan, bring it up to the boil and then boil rapidly to reduce by half. Add the stock and boil again for another 3–4 minutes.

In a wide pan over a low heat, gently fry the bacon lardons in the butter until they are golden and crisp. This should take about 4 minutes; going slowly avoids burning the butter. Add the shallots, turning them to coat in the butter, then pour over the red wine and bring up to a gentle simmer. Season the pike fillets with salt and black pepper and drape them over the top of the shallots and bacon. Cover the pan and gently cook the fish fillets for about 5–6 minutes or until the fillets are opaque.

Meanwhile, with the tips of your fingers, rub together the chopped parsley and garlic. Carefully transfer the fillets from the pan onto warmed plates, spoon the sauce, bacon and shallots over the fish and sprinkle the parsley and garlic over the top.

Albacore tuna, and other big fish

Ask a fisherman what fish counts as game and he is highly likely to refer to large, deep-sea species such as marlin and swordfish. These fearsome animals are not shy of conflict, and have been known to attack small boats, mistaking them for whales. Quite what swordfish have against vegetarian mammals like whales is anyone's guess but, if hunting for sport is your bag, you probably want an aggressive opponent. It just so happens that the meat on swordfish or marlin is highly prized, and not just in those parts of the world where it is fished. You may well have come across swordfish in British fishmongers and supermarkets, as it has become a popular choice. The flesh is unlike that on any other type of fish. It's decidedly dense and meaty. However, swordfish is nothing like as popular as tuna, which lines the shelves of our food shops in myriad forms: in tins, jars, draped over sushi, or cut into steaks on the fish counter. There are many species of tuna, but the most widely eaten are blue fin, yellow fin and skipjack.

Neither swordfish nor marlin, nor most types of tuna are fished in our waters. Strictly speaking, we were not going to deal with exotic game in this book. As cooks we have always prided ourselves on using as much British produce as possible. We are probably most strict about this rule when it comes to fish and seafood. Quite apart from the fact that British seafood is superb, we like to support smaller inshore fisheries. A few years ago one of our fish suppliers started talking to us about 'Cornish tuna'. We tried some and liked it immensely.

The tuna in question is known as albacore, or long fin. It is one of the smaller members of the tuna family, usually weighing in at about a quarter of the size of blue or yellow fin. As a result, the meat is paler and less dense than those larger versions. Albacore likes cool waters and will swim into the North Atlantic, which is when Cornish fishermen land it between June and September. It's a compact and highly sustainable fishery. The albacore are line caught and seasonal. What's not to love?

If you love tuna, try switching from buying it year-round, from any old where, to Cornish albacore. We used it as the inspiration for all the following recipes, although you can swap in other types of tuna, as well as swordfish and marlin.

How to prepare albacore tuna

Owing to the size of these types of fish, you are highly unlikely to be faced with the whole thing. If you have ever been lucky enough to see tuna being prepared at markets like Tsukiji in Tokyo, you cannot fail to notice that filleting whole tuna is a three-man job, done with swords! Albacore tuna is smaller than most of the types favoured in Japan, but it is just as hazardous to fillet due to the complex bone structure and the hard skin. Please get an expert to joint and fillet tuna for you, even if you buy it whole. This is a bit of a moot point because the tuna you usually find for sale is loin meat, which has been taken off the bones from either side of the tuna's back, much like sirloin steak. All the recipes in this chapter call for tuna loin, bar one, which is for confiting the belly. You will probably have to ask a fishmonger to get this in advance for you (see page 228). Tuna loins are sold boned and skinned, because tuna skin is hard and leathery, and the bones are very robust, which makes them both hazardous to remove at home. If you do come across tuna loin with the skin or bones on, be sure to ask the fishmonger to remove them. Or, if you have to do it at home, use a very sharp, long-bladed filleting knife and a chopping board, with a damp cloth underneath it (to act as a slip mat).

If you are following the recipes in this chapter using swordfish and marlin, they might come with the skin on. Swordfish skin is softer than tuna's and there is no need to skin the loin. Swordfish and marlin are best cooked 'skin on'.

No Legs

Seared rare tuna and peppercorns

You must use the freshest tuna you can get for this dish, which is almost raw like sashimi.

serves 4–6

900g tuna loin – ask the fishmonger to cut it near the tail end, if possible. You want it in 1 or 2 pieces, about 6cm thick across the width (it will look like a mini fillet steak)
½ teaspoon salt
2 tablespoons whole black peppercorns
1 tablespoon aromatic seeds: choose between fennel and coriander
3 tablespoons mild olive oil for cooking

Rub the tuna all over with the salt and set it aside while you crack the peppercorns and your chosen aromatic. This is best done in a pestle and mortar or coffee grinder.

Shake the peppercorns and seeds into a large mixing bowl. Roll the tuna fillet in this seasoning mix, then transfer it to the fridge for half an hour. Heat the oil in a wide-bottomed frying pan and, when it is really hot, sear the tuna fillet very briefly on all sides. You literally want to give it about 20 seconds per side, as you are just colouring it. As soon as you take it from the pan, wrap it tightly in clingfilm, as if you were making it into a tuna sausage. Chill the tuna for another 30 minutes before taking it from the clingfilm and carving it as thinly as possible. You can serve the tuna unadorned, but it is delicious with a salad leaf of your choice, or slices of avocado pear, dressed with a simple vinaigrette.

No Legs

Grilled tuna steaks

This is a great way to treat tuna, marlin or swordfish if you own a ridged griddle pan. It can also be transcribed to an outdoor barbecue. Incidentally, if you don't have a griddle pan, you can use a well-seasoned, preferably cast-iron frying pan, too.

serves 4

4 tuna steaks, weighing 180g each
salt and freshly ground black pepper
2 tablespoons olive oil

Season the tuna steaks with salt and pepper and rub them with the olive oil. Carefully place the fish on the grill and cook over the highest heat for 2 minutes. Don't try to move the steaks until they are coming away from the grill, or the flesh might stick to the bars or the base of the pan, and can easily burn. Flip the steaks over and cook for a further 2 minutes. This will result in medium-rare tuna, which is the best way to eat it. If you want to cook it through, increase the cooking time by minute on either side.

Over the following four pages we have included a few of our favourite accompaniments for grilled or seared tuna. They would also complement the Seared Rare Tuna and Peppercorns recipe on page 220.

Salmoriglio

This is a classic Italian sauce for grilled fish. It is perfect for tuna, but works well with bass and mullet too.

serves 4

50g fresh oregano
50g flat-leaf parsley
1 garlic clove, peeled
½ teaspoon salt
juice of 1 lemon
100ml olive oil

Put the herbs, garlic and salt in a pestle and mortar and pound until you have a smooth paste. Add the lemon juice, and then slowly pour in the olive oil until it has all been incorporated. You can adjust the seasoning now, a little more lemon if you like a sharper sauce, or a touch more oil to loosen it. Alternatively, you can pulse the herbs in the bowl of a food processor and add the lemon, then the oil in a thin stream.

Season the finished sauce to your liking and spoon it over the fish, straight from the pan or grill. The sauce keeps well in the fridge for up to a week, but it will discolour slightly because of the lemon.

Orange and balsamic sauce

This recipe works particularly well with savoury, sharp oranges. If the oranges you have are very sweet, then substitute one with a lemon. This is a good sauce for barbecues. The recipe also works well with swordfish, marlin, bream or bass. You can make the sauce in advance. It would be fine for a couple of days in the fridge. Take it out of the fridge at least half an hour before using it as the oil will go cloudy and thicken slightly.

serves 4

2 cloves garlic, peeled and left whole
4 small sprigs of thyme
4 oranges
½ teaspoon brown sugar or honey
2 teaspoons balsamic vinegar
4 tablespoons extra-virgin olive oil
mild olive oil for cooking
4 tuna steaks (or other fish steaks)
    cooked as per the recipe on page 222

Peel and bruise the garlic, but don't chop it. Pull the thyme leaves from their sprigs. Squeeze the oranges into a small saucepan, add the thyme and garlic and stir in the sugar or honey. Heat the juice until it reduces slightly and goes syrupy. This will only take a couple of minutes. Stir in the balsamic vinegar and extra-virgin olive oil. Pour the sauce over the tuna steaks as soon as you take them off the grill or pan.

No Legs

Spinach, pine nuts and raisins

Serving grilled fish with a mix of spinach, pine nuts and raisins is common in northern Spain, and the Catalans are famous for it. This recipe works as well with swordfish as it does with tuna or marlin.

serves 4

2 tablespoons mild olive oil for cooking
30g pine nuts
1 garlic clove, finely chopped
30g raisins, soaked in hot water for
  1 hour, then drained
4 anchovy fillets
1kg fresh spinach, trimmed of the large
  stalks
juice of 1 lemon
4 tuna steaks (or other fish steaks)
  cooked as per the recipe on page 222

Heat a wok or large frying pan over a medium flame and add the olive oil. When it is hot add the pine nuts and garlic and cook until they take on a golden colour. Stir in the drained raisins and the anchovies and cook for 30 seconds, stirring and breaking up the anchovies as you go. Add the spinach and toss until it starts to wilt, then season with salt and pepper and the lemon juice. Pile the mixture on to 4 warmed plates.

Preheat a ridged grill pan or a barbecue. Grill the swordfish steaks following the instructions for Grilled Tuna Steaks on page 222 and transfer them to the warm plates alongside the spinach.

Chermoula-grilled fish steaks

Chermoula is a fairly powerful, aromatic north African paste. It's often used as a marinade for meat and, particularly, fish. Any chermoula paste left over from this recipe will keep well, covered, in the fridge for a week. Be sure to grill over a medium heat as the spices can easily char.

serves 4

4 garlic cloves, chopped
1 teaspoon ground cumin
1 teaspoon ground coriander
1 teaspoon smoked sweet paprika
1 red chilli, seeded and chopped
a pinch of saffron threads
1 small bunch of coriander
juice of 1 lemon
5–6 tablespoons of extra-virgin olive oil
1 teaspoon sea salt
1 lime
4 tuna, swordfish or marlin steaks

Blend all the ingredients together in a food processor to create a thick paste.

Rub 1 tablespoon of the chermoula paste over each fish steak, cover and leave to marinate in a cool place for at least 1 hour.

Preheat a ridged grill pan or a barbecue to a medium-high heat. Place the fish on the grill and cook for 1–2 minutes either side. Don't try to turn the fish until it is ready to come away from the bars; you're in danger of leaving the spicy crust behind. When the fish is ready, squeeze the lime over the steaks just before taking them off the grill. This dish is delicious with a sharp salad and a glass of cold, dry white wine.

Speidini

'Speidini' is the Italian word for skewer. All over Italy you'll find various tit bits skewered and grilled as snacks or part of a meal. You could easily use bamboo or metal skewers for this dish, but using rosemary stalks gives the fish a deep flavour, really permeating the flesh. Any solid, meaty fish favours this method, so feel free to substitute marlin or swordfish in place of the tuna.

serves 4

4 rosemary stalks, around 18–20cm in length
4 tuna steaks, weighing around 200g each
salt and freshly ground black pepper
4 tablespoons extra-virgin olive oil
12 fine slices of pancetta, preferably from the belly
2 lemons

Strip the leaves from the rosemary stalks, leaving only the top few tufts, then carefully cut the other end of the stalk into a sharp point. Take 1 tablespoon of the rosemary leaves and chop them finely. Keep the remaining leaves for another dish.

Cut the fish steaks into 3cm cubes and place them into a glass or ceramic bowl. Ideally you will have cut 6 cubes from each steak. Season with a good pinch of salt and a grind of pepper, then add the chopped rosemary. Drizzle over the olive oil, gently stir and leave to marinade for 15–20 minutes.

Cut each of the pancetta slices in half lengthwise, so you have 2 strips per slice and fold them each in half. Begin each skewer by threading on one piece of pancetta followed by a fishy cube. Repeat the process until you have 6 pieces of pancetta alternating with 6 fishy cubes on each stalk.

Preheat a griddle pan, grill or barbecue to high heat. When the bars are good and hot, place the skewers on and grill for 2 minutes, or until the fish has sealed on the underside. Carefully turn the skewers over, don't try to move them before they are ready, they will lift easily when they are sealed. Continue to cook for another 2–3 minutes. The fish should be just cooked through and the pancetta nice and crisp.

Serve with wedges of lemon.

Confit of tuna Niçoise

If you have access to a good fishmonger, you can ask him or her for tuna belly; it is not as expensive as the leaner loin meat that most recipes call for. The tuna confit keeps for a week or so in the fridge. It can then be used for this brilliant tuna Niçoise or the Confit of Tuna with White Beans and Chorizo on page 228.

serves 4

For the confit of tuna
1kg tuna belly
½ teaspoon salt
500ml mild olive oil for cooking
6 whole peppercorns
2 bay leaves
2 strips of lemon zest

Skin the tuna belly (or ask the fishmonger to do it for you). Season it by rubbing the salt all over the meat. Heat the oil to simmering point in a large pan and then immerse the tuna belly in the oil, along with the peppercorns, bay leaves and lemon zest. Bring the oil back to a gentle simmer, but do not allow it to boil. Simmer for about half an hour, and then remove from the heat and leave to cool completely. The tuna must be entirely covered by the oil. When the fish is cold, you can remove any skin and bones you might have missed the first time. Return the fish to the oil if you do not wish to use it immediately and keep refrigerated until required.

For the salad Niçoise
400g small, waxy new potatoes
100g runner or dwarf beans
4 eggs
4 tomatoes
75ml extra-virgin olive oil
1 tablespoon Dijon mustard
1 tablespoon white wine vinegar
200g cooked haricot or canellini beans
   (about half an average-sized tin)
1 cos lettuce or 2 Little Gem lettuces
200g confit of tuna (or tinned tuna in
   oil)
100g black olives
2 tablespoons capers
a small handful of basil leaves
8 anchovy fillets
salt

First of all, scrub and then cook the potatoes until tender. Leave them to cool. Unless they are tiny, break them up by hand, rather than slicing them. This creates little crumbs that fall into the dressing and emulsify it ever so slightly. It is just a suggestion, and if you want your salad very pretty, by all means slice them neatly instead. Next, cook the beans. Runners should be sliced and given a good 5 minutes at a rolling boil; dwarf (aka bobby) beans need no more than 1–2 minutes.

Bring a pan of water to the boil, carefully put in the eggs, then cover and cook them for exactly 6 minutes. Cool the cooked eggs immediately by plunging them into cold water. Peel them as soon as possible, as the shell comes off most easily just after they have been cooked. Cut them into quarters.

Deseed the tomatoes: cut them in half from top (stalk end) to bottom, and scoop out the seeds with a spoon. Cut each half of tomato by half into quarters.

The rest of the preparation of this salad is about throwing it together. Whisk up the oil, mustard and vinegar and use half of the mix to dress the potatoes. Doing this while they are slightly warm is good, as they will absorb it better. If you have broken, rather than sliced them as suggested, this is particularly prudent. Then toss everything else except the eggs and anchovies together in a large bowl with the remaining dressing. Now season the salad to your liking with salt. Top it off with the eggs and anchovy fillets.

(Illustrated oppsite is the Confit of Tuna with White Beans and Chorizo on page 230.)

No Legs

Confit of tuna with white beans and chorizo

You can make this dish with the tuna confit from the preceding recipe or, if you prefer, a shop-bought version. The best tinned tuna comes in olive oil, not brine!

serves 4

200g dried white beans such as
    canellini
2 tablespoons of olive oil
3 cloves of garlic
1 bay leaf
salt and freshly ground black pepper
a good chorizo sausage, around 200g
    in weight
2 ripe tomatoes
2 spring onions, finely sliced
2 tablespoons chopped flat-leaf parsley
1 small head of trevisse
1 small head of frisée curly endive
600g tuna confit (see recipe on page
    228) or good tinned tuna in olive oil
the juice of the lemon you pared for
    the confit on page 228
100ml of olive oil from the tuna confit

Put the beans in a bowl. Add enough water to amply cover them and leave to soak for around 12 hours, or overnight.

Drain the beans and rinse them under cold running water. Put them in a heavy-based pot and pour in enough fresh water to cover them by 10cm. Bring the beans to the boil, skim off any scum that forms on the surface, add the olive oil, garlic and bay then turn the heat down to low and simmer until the beans are soft, around 1–1½ hours. If the liquid evaporates and the beans become dry, just top up with a little more water. When the beans are nice and soft, pick out the bay, crush the garlic through the pot, season well with salt and pepper and keep the beans in their liquid.

The rest of the preparation of this salad is simply throwing it all together. Dice the chorizo into 1cm cubes, and then do the same with the tomatoes. Pop them into a bowl along with the spring onions and parsley. Drain the white beans, though not completely, leave a couple of tablespoons of their cooking liquor as it really helps to amalgamate the salad. Add the beans to the bowl, then after tearing the trevisse and frisée into manageable pieces, toss them through. Lightly flake the confited tuna over the top of the salad. Whisk up the lemon juice and olive oil with another pinch of salt and pepper to dress the salad. Toss lightly until well combined.

Confit tuna fishcakes

A recipe that comes via Trish's Mum. She always uses tinned tuna, but this works even better with the leftovers of your own homemade tuna confit.

serves 4

500g floury potatoes, peeled and cut
    into 4cm chunks
400g tuna confit, drained of olive oil
    (see page 227)
4 spring onions, finely sliced
2 tablespoons chopped parsley
salt and freshly ground black pepper
a squeeze of lemon juice
100g of plain flour
vegetable oil, for frying

Bring the potatoes to the boil in plenty of salted water, then lower the heat and simmer until tender. Drain well and leave in a colander to dry for a few minutes, then return the spuds to the pan and mash until smooth. Set aside. Flake the drained tuna into the mashed potato, mix in the spring onions and parsley, and then season with salt, pepper and lemon juice to taste. Divide the mixture into 8 balls, and then shape them into cakes. Season the flour with a good pinch of salt and a twist of black pepper. Roll the cakes in the flour and shake off any excess.

Heat the oil in a large frying pan, covering the base by about ½ a centimetre, and fry the cakes over a moderate heat for about 5 minutes per side, until they are crisp and brown. Trish's Mum serves these fishcakes with tomato ketchup seasoned with a dash of Worcester sauce.

trimmin&condime

Meat stuffings

The word forcemeat comes from the French *farci*, meaning to stuff. It is usually made up of fatty meat from pork bellies, hocks and trotters, or the trimmings of prime cuts of meat or poultry. For the sake of simplicity in the following recipes we recommend pork belly. Of course, if using wild boar, you can use the belly on one of these fine beasts in place of domestic pork. We don't recommend stuffing the cavities of small game birds with forcemeat stuffings, since the long cooking time required to heat the stuffing safely will dry out the meat. You are better off cooking the stuffing separately in a baking dish. The cooking times for each stuffing will appear in the recipes.

Classic forcemeat stuffing

1 tablespoon duck fat or butter
1 small onion, finely diced
½ teaspoon sea salt
200ml red wine
4 rashers of streaky bacon
300g minced belly of pork
100g of chicken livers, as well as the
    livers from the bird you are cooking
10 sprigs of thyme
2 tablespoons parsley
1 large clove of garlic
3 tablespoons brandy
¼ teaspoon freshly ground black pepper

Warm the duck fat or butter in a small saucepan and add the onion, along with a pinch of salt. Sweat the onion over a low heat for 5 minutes until it is slightly softened, then add the wine. Leave the pan over the lowest heat until the wine has completely reduced. Take the pan from the heat and let the onion cool.

Finely chop the bacon rashers and add them to a bowl with the pork mince. Clean the chicken or game livers by trimming off the white sinew that holds the two lobes together. Slice each liver into 3 or 4 pieces, depending on their size; they want to be a good 2mm thick. Add them to the bowl. Strip the leaves from the thyme sprigs and chop them along with the parsley. Crush the garlic and add it to the bowl. Pour in the brandy, along with the salt and pepper and give everything a really good stir.

Set the oven to 180°C / Gas Mark 4. Grease a small baking dish and fill it with the stuffing mix. Cook for 35 minutes, and then check it. The stuffing is ready when it has cooked through and set. Test it with a probe thermometer if you wish, and it should be at least 70°C in the middle.

Chestnut and onion stuffing

Unless you are a dab hand at roasting and shelling your own chestnuts, we highly recommend buying them ready-cooked and peeled for this stuffing. The best ones are completely natural and come vacuum packed, rather than tinned or dried. They are available in most supermarkets.

3 rashers smoked streaky bacon
300g minced pork belly
1 small bunch parsley
2 cloves of garlic
100g cooked, peeled chestnuts
2 onions
50g unsalted butter
3 tablespoons brandy
½ teaspoon salt
¼ teaspoon freshly ground black pepper

Finely chop the bacon rashers and add them to a bowl with the pork mince. Strip the leaves from the parsley and finely chop them together with the garlic. Add the chestnuts to the chopping board and roughly chop them, too. They don't want to be too finely chopped or they will become a purée. Stir them into the herbs and garlic before adding them to the bowl. Peel and finely slice the onions; heat the butter gently in a small pan and fry the onions until soft. Do not let them brown. Let them cool and add them to the bowl with the brandy, salt and pepper. Mix the stuffing thoroughly, then chill until needed. Set the oven to 180°C / Gas Mark 4. Grease a small baking dish and fill it with the stuffing mix. Cook for 35 minutes, and then check it. The stuffing is ready when it has cooked through and set. You can test it with a probe thermometer if you wish, and it should be at least 70°C in the middle.

Trimmings and condiments

Sage and breadcrumb stuffing

2 slices of stale bread (we prefer
   sourdough)
2 cloves garlic
a small sprig of sage
1 small bunch parsley
6 anchovy fillets
3 rashers smoked streaky bacon
300g minced pork belly
1 egg
2 tablespoons mild olive oil
salt and freshly ground black pepper

Blitz the bread into rough crumbs.
If you don't have a food processor, you
can grate really dry stale bread like
Parmesan cheese. Peel and chop the
garlic as finely as possible with the
picked leaves of the sage and parsley.
Chop the anchovies to a near paste and
add them to the herbs. Cut the bacon
into thin strips. Mix the bacon, anchovy
and herbs with the pork. Beat the egg
and fold it into the stuffing, along with
the breadcrumbs and the oil. Check the
seasoning.

Set the oven to 180°C / Gas Mark 4.
Grease a small baking dish and fill it with
the stuffing mix. Cook for 35 minutes,
and then check it. The stuffing is ready
when it has cooked through and set.
You can test it with a probe thermometer
if you wish, and it should be at least
70°C in the middle.

Prune and pistachio stuffing

3 rashers smoked streaky bacon
300g minced pork belly
1 sprig of rosemary
2 cloves of garlic
75g of shelled pistachio nuts
100g pitted prunes
3 tablespoons brandy
½ teaspoon salt
¼ teaspoon freshly ground black pepper

Finely chop the bacon rashers and add
them to a bowl with the pork mince.
Strip the leaves from the rosemary
sprig and finely chop them together
with the garlic. Add the pistachios to
the chopping board and run your knife
through them, (they don't want to be
too finely chopped), along with the
herbs and garlic, before adding them to
the bowl. Slice the prunes into quarters
then add them to the bowl with the
brandy, salt and pepper. Mix thoroughly
then chill until needed.

Set the oven to 180°C / Gas Mark 4.
Grease a small baking dish and fill it with
the stuffing mix. Cook for 35 minutes,
and then check it. The stuffing is ready
when it has cooked through and set.
You can test it with a probe thermometer
if you wish, and it should be at least
70°C in the middle.

Liver parfait

This parfait, using chicken or duck
livers, or indeed the livers from
whichever game bird you are roasting,
is a wonderful accompaniment for
classic roasts, spread on a small piece
of toast and placed either under or next
to the roast meat. It can also be served
as a starter, before a classic game roast.
Melba toast is the classic partner, but

consider serving the parfait with boozy
prunes (see page 241) or any of the
pickled fruits on pages 239–241.

500g free-range chicken or duck livers,
   as well as the livers from the birds
   you are cooking
¼ teaspoon salt
¼ teaspoon pepper
¼ teaspoon four-spice mix sometimes
   sold as 'quatre epices' (black pepper,
   nutmeg, cinnamon and clove)
1 tablespoon duck fat or soft butter
50ml Madeira wine
1 tablespoon brandy
1 egg yolk
100g cold butter

Trim and clean the chicken, duck,
and/or game livers by trimming off the
white sinew that holds the two lobes
together. Season them by tossing with
the salt, pepper and four-spice mix.
Heat the duck fat or butter in a pan.
If using butter, you can pinch it from
the butter mentioned later in the recipe
(none of the amounts here need to be
too exact). When the fat is good and
hot, fry the livers for just a minute on
either side. Remove them with a slotted
spoon and deglaze the pan with the
Madeira and brandy. It will probably
flambé a bit so stand back! Pour the
juices over the livers. Now purée them
in a food processor. Add the egg yolk
and butter, cut as small as possible.
Blitz again until very smooth. Check the
seasoning. Pass the parfait through a
fine sieve. You might want to help push
it through with the rounded base of a
ladle or a wooden spoon. Check the
seasoning. You might want more salt
or pepper. Don't add any more booze.
You can chill the parfait to set it in a
storage box or, if you plan to serve it
in its own right as a starter, use a
terrine mould lined with clingfilm or
silicone paper.

Two meat-free stuffings

The two stuffings that follow can be put into the cavity of game birds, as they will not require increasing the cooking time. Both are delicious with partridge, quail, pheasant and guinea fowl. We also recommend the mushroom stuffing with darker meat such as that of pigeon and wild duck. Never, ever, ever stuff a grouse!

Dried mushroom stuffing

25g dried wild mushrooms
2 red onions
1 clove garlic
25g unsalted butter
2 tablespoons mild olive oil
juice of half a lemon
salt and freshly ground black pepper
50g fresh mushrooms of your choice
25g dry breadcrumbs

Soak the dried mushrooms in 300ml of hot water, straight from a boiled kettle, for about half an hour. After this time drain them, reserving the water. Strain the water through a fine sieve lined with muslin or kitchen towel and set it aside. Wash the dried mushrooms under a running tap, then squeeze them dry. Chop them roughly and set aside. Peel and dice the onions and garlic as finely as possible. Heat the butter and olive oil gently and fry the onions and garlic for about a minute, then stir in the lemon juice, with about half a teaspoon of salt. Sweat the onions until they are soft. Don't let them brown.

Chop the fresh mushrooms finely and add them to the onions. Fry them uncovered until they are also tender and juicy. Add the dried mushrooms to the pan, with the breadcrumbs, and remove it from the heat. Transfer to a mixing bowl. Now add just enough of the strained mushroom liquor to loosen the stuffing. You might not need all of it if the fresh mushrooms produced a lot of juice in the pan. Check the seasoning. You can now either stuff the mushroom mix into a bird of your choice or grease a small baking dish with butter and bake the stuffing alongside your roast. It will take about 20 minutes in a hot oven. You can also grill the stuffing. If you have a cooking cheese like Parmesan or Gruyère, use it to grate over the top of the dish.

Lemon and mascarpone stuffing

zest of one lemon
6 sprigs thyme
150g mascarpone cheese
50ml brandy
salt and freshly ground black pepper

Finely grate the lemon zest and pull the thyme leaves from their stalks. Chop the leaves as finely as possible. Mix the lemon and thyme with the mascarpone and brandy, and then season to your liking with the salt and pepper. Spoon the mixture into the cavities of your chosen birds, then truss the cavities with string before following the cooking methods we have given in the 'classic roast' section of each chapter.

Trimmings and condiments

Three classic sauces

Bread sauce

1 onion
3 cloves
500ml whole milk
80g unsalted butter
1 bay leaf
1 sprig thyme
50ml double cream
120g fresh white breadcrumbs
salt and freshly ground black pepper

Peel the onion and leave it whole.
Stud the onion with the cloves. Heat the
milk and butter in a saucepan and add
the studded onion with the bay leaf and
sprig of thyme. Simmer very gently,
without letting the milk boil, for about
10 minutes. Remove the pan from the
heat and allow the onion and aromatics
to steep, covered. This mix can now be
left for several hours, or just until it is
cooled.

Strain the mix, discarding the onion,
cloves, bay leaf and thyme. Add the
double cream and reheat the mix gently.
Don't let it come to a boil. Finally, fold
in the breadcrumbs and let the sauce
thicken up over as low a heat as
possible. This will only take a minute
or so. Season the bread sauce to your
liking and serve immediately.

Note that cold bread sauce, left over
from any roast dinner, is delicious and
can be cut into slices and fried. This is
best done in butter, again as gently as
possible.

Horseradish sauce

2cm (ish) stick fresh horseradish
juice of a quarter of a lemon
1 teaspoon Dijon mustard
250ml crème fraîche or English set sour
   cream
salt and freshly ground black pepper

Peel and grate the horseradish (we use
the same blade as you would for Parmesan
cheese or lemon zest). You might want
to do this either outside or by an open
window. Horseradish has a tendency to
clear the sinuses.

Combine the grated horseradish with
the lemon juice, mustard and crème
fraîche or sour cream, and then season
the sauce to your liking with salt and
black pepper (go easy on the pepper).
This sauce is best served immediately.
It can be kept in the fridge for several
days, but it will set, almost like butter
after a couple of hours. After a day or
so it also becomes milder. You might
like it better that way.

Cumberland sauce

1 orange
1 lemon
6 tablespoons redcurrant jelly
50ml port
1cm (ish) cube of fresh ginger
1 teaspoon Dijon mustard

Thinly peel the rinds from the orange
and lemon, avoiding as much of the
pith as you can and reserving the fruit.
You can use a really sharp pairing knife,
but a potato peeler is even better. Cut
the peelings lengthways into fine strips.
Pop them into a small pan of cold water
and bring to the boil for one minute.
Strain the peelings, discard the water and
repeat the process. This stops the peel
becoming bitter in the finished sauce.

Place the redcurrant jelly and port in
another small saucepan. Peel and cut
the ginger into long thin strips to match
the fruit zest. Add it to the port and
jelly mix. Place the pan over a low heat
and whisk as the jelly melts. Simmer
the sauce for 5 minutes or until the
sauce thickens visibly. It could take a
little longer depending on the thickness
of your pan base. Add the juice of the
orange and half the lemon, plus the
boiled strips of fruit peelings. Stir in the
mustard and allow the sauce to cool.
Cumberland sauce is ready to use
immediately, but it will keep for up to a
fortnight in the fridge.

Five favourite pickles

The following recipes will each fill a 1-litre kilner jar. To ensure that the pickles do not spoil, it is essential that you sterilise the jars just before using them. Wash the jars in hot soapy water, then rinse them with equally hot water, being careful not to touch the insides. Transfer the jars, still hot and wet, to an oven preset at 140°C / Gas Mark 2. Set them upside down to dry. Leave them in the oven for a couple of minutes, or until you are ready to fill them whilst they are still nice and hot. Once sealed, don't forget to wipe down the jars, in case any of your sticky pickling juices have run down the sides.

Pickled quinces or pears

600ml white wine vinegar
400g caster sugar
½ teaspoon cloves
½ teaspoon black peppercorns
1 cinnamon stick
6 medium-sized quinces or large pears

In a heavy-based, non-reactive pan, bring the vinegar, sugar and spices to the boil. Once it has reached the boil, take the pan off the heat.

Peel the quinces or pears, cut them into quarters then eighths and core them. Add them to the hot liquid and cover the contents of the pan with a circle of baking paper that covers the surface of the liquid. Put the pan back over a high heat and bring to the boil then turn the heat down to a simmer. Poach the fruits for 15–20 minutes until they have just softened. Be careful not to over-cook them; they have a tendency to go mushy fairly quickly.

Spoon the fruits into clean sterilised jars. Now boil the vinegar for 10 minutes to reduce then pour the liquid over the fruit to cover it all. Seal the jars while they are hot and leave for at least a month before opening.

Pickled figs

600ml water
80g sea salt
1kg ripe figs
300ml white wine vinegar
1 teaspoon allspice berries
1 teaspoon cloves
550g golden caster sugar

Bring the water to the boil in a stainless steel pot and stir in the salt. Once the salt has dissolved, remove the pot from the heat and leave to cool. Drop in the figs; weigh them down with a light plate (something like a saucer) until the fruit is completely submerged. Soak for 12 hours or overnight.

To make the pickling mixture, bring the vinegar, allspice, cloves and half the sugar to the boil, then turn the heat down and simmer for 10 minutes. Add the figs and poach over the lowest heat for 40 minutes. Carefully spoon the fruit into clean sterilised jars.

Add the remaining sugar to the syrup and boil for 10 minutes. Pour this over the figs until they are completely covered. Seal the jars while they are still hot and leave for at least a month before opening.

Pickled plums, damsons or greengages

1kg plums, damsons or greengages
600ml white wine vinegar
400g caster sugar
1 cinnamon stick
2cm (ish) piece fresh ginger

Wash the plums and dry them thoroughly. Place them in a washed and sterilised kilner jar, being careful not to squash them as you fill the jar. In a heavy-based, non-reactive pan, bring the vinegar, sugar and spices to the boil. Once it has reached the boil, take the pan off the heat. While it is still piping hot, pour the solution directly over the fruits. Seal the jar whilst still hot and leave this pickle for a month before opening.

Pickled cherries

1kg cherries
600ml distilled malt vinegar
400g caster sugar

Wash the cherries and pat them dry. Pack them into the sterilised kilner jar, being careful not to squash the fruits. Heat the vinegar and sugar in a heavy, non-reactive pan, bring them to the boil and simmer until the sugar has dissolved. Once this has happened, and whilst still piping hot, pour the solution over the cherries. Seal the jar immediately. Leave this pickle for a month before opening.

Boozy prunes

Whenever you need prunes, we highly recommend sourcing wonderful (if pricy) Agen prunes from France. These are fatter and somehow plummier than other varieties. You don't need a kilner jar for this pickle, and it is ready to use almost as soon as the mix has cooled. We keep ours happily in the fridge, in a Tupperware container.

1kg prunes, either dried or ready to eat
1 litre water
2 tea bags (we use breakfast tea, don't go for anything too aromatic)
100g caster sugar
250ml brandy

Stone the prunes and pop them into your chosen container. Boil the water, pour it into a mixing jug and add the teabags, plus the sugar. Basically you are making an over sized, over stewed, over sweetened cup of tea here. Let it steep for 10 minutes, then remove the tea bags. Don't forget to do this! A teabag in amongst a batch of boozy prunes is a well-camouflaged booby trap. Pour the tea over the prunes and let the mix go cold. This doesn't take long but, if you can, leaving the prunes to go cold in the tea overnight is ideal.

Once they are cold, douse the prunes in the brandy. Mix the brandy through the now syrupy juices around the prunes. Do this carefully to avoid smashing the fruit. Your prunes are now boozy, and ready to eat.

Four other trimmings

Spiced breadcrumbs

2 slices stale white bread (sourdough is best)
1 tablespoon olive oil for cooking
2 cloves garlic, peeled and chopped
1 small red chilli, deseeded and chopped
1 teaspoon capers, chopped
2 anchovy fillets, chopped almost to a paste
1 sprig rosemary, destalked and chopped

Tear the bread into chunks and bake in a moderate oven until fully dry and crispy. Transfer it to a food processor and blitz to fairly fine breadcrumbs. In a wide frying pan, heat the oil and, when it is only just warm, gently fry the garlic, chilli, capers, anchovies and rosemary until you just begin to get the aromas. This takes less than a minute or so. Now add the crumbs and fry gently until they look good and golden. Dry them on kitchen paper and reserve them for scattering all over your gratin (or choice of vegetables). These will keep for three to four days in an airtight container in the fridge.

Game chips

We should point out that it is perfectly possible to buy a really good brand of potato crisps to serve as game chips. You might want to choose this option if you don't own a deep-fat fryer.
3 medium-sized potatoes (approx weight 600g) – we recommend King Edwards, Maris Piper, Spunta or Golden Wonder
mild vegetable oil for deep-frying
sea salt

Peel and slice the potatoes as thinly as you can. Use a mandoline if you have one. Soak the slices in cold water for about 20 minutes to remove the excess starch. Drain them and pat thoroughly dry. Heat the oil to 190°C if you have a fryer or thermometer. If not, test the oil by dropping in a cube of fresh bread. If it fizzes healthily and goes golden in under a minute you are good to go. Fry the potatoes in at least three batches until they look like good, gold coloured crisps. Don't let them go brown as this makes them bitter. Drain each batch and dry on kitchen paper. Sprinkle with sea salt whilst still hot. You can serve game chips immediately, or keep them warm in a very low oven until you are ready to dish up. It's a traditional no-no, but we think room temperature game chips are fine, if you are serving them as part of a spread and already have a full oven.

Celeriac and apple purée

This is a rich and wintry purée that falls somewhere between a mash and a sauce. It goes well with just about any roast meat, but especially game. It can be made in advance and kept for up to two days in the fridge, which makes it a handy dish for busy periods like Christmas. This recipe should make for enough for four to six people.

2 medium-sized, floury potatoes (approximately 400g)
1 smallish celeriac (approximately 500g)
2 eating apples
juice of half a lemon
250ml double cream
100ml milk
50g unsalted butter
salt, to taste

Peel and roughly dice the potatoes and celeriac. Peel, core and dice the apples. Toss the apple and celeriac pieces with the lemon juice and set them aside. Cover the potatoes with plenty of salted water and boil them until they are tender enough to mash. Make sure they really are cooked, as you want this purée to be super smooth, without lumps. Once they are done, pass them through a ricer or mash them until smooth. Whatever you do, don't blend them, as this will make the purée gluey. Meanwhile, bring the cream, milk and butter to a simmer in a pot large enough for the apples and celeriac. When all the pieces of butter have melted, pop the apple and celeriac pieces into the pot. Simmer very gently until they are both very tender. Once cooked, purée the mixture, cream and all (you can do this with a blender). Now fold the potatoes carefully through the creamy celeriac mix, adjust the seasoning and serve.

Beetroot purée

Beetroot purée is sweet and sour. It is perfect with any game, but especially pigeon, squab, venison and hare. For a short cut you can buy ready-cooked beetroot (though avoid the pickled stuff in a jar). The best are vac-packed. Most supermarkets sell them. A good greengrocer often does his or her own. This recipe should make enough for four people.

500g cooked beetroot
1 tablespoon olive oil
1 large onion, sliced
1 clove of garlic, crushed
2 tomatoes
3 tablespoon red wine vinegar
sea salt and pepper
2 tablespoons crème fraîche

Peel the skin from the beetroots and cut them into 2cm cubes. Heat the olive oil in a saucepan and add the onions and garlic with a pinch of sea salt. Sauté the onions over a medium to low heat for about 5 minutes until they have softened. In the meantime, skin the tomatoes. You can do this by scoring the skin around the core, putting them in a bowl and pouring over boiling water and then leaving for about 1 minute until the skin has loosened. Run the tomatoes under cold water and slip the skins off. Chop the tomatoes into 2cm dice and add them to the pan along with the cubed beetroot. Pour in the vinegar, season with sea salt and pepper and add 200ml of water. Cover and cook over a gentle heat for 40 minutes. When the beetroots are quite soft, take the pan from the heat and leave to cool a little. Purée the beets in a blender with the crème fraîche and keep warm until you require the purée. This sauce can be kept in the fridge for up to three days.

Trimmings and condiments

Game stocks

Homely, broth type stocks from cooked bones

The most basic, homely way to get a stock going is to use the carcasses of leftover roasts. Chefs often buy bones to make stocks, and roast them before they go into the pot, so with a pre-cooked carcass you have a head start. A word about the nature of the stock. Pheasant, guinea fowl, partridge, rabbit and quail bones create a subtle, but comforting broth and, if reduced, quite a blonde gravy. Wild duck and grouse bones will give you stronger tasting stock. Pack whatever bones you choose as tightly as you can into a pan with depth, rather than width, and side handles if possible (once filled with stock it will be heavy). You should cover the bones with water by about 4 cm (2 inches) and bring it to a simmer, not a boil. Skim off any froth or scum that forms on the top and, after doing this for 10 minutes or so, add some vegetables. A couple of carrots, a stick or two of celery and an onion would be fine. Don't peel the onion, as its skin will add a lovely golden colour to the finished stock. How long you cook the stock for is really up to you. Half a day or so will give you really intense results. One foolproof way to see if you have got the most out of a carcass is to pull one out of the stock. If it falls apart in front of you, the stock is definitely ready to strain.

To strain the stock, use as fine a sieve as you can. If you like making stock, a conical 'chinoise' is a good investment. Once the stock is strained, and only then, you can increase the heat underneath it and give it quite a vigorous simmer to reduce it by about half. Keep skimming it of any fat that comes to the surface.

The results should then set to a golden jelly once refrigerated.

Darker, moodier stocks from raw bones

The really strong, gamey tasting stocks that chefs love to reduce into glossy jus (posh gravy) are best made from the bones of darker meat. If you have butchered venison or hare and have bones left over, or if you have filleted the breasts from pigeon or rooks, this method of making stock is for you. Set the oven to its highest setting. Lay the bones out on as wide a roasting tray as possible and bake them for half an hour. Be sure to check on them so that they don't burn.

Remove the bones from the roasting tray and transfer them to the stockpot. Replace the bones, in the same roasting tray, with a couple of onions, quartered, 3 or 4 whole carrots, and 2 or 3 stalks of celery. It really doesn't matter if one of these vegetables is missing; you can get away with a combination of a couple of them. Roast the vegetables for 15 minutes or so, until they wrinkle and caramelise slightly. Transfer them to the stockpot. Now just cover the bones with cold water, by about 2 centimetres (an inch). Bring it to a simmer, not a boil and skim any scum that forms on the surface. More so than with small bird bones, you might get fat blobbing up to the surface, too, and you should skim this as well. Simmer this stock for 3 hours, or for half a day if possible.

When it comes to straining, if you used big venison bones, it is probably easier to lift them out of the stock with a large spatula or tongs. Then pass the boneless stock through a sieve or chinoise.

Return it to the heat and allow the stock to simmer vigorously until reduced by half. Keep skimming it of any fat that comes to the surface.

Storing stocks

Stock contains meat proteins and is at risk of harbouring pathogens at ambient temperatures, so cool any finished stock as fast as possible, then either refrigerate or freeze it until you plan to use it. In the fridge a stock is good for about 5 days; it goes without saying that it will last longer in a freezer.

If you keep a stock in the fridge, you get an extra chance to skim it of any last fat that rises to the surface and sets. We scrape it off with a spoon or palette knife.

Old-fashioned gravy

This is a recipe for old-fashioned gravy, as opposed to the pure reduction of stocks often called 'jus' by chefs. To achieve a jus, you would continue to reduce one of the strained and skimmed stocks on page 243 by at least two thirds, until it becomes what we can only describe as sticky and slightly silky when rubbed between two fingers. This stickiness is the concentration of gelatine in the stock, which comes from the bones. So a jus, when chilled, sets pretty firmly. You then season a jus to your liking and simply reheat it as and when it's needed. Be warned that this process takes at least a whole day. This is why posh restaurants are always making huge amounts of stock; whatever they produce gets reduced down to a thimble's worth of jus!

Gravy is thickened with a little flour and relies on flavoursome, but not necessarily reduced stock. It is further seasoned with the juices from a roast joint of meat. It's a far more homely product and it takes way less time to make. If, for some reason, you can't use flour in your cooking, you can omit it and have thinner gravy, which will still taste great. Another option is to use a gluten- free thickener such as arrowroot or potato flour.

However long you roast any meat for, it is very important to rest it in the roasting tray for several minutes before serving. We have detailed this resting time in the classic roast sections of each chapter. Don't skip it! The rest is essential for tender meat and good gravy!

After the resting time, remove the roast from its tray and pop it onto a serving dish. The tray is now the key to your gravy. Place the roasting tray over a medium heat. Add one level tablespoon of flour to the juices in the tray and stir it in vigorously. What you see looks pretty unpromising, but never fear. Keep stirring until the flour has grabbed all the detritus on the roasting tray. Now add about 500ml of your chosen stock, bit by bit, stirring it in as you go. Keep stirring until the gravy starts to thicken. You might decide you want more stock (it depends on how thick you like gravy). Check the seasoning of your finished sauce and pass it through a sieve into a gravy jug just before serving.

legwork

1

Game meal planners for winter and summer

A gamey Christmas

With such a plethora of game available during the festive season it makes perfect sense to make a feature of your favourite bird or joint at this time of year. Any of the classic roasts and suggested trimmings from the recipe section of this book will work as Christmas dinner. If you don't relish the idea of December 25th without its traditional turkey, why not try a game-based meal on one of the other holidays (Christmas eve or new year's eve, for example)? Feel free to mix and match from the following suggestions.

A fairly traditional spread

Classic Roast Pheasant (page 24)
Sage and Breadcrumb Stuffing (page 236)
Bread Sauce (page 238)
Savoy Cabbage, Chestnuts and Bacon (page 30)
Pickled Quince (page 239)

A ducky dinner

Classic Roast Mallard (page 84)
Prune and Pistachio Stuffing (page 236)
Celeriac and Apple Purée (page 243)
Add to the above your favourite seasonal greens. We love brussels tops and curly kale

A less conventional pot roast

Starter
Wild Boar Proscuitto (page 193)
Main course
Seven-hour Venison Shoulder and Gratin Dauphinoise (page 158)
Dried Mushroom Stuffing (page 237)

A barbecue on the wild side

The summer is not well known for gameyness, but with the availability of some types of deer, not to mention rabbit and wood pigeon, you can do some experimenting over the coals come the warmer months. Here are some recipes from this book that will work as barbecues.

Spatchcocked Quails with Aioli (page 45)
Venison Burger (page 172)
Grilled Albacore and Salmoriglio (page 222)
Seared Albacore and Peppercorns (page 220)

Legwork

A guide to storing and freezing game

We should state upfront that we think the best approach to buying all game is to purchase only what you need and use it straight away. This is slightly idealistic and, you might argue, easy to say if you work in a restaurant with a regular supply line. If you are lucky enough to be offered a few brace of small game or a carcass of something larger, then you might have to turn to the fridge or freezer for help.

Hanging

Hanging game is not the same as keeping it in the fridge. We don't recommend hanging your own game unless you are quite experienced at it and have access to a large (ish) space where you can guarantee properly cool conditions. Ideally the air in a hanging space should be between 6 and 10 degrees centigrade. A garden shed (with a high enough ceiling) would be perfect, as would a cellar or properly cool larder (aka pantry). Check up on any hanging meat daily. You'll need to pluck (or skin) and draw it at the first sign (or smell) of spoilage. Perhaps most importantly, the space needs to be kept insect free. Stop hanging all game as soon as you see any flies or other nasties lurking near the carcasses.

Refrigeration

All meat should be refrigerated at 4 degrees centigrade or lower. We might be risking the ire of the clingfilm brigade, but we believe that the short-term storage of all game is best done in something which allows the meat to breathe a little. Baking parchment is ideal, as is muslin. Make sure all game is totally plucked (or skinned) and drawn before you put it in the meat draw of the fridge. If you have no meat draw, make sure the meat is not in contact with anything else in the fridge, especially cooked food or dairy. Don't keep the meat even remotely near anything like onions or garlic (especially if peeled) as they can affect its flavour. If you have a number of small birds or small carcasses like rabbit, wrap each one in an individual piece of paper or cloth. Don't wrap too tightly and change the wrapping after two days if you need to keep the meat for any longer than that.

If you need to keep anything for longer than five days, it is probably best to turn your thoughts to cooking it or freezing it.

Freezing

First up we should say that it might be more fun and rewarding to think about curing some cuts of game before turning to the more obvious option of freezing them. We have included recipes for hams, terrines and other types of charcuterie throughout the book and you can use the index to find them.

If you don't fancy putting up a store of game meat this way, the good news is that lots of game freezes well. Its leanness works in its favour, as it is fat that limits the freezing time of most meat. Do not freeze game that has not been plucked (or skinned) and drawn. Ensure that the freezer maintains a temperature of -18° centigrade or lower. For the freezer we prefer to use clingfilm rather than any other wrapping. Wrap birds or small mammals individually, using a double layer of clingfilm to prevent freezer burn. Do the same for joints of larger animals. We don't recommend freezing any meat for more than three months, especially if you want to roast it once thawed. Anything lingering longer is best pot-roasted, casseroled or put into a pie.

Legwork

Ethical and environmental concerns surrounding game

The moral and ethical issues surrounding game are too varied and complex to deal with comprehensively in what is, essentially, a cookbook. Our field of expertise is a narrow one: we are both simply cooks, and the only information we can pass on to you with absolute surety relates to what you do with any type of meat or fish once you get it into the kitchen. So far, so simple.

However, as cooks we are also consumers, and what we choose to buy for our kitchens, or recommend to you as foodstuffs does have an impact on the lives and welfare of this country's wild animals and their environment.

In the internet age, comprehensive information pertinent to animal welfare, and the environmental impact of food production is constantly updated at great speed. Without wanting to sound like we are copping out, we honestly believe that making any vehement statements about the impact of what you choose to buy, cook and eat is, if not pointless, then at least likely to be out of date by the time this book goes to print. Therefore, we can only really pose the kinds of questions we ask ourselves before we decide to put any items on our menus, or into books like this one.

If you have any ethical concerns about eating game, they are most likely to be related to your attitude towards hunting for sport.

Neither of us hunts, but we are well aware that much of the meat we buy supports those who rear animals or manage land that allows them to make commercial gains from hunting. This, in turn, enables people to hunt. That should tell you that we have no issues with other people hunting for our food, as long as the suppliers we buy it from can answer all our questions.

If you are worried about the idea of buying game from commercial shoots you might want to raise the following questions before you buy grouse, wild venison, pheasant and partridge, as well as some wild ducks and other waterfowl.

How wild are the animals? If they were reared in incubators or pens then released onto managed land, how were they reared? How were they fed? Were they inoculated or given antibiotics in their feed? How were they killed, who were they killed by, and on what scale?

The hunting of pests and vermin might bother you less than pheasants and partridges but you should still be aware that rabbit, hare, pigeon, rooks, some types of deer, some wild ducks and truly wild boar might be hunted with an element of sport involved.

When you buy any wild food you must ask the following questions: Is it remotely endangered? Is it humanely killed? And who by?

If you abhor the idea of hunting altogether, you could stick fairly safely to farmed meats labelled as game. These include guinea fowl, quail, farmed wild boar, farmed rabbit and farmed salmon, trout or charr. But these, too, come with their own ethical and environmental issues. How are the farmed animals reared? What do they eat? Are they treated with inoculations and antibiotics? What waste products does the farming produce? How does it affect the surrounding wildlife? And, last but not least, how are the animals dispatched?

We think that the best place to go for all the answers to our questions is to the suppliers themselves. We prefer not to buy any meat or fish from large retailers as a result, not because we have any problem with them, but because we like to talk to the people that produce the food first-hand. If you do rely on supermarkets, or if you like to buy food online, then make sure you have access to someone who can give you assurances about what they sell. If you feel that your questions are sidestepped, or answered dishonestly, then it is probably best to go elsewhere.

Legwork

Useful information

Here are some useful organisations that might deal with any questions you have regarding the hunting, fishing, buying and eating of wildlife.

The Game and Wildlife Conservation Trust

Well-organized and comprehensive site, with information for and about farmers, land managers and gamekeepers.

Burgate Manor
Fordingbridge
Hampshire SP6 1EF
Phone 01425 652381
www.gwct.org.uk

Game To Eat

Campaign dedicated to raising awareness of game, mainly as a foodstuff. Includes a handy section on stockists.

www.gametoeat.co.uk

River Cottage

Hugh Fearnley-Whittingstall's website aims to encourage discussion, recommend suppliers and implement River Cottage's various campaigns and projects.

www.rivercottage.net

The British Association for Shooting and Conservation

The national representative body for sporting shooting. Includes a promotional sub-site called Game's On, with recipes, articles and useful links.

www.basc.org.uk

The Low Impact Living Initiative

Non-profit organisation promoting a lifestyle with reduced environmental impact. Includes useful section on game, with the emphasis on truly wild meat not killed for sport. Excellent, non-biased list of useful links to organizations like the BASC as well as anti hunt groups.

www.lowimpact.org

Two organisations we have found useful for issues surrounding wild and farmed fish:

Fish online

The Marine Conservation Society's website can help you identify which fish are from well managed sources and/or caught using methods that minimize damage to marine wildlife and habitats.

www.fishonline.org

The Marine Stewardship Council

The MSC has an eco-labelling scheme that will be familiar to many shoppers. This site can tell you more about the work behind that.

www.msc.org

Legwork

Further reading

We found a number of reference and recipe books very handy whilst researching this book. They included:

The River Cottage Cookbook
Hugh Fearnley-Whittingstall (Collins, 2003)

The River Cottage Meat Book
Hugh Fearnley-Whittingstall (Hodder and Stoughton, 2004)

The Oxford Companion to Food
Alan Davidson (Oxford University Press, 2006)

North Atlantic Seafood
Alan Davidson (Prospect, 2003)

The Savvy Shopper
Rose Prince (Fourth Estate, 2006)

Real Flavours
Glynn Christian (Grub Street, 2005)

English Food
Jane Grigson (Penguin, 1998)

Food in England
Dorothy Hartley (Little Brown, 1999)

Nose To Tail Eating (A Kind of British Cookery)
Fergus Henderson (Bloomsbury, 2004)

Maggie's Harvest
Maggie Beer (Penguin Australia, 2007)

The Cook's Companion
Stephanie Alexander (Penguin, 2004)

Wild Garlic, Gooseberries and Me
Dennis Cotter (Collins, 2007)

Chez Panisse Café Cookbook
Alice Waters (Collins, 1999)

The River Café Cookbook
Ruth Rogers and Rose Gray (Ebury Press, 1996)

Flavours of India
Madhur Jaffrey (BBC Books, 1995)

Indonesian Regional Food and Cookery
(Doubleday, 1994)

Thai Food
David Thompson (Pavilion, 2002)

Legwork

Shopping

Here is a list of stockists, farmer's markets and internet-based suppliers that we have found very useful when buying game. The information here is highly subject to change. Our apologies if a company changes its name or ceases to trade. The following suppliers can deliver game to you but to find your nearest farmer's market or some of your local suppliers we recommend contacting one of the following:

Search sites

The National Farmer's Retail and Markets Association (FARMA)

Lower Ground Floor
12 Southgate Street
Winchester
Hampshire SO23 9EF

www.farmersmarkets.net

Bigbarn.co.uk

BigBarn Ltd
College Farm
Great Barford
Bedfordshire MK44 3JJ

Phone 01234 871005
www.bigbarn.co.uk

Suppliers

Yorkshire Game

Excellent game deliverer and the principle supplier of game to our restaurants.

Station Road Industrial Park
Brompton on Swale
Richmond
North Yorkshire DL10 7SN

Phone 01748 810212
www.yorkshiregame.co.uk

Blackface

Sister company to Yorkshire Game, excellent wild Scottish venison.

Weatherall Foods Limited
Crochmore House
Irongray
Dumfries DG2 9SF
Scotland

Phone 01387 730326
www.blackface.co.uk

Rare Breed Meat Company

Some game available, when in season. Free-range guinea fowl and quails.

Herons Farm
Colne Road
Coggeshall
Essex CO6 1TQ

Phone 01376 562500
www.therarebreedmeatcompany.co.uk

Graig Farm Organics

Good range of game, some farmed meat including wild boar. Also, sustainably caught fish.

Dolau
Llandrindod Wells
Powys LD1 5TL

Phone 01597 851655
www.graigfarm.co.uk

Legwork

Index

Index

t

u

game: a cookbook

Index

A guide to the game year

The following dates indicate a closed hunting season; the actual availability of any game will vary from year to year, especially if the animal is truly wild or migratory. You will find more detail on the seasons, habitat and availability of each type of game in the recipe section of this book. Please note that we do not include seasons here for quail, guinea fowl and wild boar because only farmed versions are currently available in the UK.

birds

grouse	12th August to 10th December
mallard	1st September to 31st January
partridge	1st September to 1st February
pheasant	1st October to 1st February
pigeon	No closed season
rooks	Usually available in May only
snipe	1st October to 31st January
teal	1st September to 31st January
widgeon	1st September to 31st January
woodcock	1st October to 31st January

furred game

hare	August 1st to March 31st
rabbit	No closed season but widely available from August through March
squirrel	No closed season
venison	Red deer available July to April
fallow deer	available October to February
roe	available April to February

fish

albacore tuna	June to September
pike	July to February (River pike fishing is restricted between March and June. Many anglers on still water impose their own close seasons.)
river trout	June to September
sea trout	June to September
wild salmon	June to September

A guide to the game year

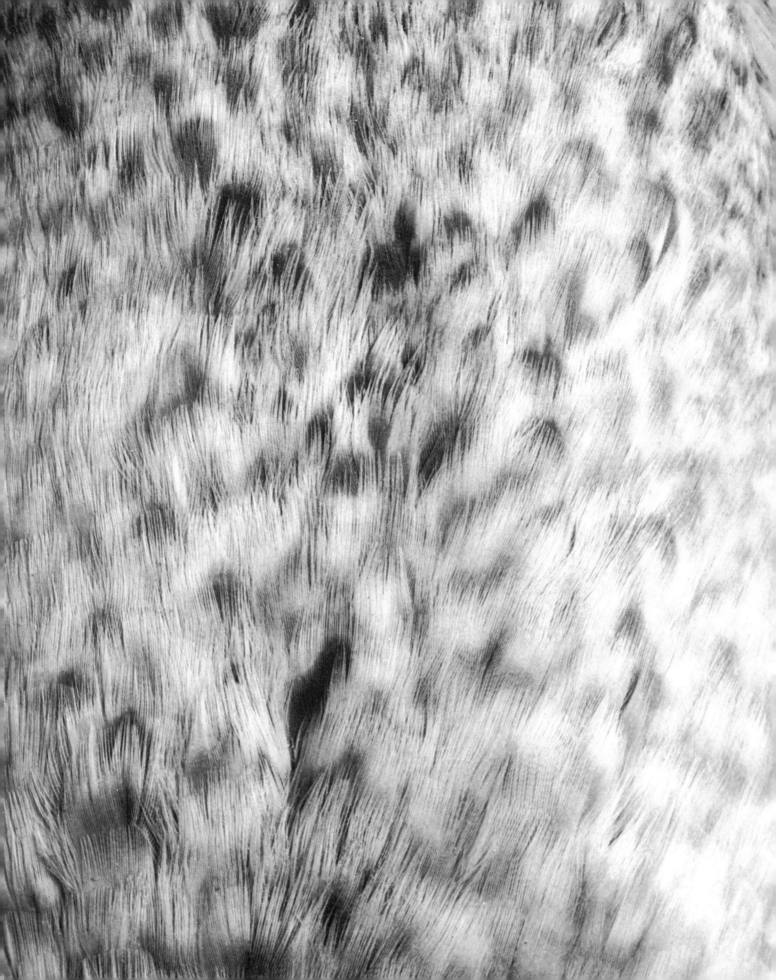

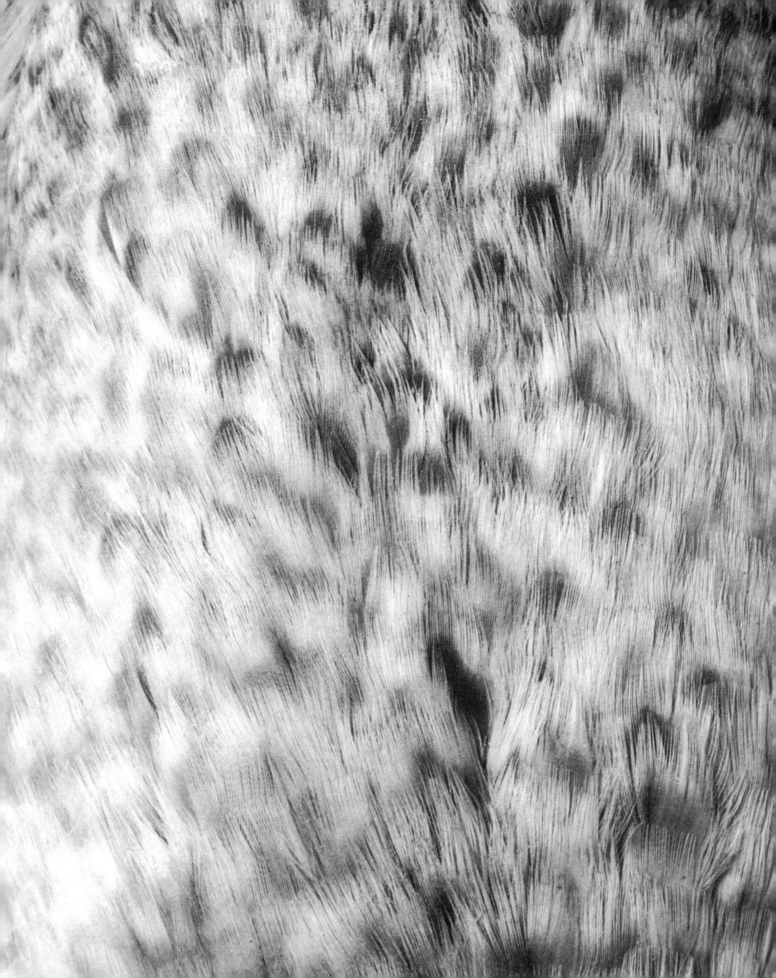

Acknowledgements

272

Many people have helped to make writing *Game* a fruitful and enjoyable endeavour.

Ben Whetherall and Lorraine Larner of Yorkshire Game provided invaluable information and most of the goodies for the illustrations.

We have been lucky enough to have the recipes in this book photographed by our good friend Jason Lowe. Working with him is always a huge pleasure.

This book simply wouldn't have been possible without the tireless support and encouragement of the following people:

Jon Croft, Matt Inwood, Meg Avent and all the team at Absolute Press; Jonathon Jones, Rob Shaw, Mike Belben, Sam Hutchins, Sam Coxhead, Warren Fleet, Matthew Lucas Young, Michael Davies and all the staff at Great Queen Street and the Anchor and Hope; Lizzy Kremer, Laura West and their colleagues at David Higham Associates; Ben Woodcraft at Ben's fish; Lincoln Barton, Dave Haskell and Chris Newton at Cove Shellfish; Steve Downey at Chef Direct; Graham, Ian and Fred at Mackanna Meats; Matthew Drennan and Angela Boggiano at *Delicious* Magazine and Helen Renshaw (formerly at *Delicious* too).

We are constantly inspired by and indebted to the following cooks and authors: Alan Davidson; Hugh Fearnley-Whittingstall; Maggie Beer; Rose Prince; Richard Corrigan; Dennis Cotter; Stephanie Alexander; David Thompson; David Eyre; Adam Robinson; Simon Hopkinson; Fergus Henderson; Claudia Roden; Carla Tomasi; Lori De Mori and Sri Owen. Last but not least, a heartfelt thank you to all the friends, family and pets who put up with our hermit-like existence and the general lack of attention that comes from anyone writing a book. You know who you are!